Young Person's Occupational Outlook Handbook

Fifth Edition

Based on information from the U.S. Department of Labor

Uncorrected Proof
Publication Month: September 2004
ISBN: 1-59357-125-9
Price: $19.95
Estimated Page Count: 336
Will include appendix and index.

jist Works
America's Career Publisher

Young Person's Occupational Outlook Handbook, Fifth Edition

© 2005 by JIST Works, an imprint of JIST Publishing, Inc.

Published by JIST Works, Inc.
8902 Otis Avenue
Indianapolis, IN 46216-1033
Phone: 800-648-JIST   Fax: 800-JIST-FAX   E-mail: info@jist.com

Visit our Web site at **www.jist.com** for information on JIST, free job search tips, book chapters, and ordering instructions for our many products!

See the back of this book for additional JIST titles and ordering information. Quantity discounts are available for JIST books. Please call our Sales Department at 1-800-648-5478 for a free catalog and more information.

Acquisitions and Development Editor: Lori Cates Hand
Cover Design: Aleata Howard
Interior Design: Lynda Preston, Rockabye Design Production
Page Layout: Trudy Coler
Illustrator: Richard Scott Morris
Proofreader: Paula Lowell
Database Administrator: Patti Deethardt

Printed in the United States of America

07 06 05 04   9 8 7 6 5 4 3 2 1

ISBN 1-59357-125-9

About This Book

This book presents information on nearly 280 major jobs. These jobs cover 88 percent of the workforce, and you are very likely to work in one or more of them during your life.

In looking over these jobs, we suggest that you consider every one that interests you. Remember that you are exploring job possibilities. The information will help you learn which classes to take and what additional training or education you will need to do that job. If a job requires more training or education than you think you can get, consider it anyway. There are many ways to finance an education, so don't eliminate any job possibility too soon.

The introduction will give you useful information to understand and use the book for career exploration. We hope this book will help you identify some new jobs to think about and some new possibilities to consider.

Contents at a Glance

Table of Contents

Professional & Related Occupations

Service Occupations

Sales & Related Occupations

Office & Administrative Support Occupations

Farming, Fishing & Forestry Occupations

Construction Trades & Related Workers

Installation, Maintenance & Repair Occupations

Production Occupations

Transportation & Material Moving Occupations

Introduction

This book was designed to help you explore a wide variety of jobs. This is important because your career choice is one of the most important decisions you will make in life. This book includes descriptions for 277 major jobs. These jobs together employ 88 percent of the American workforce. The job descriptions answer questions such as these:

* What do people in this job do all day?
* What training or education will I need to do the job?
* How much does the job pay?
* Will the job be in demand in the future?

The information in this book is based on another book called the *Occupational Outlook Handbook* (the *OOH*). The *OOH* is published by the U.S. Department of Labor and is the most widely used source of career information available. Like the *OOH,* the *Young Person's Occupational Outlook Handbook* groups similar jobs together. This makes it easy to explore related jobs you might not know about. The job descriptions in the *OOH* are more detailed than the ones in this book. You can refer to the *OOH* for more information on jobs that interest you.

Tips to Identify Jobs That Interest You

The table of contents lists all the jobs in this book, arranged into groups of similar jobs. Look through the list and choose one or more of the job groups that sound most interesting to you. Make a list of the jobs that interest you. Then read the descriptions for those jobs.

The Information in Each Job Description

Each job description in this book uses the same format. They all include eight sections:

On the Job: This section has a short description of the duties and working conditions for the job.

Subjects to Study: Here you'll find some high school courses that will help you prepare for the job.

Discover More: This section has an activity you can do to learn more about the job, or a place to go for more information.

Related Jobs: This section lists similar jobs you can consider.

Something Extra: This box has interesting, fun facts or stories related to the job.

 Education & Training: This section tells you the education and training levels most employers expect for someone starting out in the job. Almost all jobs now require a high school diploma, so we do not include "high school graduate" as an option. Instead, we list the additional training or education the average high school graduate needs to get the job.

Here are the abbreviations we've used for the levels of training and education:

Short-term OJT	=	On-the-job training that lasts up to six months.
Long-term OJT	=	On-the-job training that lasts up to two or more years.
Work experience	=	Work experience in a related job.
Voc/tech training	=	Formal vocational or technical training received in a school, apprenticeship, or cooperative education program or in the military. This training can last from a few months to two or more years and may combine classroom training with on-the-job experience.
Associate degree	=	A two-year college degree.
Bachelor's degree	=	A four-year college degree.
Master's degree	=	A bachelor's degree plus one or two years of additional education.
Doctoral degree	=	A master's degree plus two or more years of additional education.
Professional degree	=	Typically, a bachelor's degree plus two or more years of specialized education (for example, education to be an attorney, physician, or veterinarian).
Plus sign (+)	=	The plus sign indicates that you need work experience in a related job as well as formal education. For example, "Bachelor's degree +" means that you need a bachelor's degree plus work experience in a related job.

Earnings: Dollar signs represent the approximate range of average earnings for a job.

$	=	$15,000 or less per year
$$	=	$15,001 to $23,000 per year
$$$	=	$23,001 to $28,000 per year
$$$$	=	$28,001 to $50,000 per year
$$$$$	=	$50,001 or more per year
Varies	=	Between $15,000 and $50,000, depending on various factors

Job Outlook: This tells you whether the job is likely to employ more or fewer people in the future.

Declining	=	Employment is expected to decrease by 1% or more.
Little change	=	Employment is expected to decrease as much as 2%, remain about the same, or increase as much as 9%.
Average increase	=	Employment is expected to increase from 10% to 20%.
Above-average increase	=	Employment is expected to increase from 21% to 35%.
Rapid increase	=	Employment is expected to increase by 36% or more.

Using the Earnings and Job Outlook Information

Are lower earnings "bad" and higher earnings "good"? Is rapid growth in a job better than slow growth or a decline?

Many people do not consider jobs if the jobs have low earnings or are not projected to grow rapidly. But we think you should look at earnings and growth as just two of several factors when you consider your job options. Here is some advice for looking at these important measures.

Earnings Information

Median earnings for an adult worker in the United States are about $32,000 a year. A four-year college graduate has median earnings about $17,000 more than that per year. There is a clear connection between earnings and education, and it goes like this: The more you learn, the more you are likely to earn. But information on earnings can be misleading. Some people earn much more than the average, even in "low-paying" jobs. For example, some waiters and waitresses earn more than $50,000 a year, although the average earnings for these jobs are much lower. And some high school graduates earn much more than the average for four-year college graduates.

Earnings also vary widely for similar jobs with different employers or in different parts of the country. Finally, young workers usually earn a lot less than the average because they have less work experience than the average worker in the same job.

This book presents earnings information for the "average" person in the job. But you should remember that half of all people in any job earn more than average, and half earn less. So don't eliminate a job that interests you based only on its average pay.

Job Outlook Information

The U.S. Department of Labor, a part of the federal government, collects job information from all over the country. The department uses some of this information to guess which jobs are likely to grow and which will decline—and by how much. The most recent information projects job growth for the next eight years. Some jobs will grow faster than average. Others will grow slower than average. What's more, some jobs are likely to employ fewer people in eight years than they do now.

But, as with earnings, job growth should be only one of the things you consider in planning your career. For example, jobs that employ small numbers of people may have rapid growth, but they won't generate nearly as many new jobs as a slow-growing but large field like "cashier." Don't eliminate jobs that interest you simply because they are not growing quickly. Even jobs that are "declining" will have some new openings for talented people because workers leave the field for retirement or other jobs.

☞ Some Things to Consider

Choosing your career is one of the most important decisions of your life. By exploring career options now, you will be better prepared to make good decisions later. Here are some things you should consider:

Your Interests: Think about what interests you. Your hobbies, school subjects you like or do well in, sports and clubs, home and family chores, volunteer activities, and other things can be clues to possible careers. For example, if you are interested in music, you might think about a job in the music industry.

Your Values: It is important to look for a job that lets you do something you believe in. For example, if you want to help people, you will be happier in a job that allows you to do that. Or you may be able to find a hobby or volunteer job that lets you do this outside of your job. Either way, it's worth thinking about.

Education and Training: How much education or training are you willing to consider getting? Most of the better-paying jobs today require training or education beyond high school. And more and more jobs require computer skills, technical training, or other specialized skills. It's true, "the more you learn, the more you are likely to earn." So you might want to consider getting a four-year degree or technical training after high school. Either of these options can lead to jobs with high pay and good opportunities. For now, you should consider any job that interests you, even if you aren't sure whether you can afford the training or education required. If you really want to do something, you can find a way.

Earnings: What you earn at your job is important because it defines what kind of lifestyle you can afford. Higher-paying jobs usually require higher levels of training or education, or higher levels of responsibility.

Working Conditions: Do you like to work in an office or outside? Would you rather work by yourself or as part of a group? Do you want to be in charge? What kinds of people would you like to work with? These are just some of the things to consider in planning your career.

Satisfaction: You will spend hundreds of hours working each year, and you will be happier if you are doing work you enjoy and are good at. Your interests and values can give you important clues to possible jobs.

Skills: What skills do you have? What skills do you need to get the jobs you want? What skills can you learn or improve with more training or education? The skills you have already, and the skills you can develop in the future, are important parts of making good career decisions.

Self-Employment: Did you know that 8 percent of all workers are self-employed or own their own businesses today? Head to the library and you'll find lots of books and other sources of information on this topic. If self-employment appeals to you, don't let anyone tell you "you're too young." Check it out!

Getting More Information

As you can see, there are a lot of things to consider in planning your career or job options. This book can help you find the jobs that interest you. But when you're done here, you'll want to get more information. After you decide which jobs interest you, here are some places to learn more:

Check out the *Occupational Outlook Handbook:* The *OOH* has more thorough descriptions for each of the jobs in this book, so you should start there. It's available in the reference section of your library or at your local bookstore. A book called *America's Top 300 Jobs* includes all of the *OOH* job descriptions, and libraries are more likely to let you check it out.

Visit the Library: You can find the *OOH* and many other career books, magazines, and other resources at most libraries. Ask your librarian for help in finding what you want.

Talk to People: Find people who work in jobs that interest you and "interview" them. Ask what they like and don't like about the job, how to get started, what education or training you need, and other details.

The Internet: If you have access to the Internet, you can find a lot of career information online.

Your Teacher: Ask your teacher for ideas on other sources of career information. He or she might be able to help you find more information in your school library or from other sources.

Remember, this book is only the beginning of your search for "the right career." Don't rule out any jobs because they seem out of reach or because they don't pay "enough." Follow your dreams, do your homework, and you'll figure out how to get from here to there.

Management & Business & Financial Operations Occupations

Administrative Services Managers

On the Job

Administrative services managers work for large and small businesses and government agencies. They manage the services that keep businesses in business: the mailroom, food, security, parking, printing, purchasing, and payroll. In large companies, they may manage other workers. In small ones, they may be responsible for any or all of these services themselves. Facility managers plan, design, and manage workplace facilities.

Subjects to Study

English, math, speech, computer skills, business

Discover More

Divide your class into groups of four or five. Have each group take a turn planning a class activity. Groups will have to decide what supplies they need for their activity, who will bring them in, and how they will teach the activity. For example, you might teach your classmates to make paper fans or create an assembly line to produce birdhouses.

Related Jobs

Office and administrative support worker supervisors and managers; cost estimators; property, real estate, and community association managers; purchasing managers, buyers, and purchasing agents; top executives

Education & Training
Associate's degree

Earnings
$$$$$

Job Outlook
Average increase

Advertising, Marketing, Promotions, Public Relations & Sales Managers

On the Job

These workers help businesses sell their products. Before a product ever goes on the assembly line, marketing managers decide whether it will sell and who will buy it. Advertising managers decide what type of ads will work best. Promotions and sales managers design campaigns to let the public know about the product. Public relations managers help companies create a good image in the community. All of these managers travel a lot, and job transfers are common.

Subjects to Study

English, speech, writing skills, journalism, business, art

Discover More

The next time you are watching TV or reading a magazine, study the commercials or ads closely. Some are funny, some serious, others just confusing. Are they effective? Do they make you want to buy the products they are promoting? How would you change an ad to make it more effective?

Related Jobs

Actors, producers, and directors; artists and related workers; demonstrators, product promoters, and models; market and survey researchers; public relations specialists; sales representatives, wholesale and manufacturing; writers and editors

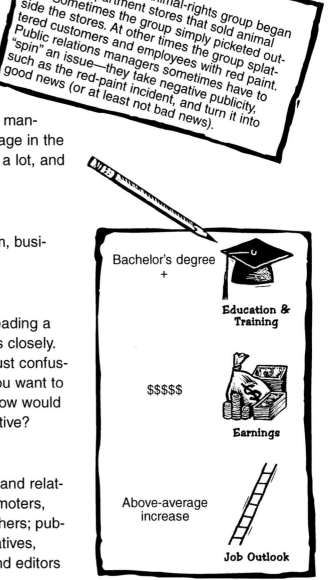

Bachelor's degree +

Education & Training

$$$$$

Earnings

Above-average increase

Job Outlook

Computer & Information Systems Managers

On the Job

Computer and information systems managers plan and direct computer labs in large and small companies and for the government. They hire computer programmers and support specialists. They manage and review the work in a business and help determine salaries. They also decide what workers and equipment are needed to do certain jobs.

Subjects to Study

Math, physics, chemistry, computer skills, speech, business

Discover More

Take a tour of your school's computer lab. Does the lab instructor keep the computers in running order, or does the school use an outside contractor for that job? How often are the computers "defragged"? Are they checked regularly for viruses? These are just a few of the questions a computer systems manager must answer.

Related Jobs

Computer programmers; computer software engineers; computer systems analysts, database administrators, and computer scientists; computer support specialists and systems administrators; top executives

Bachelor's degree +

Education & Training

$$$$$

Earnings

Rapid increase

Job Outlook

Construction Managers

On the Job

Construction managers plan and direct construction projects. On small projects, they are responsible for all the people, materials, and equipment at a job site. They hire and schedule workers, make sure materials are delivered on time, and oversee the safety of the work site. They often work outdoors, and may be on call 24 hours a day to deal with delays, bad weather, and emergencies.

Something Extra

Did you ever wonder how builders choose what materials to use? Sometimes the environment dictates the materials. In China, for example, builders use stone and brick for construction because much of the land is treeless. In Northern California, builders cannot use wood-shingled roofs on houses because of fire hazard. In Mexico, houses are built from mud bricks called adobe, which keeps them cool in the hot sun.

Subjects to Study

Math, shop, computer science, drafting, technology, business courses

Discover More

Taking shop courses at school, building small projects at home, and apprenticing with a skilled craft worker are some ways you can learn more about the construction industry.

Related Jobs

Architects, except landscape and naval; civil engineers; cost estimators; landscape architects; engineering and natural sciences managers

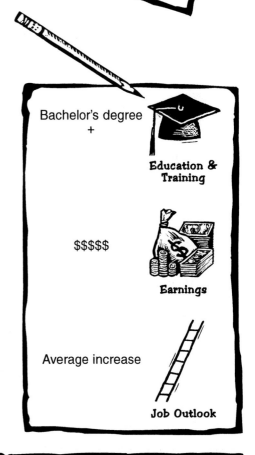

Bachelor's degree +

Education & Training

$$$$$

Earnings

Average increase

Job Outlook

Education Administrators

On the Job

Education administrators are like the managers of schools, colleges, and universities. They develop programs, monitor students' progress, train teachers, and prepare budgets. They must communicate with parents, students, employers, and the community. They might be school principals, college presidents or deans, or school-district superintendents.

Subjects to Study

English, speech, computer science, statistics, psychology, college-prep courses

Discover More

Ask the principal or dean at your school if you can "apprentice" with him or her for a day or two, watching, asking questions, and helping out as needed. Does the workday end when school is out? Will you have to attend evening meetings? Are there aspects of the job you like or dislike?

Related Jobs

Administrative services managers; office and administrative support worker supervisors and managers; human resources/training, and labor relations managers and specialists; archivists, curators, and museum technicians; counselors; librarians; instructional coordinators; teachers—preschool, kindergarten, elementary, middle, and secondary; teachers—postsecondary

Education & Training
Master's degree +

Earnings
$$$$$

Job Outlook
Above-average increase

Engineering & Natural Sciences Managers

On the Job

Engineering and natural science managers plan and direct research, development, and production in large and small companies and research labs. They hire engineers, chemists, and biologists. They manage and review the work in a business or lab and help determine salaries. They also decide what workers and equipment are needed to do certain jobs.

Subjects to Study

Math, physics, chemistry, shop and technology courses, computer skills, speech, business

Discover More

Ask to shadow your own school lab coordinator for a day or two. What kinds of jobs does he or she perform on a regular basis? This might include supervising other workers and volunteers, keeping track of chemicals and other supplies, preparing workstations for students, and defragging computers, in addition to teaching students.

Related Jobs

Engineers, mathematicians, agricultural and food scientists, biological and medical scientists, conservation scientists and foresters, atmospheric scientists, chemists and materials scientists, environmental scientists and geoscientists, physicists and astronomers, computer programmers, top executives

Something Extra

Twenty years ago, the title engineering manager almost always brought up the image of a man in a lab coat. But in the last two decades, the field has begun opening to women. In fact, today's engineering companies are actively recruiting women at all levels of employment. Current statistics show the results: Nearly 25 percent of all engineering and science managers today are women. Although that's still below the average of 45 percent for all occupations, it's a long way from the old stereotype.

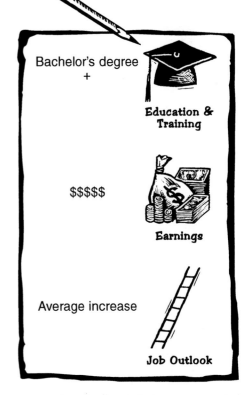

Bachelor's degree +

Education & Training

$$$$$

Earnings

Average increase

Job Outlook

Farmers, Ranchers & Agricultural Managers

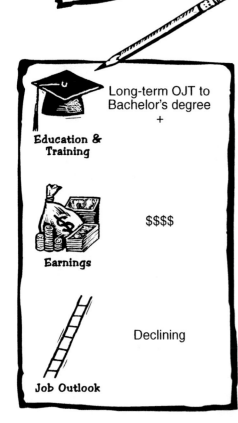

Education & Training

Long-term OJT to Bachelor's degree +

Earnings

$$$$

Job Outlook

Declining

On the Job

Because of the chemicals and equipment used, farming and ranching are dangerous jobs. Farmers on crop farms work dawn to dusk through the growing season to produce the grains, fruits, and vegetables that feed the country. During the rest of the year, many work second jobs. On ranches, animals must be fed and watered every day and fences must be inspected regularly. Farmers and ranchers must also have good business skills.

Subjects to Study

Life sciences, mechanics and shop courses, math, business, computer skills, agriculture, physical education

Discover More

Planting, tending, and harvesting your own vegetable or flower garden is a good way to learn about crop farming. To learn more about animal farming, you could raise a small animal through the 4-H program in your community.

Related Jobs

Agricultural engineers; agricultural and food scientists; agricultural workers; purchasing managers, buyers, and purchasing agents

Financial Managers

On the Job

Financial managers work for all kinds of businesses. Many work for banks, credit unions, or insurance companies. They prepare financial reports and make sure the business pays its taxes and has enough money to operate. They watch over the cash flow, manage the company's stocks, and communicate with investors. They also decide whether the business needs to borrow money, lend money, or invest in stocks and bonds.

Something Extra

Did you know that in Japan, people often bow slightly to each other? Or that in Singapore, it's considered rude to look another person directly in the eye? In today's economy, U.S. companies are doing more and more business in other countries. Understanding those cultures can mean the difference between success and failure.

Subjects to Study

Math, English, business, accounting, writing and computer skills, speech, foreign languages

Discover More

Learn more about investing in the stock market by checking out these sites on the Internet:

The Young Investor
www.younginvestor.com
Kids' Money
www.kidsmoney.org
EduStock
http://library.thinkquest.org/3088/

Related Jobs

Accountants and auditors; budget analysts; financial analysts and personal financial advisors; insurance underwriters; loan counselors and officers; securities, commodities, and financial services sales agents; real estate brokers and sales agents

Bachelor's degree

Education & Training

$$$$$

Earnings

Average increase

Job Outlook

Food Service Managers

On the Job

Food service managers select and price the food on a restaurant's menu. They hire and train workers and manage staffing, payroll, and bookkeeping. They also oversee the preparation of food, order supplies and ingredients, and make sure the restaurant is clean and well maintained. Many managers work nights and weekends, often under stressful circumstances.

Subjects to Study

Math, English, business, nutrition, home economics, psychology, accounting

Discover More

The best way to learn about the food industry is to work in it. Consider taking a summer job at a local restaurant, waiting tables, busing tables, or washing dishes. Talk to someone who works in a restaurant.

Related Jobs

Lodging managers, sales worker supervisors, food and beverage serving and related workers

Education & Training
Voc/tech training to Bachelor's degree

Earnings
$$$$

Job Outlook
Average increase

Funeral Directors

On the Job
Funeral directors, also called morticians or undertakers, prepare bodies for burial or cremation. When someone dies, they help the family plan the funeral, prepare the obituary notice, and handle the paperwork. Most are licensed embalmers. Funeral directors are also businesspeople: They prepare bills, keep financial records, and hire and manage a staff. Most work long, irregular hours.

Something Extra
More and more people are opting for cremation these days. And people sometimes choose unusual ways to deal with their ashes. "Star Trek" creator Gene Roddenberry's ashes were carried into space on the space shuttle; 1960s rock icon Janis Joplin's were scattered off the California coast; and John Lennon's were wrapped as a Christmas gift and delivered to his wife, Yoko Ono.

Subjects to Study
Business, English, biology, chemistry, psychology, speech

Discover More
Take a class trip to a local funeral home. Ask the director about his or her job: Does the director do much counseling with grieving families? Does he or she also do embalming—preparing bodies for burial? Does the funeral home offer cremation services as well? Has the director had clients who have made unusual requests for their ashes?

Related Jobs
Clergy, social workers, psychologists, physicians and surgeons

Voc/tech training

Education & Training

$$$$

Earnings

Little change

Job Outlook

Human Resources, Training & Labor Relations Managers & Specialists

On the Job

These workers find the best employees they can and match them with jobs in their company. They interview job candidates and train new workers. They may travel to college campuses to find the best job applicants. They also help to resolve conflicts among workers or between workers and management.

Subjects to Study

English, business, psychology, sociology, communications, writing skills, computer skills, foreign languages

Discover More

If your school has a conflict-resolution team, volunteer to participate. If it does not, set up a team in your classroom. The team's job is to help out when two students are involved in a dispute. Team members hear both sides and come up with a fair solution. They might also teach conflict-resolution skills to other students.

Related Jobs

Counselors, education administrators, public relations specialists, lawyers, psychologists, social and human service assistants, social workers

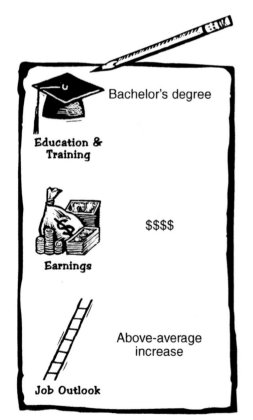

Bachelor's degree

Education & Training

$$$$

Earnings

Above-average increase

Job Outlook

Industrial Production Managers

On the Job

These workers direct scheduling, staffing, equipment, quality control, and inventory in factories. Their main job is to get goods produced on time and within budget. They decide what equipment and workers to use and in what order. They also monitor the production run to make sure it stays on schedule and to fix any problems that arise.

Subjects to Study

Math, English, shop and technology courses, computer skills, business

Discover More

Plan an assembly-line process for making a craft. How many workers do you need? What materials and equipment will you use? How long will it take to make the item? How much will it cost? These are the questions a manager must answer.

Related Jobs

Engineers, management analysts, operations research analysts, top executives, industrial engineers, including health and safety

Something Extra

You have to have 10,000 widgets ready by next Tuesday. Your widget painter cannot run at the same time as your widget packer. Your widget tops are arriving tomorrow, but the bottoms won't be in until the next day. On top of that, your widget-assembling workers charge double time if they have to work nights. You must decide the best way to run the assembly line and when to run each machine. You also have to decide whether to have your workers work overtime or to hire temporary helpers. And you must decide it all by noon. You're a production manager!

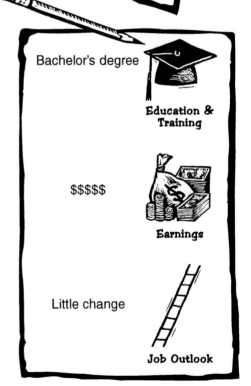

Bachelor's degree

Education & Training

$$$$$

Earnings

Little change

Job Outlook

Lodging Managers

On the Job

Lodging managers hire, train, and supervise the people who work in hotels, motels, and even bed-and-breakfast inns. They set room rates, handle billing, order food and supplies, and oversee the day-to-day operations of business. Managers who work for hotel chains may organize and staff a new hotel, refurbish an older one, or reorganize one that is not operating well. Most work more than 40 hours a week, often at night and on weekends.

Subjects to Study

English, foreign languages, business, math, accounting, computer skills

Discover More

Call a local hotel and ask if you can "shadow" the front desk manager for a day. Ask about job responsibilities. What kinds of hours are required? How does the manager handle unpleasant customers? What emergencies has he or she faced in the last year?

Related Jobs

Food service managers; sales worker supervisors; property, real estate, and community association managers

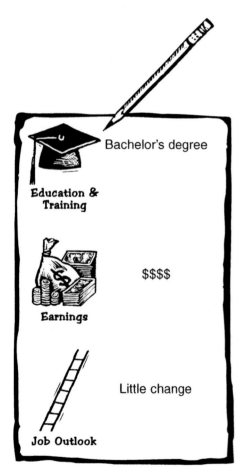

Bachelor's degree

Education & Training

$$$$

Earnings

Little change

Job Outlook

Medical & Health Services Managers

On the Job

Medical and health services managers plan, organize, and supervise the delivery of health care. They determine staffing and equipment needs and direct the public relations, marketing, and finances of hospitals, nursing homes, HMOs, clinics, and doctor's offices. They may be in charge of an entire organization or only one department within it. These managers earn high salaries, but they often work long hours.

Something Extra

Imagine it's 10 degrees below zero outside, and half of the staff members of your nursing home can't make it to work. Most of the elderly residents have the flu. The doctor on call is stuck in the snow somewhere. Whose responsibility is it to make sure the residents are safe, fed, and well cared for? If you're the manager, it's your job!

Subjects to Study

Math, English, speech, writing skills, business, psychology, health

Discover More

To learn more about careers in the health-care field, try volunteering at a local nursing home or hospital in your community. Many have volunteers who read to or visit with patients and make small deliveries.

Related Jobs

Insurance underwriters

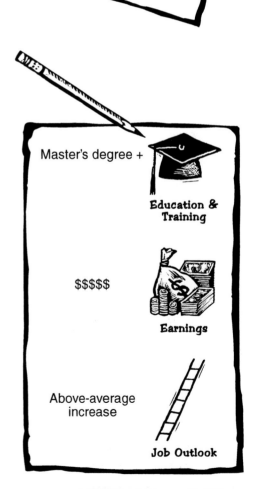

Master's degree +

Education & Training

$$$$$

Earnings

Above-average increase

Job Outlook

Property, Real Estate & Community Association Managers

On the Job
Property and real estate managers oversee apartment buildings, rental houses, businesses, and shopping malls. They sell empty space to renters, prepare leases, collect rent, and handle the bookkeeping. They also make sure the property is maintained, and they handle complaints from renters. Community association managers work for condominium or neighborhood owners' associations.

Subjects to Study
Math, English, foreign languages, writing and computer skills, business, accounting, shop courses

Discover More
Visit an apartment complex in your community and spend a day with the manager. Ask about the best and worst parts of the job, problems he or she sees in a typical week, and what kind of training you need for this job.

Related Jobs
Administrative services managers, education administrators, food service managers, lodging managers, medical and health services managers, real estate brokers and sales agents, urban and regional planners

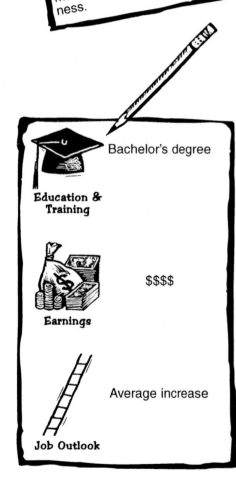

Education & Training — Bachelor's degree

Earnings — $$$$

Job Outlook — Average increase

Purchasing Managers, Buyers & Purchasing Agents

On the Job

These workers look for the best merchandise at the lowest price for their employers. They find the best products, negotiate the price, and make sure the right amount is received at the right time. They study sales records and inventory levels, identify suppliers, and stay aware of changes in the marketplace. Many spend several days a month traveling.

Something Extra

Were you born to shop? Do you love the mall? Are you a trendsetter? Buyers for department stores travel the world, attending fashion shows, visiting garment factories, and checking out small boutiques. They haggle for the best possible prices. And when their work is done, they can stroll through the malls and see their choices on clothes racks, in store windows, and on other shoppers!

Subjects to Study

Math, business, economics, English, speech, home economics, computer skills

Discover More

Think of your family as a business. Help your parents compile a weekly "supplies" list. Then do some comparison-shopping. Call or visit several stores to see who offers the best prices on the things your family needs. Will you save money if you buy in bulk? Should you buy from more than one source? How much can you save using coupons? See how much money you can save your family business in one week.

Related Jobs

Advertising, marketing, promotions, public relations, and sales managers; food service managers; insurance sales agents; lodging managers; sales engineers; sales representatives, wholesale and manufacturing

Bachelor's degree

Education & Training

$$$$-$$$$$

Earnings

Little change

Job Outlook

Top Executives

On the Job

Top executives make policies and direct operations at businesses and government agencies. They decide a company's goals and make plans to meet them. They meet with other executives, boards of directors, government heads, and consultants to talk about things that could affect their business. They are responsible for the business's ultimate success or failure.

Subjects to Study

Math, English, business, accounting, speech, computer science, psychology

Discover More

You can learn more about being a leader by running for the student council at your school, taking a leadership position in a club or organization, or helping to plan activities at your school, church, or home.

Related Jobs

Administrative services managers; education administrators; financial managers; food service managers; advertising, marketing, promotions, public relations, and sales managers

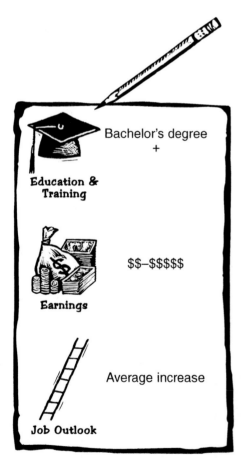

Education & Training — Bachelor's degree +

Earnings — $$–$$$$$

Job Outlook — Average increase

Accountants & Auditors

On the Job

Accountants and auditors prepare and check financial reports and taxes. They work for businesses and banks, the government, and individuals. Some are self-employed, working as consultants or preparing people's tax returns. Most use computers in their work.

Something Extra

In the 1920s, a big-talking gangster named Al Capone boasted that he owned the city of Chicago, and he was nearly right. The police seemed helpless to bring him down—until government accountants saved the day. Capone was finally convicted, not of the murders he ordered or the illegal drug-running he planned, but of tax evasion.

Subjects to Study

Math, speech, business, economics, computer skills

Discover More

With your teacher's help, set up a banking system in your classroom. You can earn "class dollars" for good behavior, turning in work on time, and good attendance. You can spend those dollars on items from the "class store" or maybe on special privileges. Keep your bankbook up to date, recording each dollar you earn and each one you spend at the class store.

Related Jobs

Budget analysts; cost estimators; loan counselor's and officers; financial analysts and personal financial advisors; tax examiners, collectors, and revenue agents; bill and account collectors; bookkeeping, accounting, and auditing clerks; computer programmers; computer software engineers; computer support specialists and systems administrators

Bachelor's degree

Education & Training

$$$$

Earnings

Average increase

Job Outlook

Budget Analysts

On the Job

Budget analysts help businesses decide how much money they need to run and how to spend that money. They check reports and accounts during the year to make sure the business is staying within its budget and spending its money wisely.

They also look for ways companies can save money and use it more efficiently.

Subjects to Study

Math, business, economics, computer skills, statistics, accounting

Discover More

Imagine you are starting a business making widgets. Give yourself $10,000 to start, and then decide how to spend the money. Do you need employees? How much will you pay them? What equipment and supplies do you need? Do you have to rent work space? Make a budget for your business. Can you make a profit?

Related Jobs

Accountants and auditors, cost estimators, economists, financial analysts and personal financial advisors, financial managers, loan counselors and officers, management analysts

Education & Training — Bachelor's degree

Earnings — $$$$$

Job Outlook — Average increase

Claims Adjusters, Appraisers, Examiners & Investigators

On the Job

Insurance claims adjusters and claims investigators check to make sure that claims filed are covered by their company's policies. Then they decide how much should be paid and okay the payment. If the claim is not covered, they deny payment. Appraisers travel to see damaged property and assess how much the damage is worth. Sometimes investigators check out suspicious or unusual claims for fraud.

Something Extra

Sometimes people run away from their bills. This used to be called "skipping out," which led to the term "skip-tracing." Insurance investigators and collectors skip-trace people by checking with post offices, telephone companies, and credit bureaus. They may even question family members, coworkers, and former neighbors to get information.

Subjects to Study

Math, English, computer skills, economics, business, accounting, foreign languages, psychology, health

Discover More

Ask your parents if they have ever filed a claim on their car, home, life, or health insurance. Find out what they did to file the claim. Did they talk to an adjuster?

Related Jobs

Cost estimators; bill and account collectors; medical records and health information technicians; billing and posting clerks and machine operators; credit authorizers, checkers, and clerks; bookkeeping, accounting, and auditing clerks; construction and building inspectors; accountants and auditors; private detectives and investigators; automotive body and related repairers; automotive service technicians and mechanics

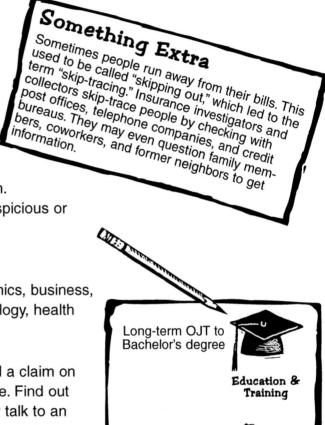

Long-term OJT to Bachelor's degree

Education & Training

$$$$

Earnings

Average increase

Job Outlook

Cost Estimators

On the Job

When a company is thinking about developing a new product, the owner needs to know how much it will cost to produce. What new machinery will be needed? How much will materials cost? How many workers will be hired? A cost estimator finds the least-expensive way to make the best product. Cost estimators decide what supplies to use, find the best prices, estimate labor costs, and report back to the owner.

Subjects to Study

Math, computer science, technology programs, business, English, economics, statistics

Discover More

Plan a business making birdhouses from craft sticks. Decide how many you will make, then find the total cost of producing them. Include all your building materials (craft sticks, glue, and paint, for example), supplies (how about a hot-glue gun?), and labor costs (what you pay your helpers). Call several stores to find the best prices on materials. How much must you charge for your birdhouses to make a profit?

Related Jobs

Accountants and auditors; budget analysts; claims adjusters, appraisers, examiners, and investigators; economists; financial analysts and personal financial advisors; insurance underwriters

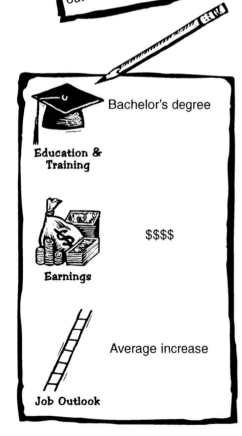

Education & Training
Bachelor's degree

Earnings
$$$$

Job Outlook
Average increase

Financial Analysts & Personal Financial Advisors

On the Job

Financial analysts help businesses decide how to invest their money safely and wisely. Many are employed full-time by the companies they advise; others work as consultants, helping many different companies. Personal financial advisors provide the same kinds of services to individuals. Many personal advisors are self-employed. These workers often put in more than 40 hours a week and may teach classes and seminars as well.

Subjects to Study

Math, English, business, accounting, writing and computer skills, speech, foreign languages

Discover More

A good way to learn about investing is to invest— with money. Look through the financial pages of your newspaper or the *Wall Street Journal.* Pick two or three stocks—ones that look like safe investments or ones that seem to be growing. Pretend that you've invested $1,000 in each, then track them for a month. Will you make money or lose it?

Related Jobs

Accountants and auditors; financial managers; insurance sales agents; real estate brokers and sales agents; securities, commodities, and financial services sales representatives

Something Extra

Have you heard of Enron? It used to be one of the largest companies in the U.S., employing thousands of people. And most of those people, at the urging of their bosses, invested their retirement savings in the company's stock. In 2001, Enron collapsed in a sea of debt and bad deals. The top bosses came out with fat bonus checks, but the people who had invested in company stock were left with nothing. Enron is a classic example of why financial advisors say it's a bad idea to invest all of your money in one stock. The key word in investment? Diversify!

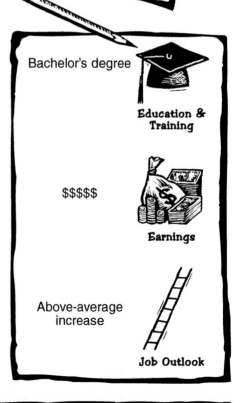

Bachelor's degree

Education & Training

$$$$$

Earnings

Above-average increase

Job Outlook

Insurance Underwriters

On the Job

How much should an insurance company charge for insurance? That depends on how likely a customer is to have an accident. Using national statistics, underwriters decide whether a person applying for insurance is a good risk. They also help the company decide how much to charge. If they set the rates too low, the company will lose money. Too high, and the company will lose business to competitors.

Subjects to Study

Math, statistics, economics, English, business, speech, accounting

Discover More

Talk with an insurance agent in your community. Ask about the company's insurance rates. Are rates higher for those under 21? Are there other groups the company considers high-risk? Do people who live downtown pay higher rates than those in the suburbs? Are rates higher for people who own sports cars or minivans? Why?

Related Jobs

Accountants and auditors; actuaries; budget analysts; cost estimators; financial analysts and personal financial advisors; financial managers; loan counselors and officers; insurance sales agents; claims adjusters, appraisers, examiners, and investigators

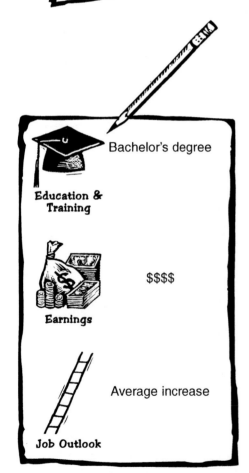

Education & Training — Bachelor's degree

Earnings — $$$$

Job Outlook — Average increase

Loan Counselors & Officers

On the Job

When you apply for a loan, you must provide information on your work, your assets and debts, and your credit rating. A loan officer will meet with you and help you fill out the application. Then he or she looks through your information and helps the bank decide whether to loan you the money. Some loan counselors contact borrowers who are behind in repaying their loans and help them find a way of making payments.

Something Extra

If you plan to go to college, you'll probably need a loan. Most college students need some kind of help paying for school. Schools, banks, and the federal government all have loan programs to help students. A loan counselor will walk you through the process of applying for a loan, tell you how much you can borrow, and work out a payment plan after you have graduated.

Subjects to Study

Math, accounting, English, speech, writing and computer skills, business, psychology

Discover More

Ask for a loan application from your parents' bank or credit union. Fill it out completely, including all of your sources of income, your savings, and your debts. Are you a good credit risk? Would you loan yourself money?

Related Jobs

Securities, commodities, and financial services sales agents; financial analysts and personal financial advisors; real estate brokers and sales agents; insurance sales agents

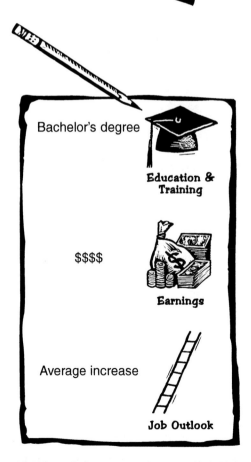

Bachelor's degree

Education & Training

$$$$

Earnings

Average increase

Job Outlook

Management Analysts

On the Job

Companies hire management analysts to solve problems. The work varies with each client and from project to project. When a management team realizes there is a problem, it may call in a consultant to collect and review information, figure out where and why the problem is happening, and decide how to fix it. The job may require frequent traveling. Some management analysts work for consulting firms. Others are self-employed consultants.

Subjects to Study

English, math, business, economics, accounting, journalism, speech, writing, business skills

Discover More

Many consultants are self-employed. Interview people you know who are self-employed. How do they find their clients? Do they advertise? What do they like and dislike about being self-employed?

Related Jobs

Accountants and auditors; budget analysts; cost estimators; financial analysts and personal financial advisors; operations research analysts; economists; computer systems analysts, database administrators, and computer scientists; administrative services managers; financial managers; human resources, training, and labor relations managers and specialists; top executives

Bachelor's degree to Master's degree +

Education & Training

$$$$$

Earnings

Above-average increase

Job Outlook

Tax Examiners, Collectors & Revenue Agents

On the Job

Tax examiners, collectors, and revenue agents work for the federal, state, and local governments. They review tax returns to make sure people and businesses are paying the right amount, send notices to those who have made mistakes, and track down those who are trying to avoid taxes altogether. Most work 40-hour weeks, except from January to April, when overtime (and angry clients) are common.

Subjects to Study

Math, business, accounting, computer science, English, foreign languages

Discover More

From January until April, your local library stocks tax forms of all kinds. Pick up a 1040 form and ask your parents or a teacher to help you fill it out based on your allowance or job earnings. Read through all of the deductions carefully—you never know which ones you will qualify for!

Related Jobs

Accountants and auditors, budget analysts, cost estimators, financial analysts and personal financial advisors, financial managers, loan counselors and officers

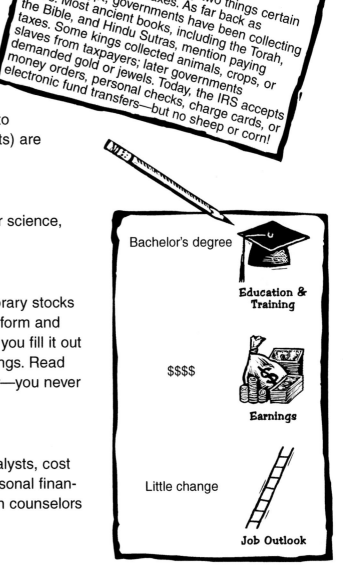

Something Extra

Someone once said, the only two things certain in life are death and taxes. As far back as ancient Egypt, governments have been collecting taxes. Most ancient books, including the Torah, the Bible, and Hindu Sutras, mention paying taxes. Some kings collected animals, crops, or slaves from taxpayers; later governments demanded gold or jewels. Today, the IRS accepts money orders, personal checks, charge cards, or electronic fund transfers—but no sheep or corn!

Bachelor's degree

Education & Training

$$$$

Earnings

Little change

Job Outlook

Professional & Related Occupations

Actuaries

On the Job

Actuaries design insurance plans that will help their company make a profit. They study statistics and social trends to decide how much money an insurance company should charge for an insurance policy. They predict the amount of money an insurance company will have to pay to its customers for claims. Some actuaries are self-employed and work as consultants.

Subjects to Study

Math, calculus, accounting, computer science, writing skills

Discover More

Take a survey in your class. How many of your classmates have broken a bone or sprained an ankle? How many have stayed overnight in a hospital? How many have had their tonsils or appendix removed? Now separate the answers by boys and girls. Which group has had more medical emergencies?

Related Jobs

Accountants and auditors, budget analysts, economists, market and survey researchers, financial analysts and personal financial advisors, insurance underwriters, mathematicians, statisticians

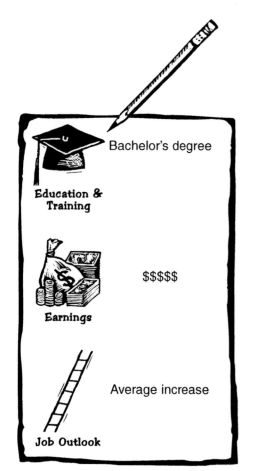

Education & Training — Bachelor's degree

Earnings — $$$$$

Job Outlook — Average increase

Computer Programmers

On the Job

Computer programmers write, update, test, and maintain the software that makes computers work. They provide detailed, step-by-step instructions for the computer. If the software does not produce the desired result, the programmer must correct the errors until the program works effectively. Some may work nights so that the computers they work on are available to businesses during the day.

Something Extra

Do you like to play computer games like Mortal Kombat, Tony Hawk's Pro Skater, Crash Bandicoot, or maybe Final Fantasy? Did you ever wonder who makes up games like these? It's computer programmers. Programmers work for computer game publishers—many of them on the West Coast—writing new games and adding new twists to old games—all of them hoping to create the next big game on the market.

Subjects to Study

Computer skills, computer programming, data processing, math, physics, keyboarding, electronics

Discover More

The image you see on a computer monitor is made up of thousands of tiny dots. Color monitors use red, green, and blue dots. Use a magnifying glass to look at the screen, or use a drop of water to act like a lens. Get a tiny drop of water on your fingertip and touch it to your computer screen. (Be careful not to drip!) Do you see the dots?

Related Jobs

Computer software engineers; computer systems analysts, database administrators, and computer scientists; statisticians; mathematicians; engineers; financial analysts and personal financial advisors; accountants and auditors; actuaries; operations research analysts

Bachelor's degree

Education & Training

$$$$$

Earnings

Average increase

Job Outlook

Computer Software Engineers

On the Job

Computer software engineers do research, design computers, and find new ways to use them in business. They may identify problems in business, science, and engineering. Then they use computers to solve the problems. This kind of work can result in eyestrain, backaches, and hand and wrist problems.

Subjects to Study

Math, physics, computer science, communication skills, shop and technology courses

Discover More

Did you know your computer gives out radio waves? Try this experiment and see. Get a small radio and set it on AM. Turn it on and find a spot between stations, so you just receive static. Now turn the radio up high and put it next to your computer. You should hear sounds from your computer on the radio!

Related Jobs

Computer systems analysts, database administrators, and computer scientists; computer programmers; financial analysts and personal financial advisors; computer hardware engineers; computer support specialists and systems administrators; statisticians; mathematicians; management analysts; actuaries; operations research analysts

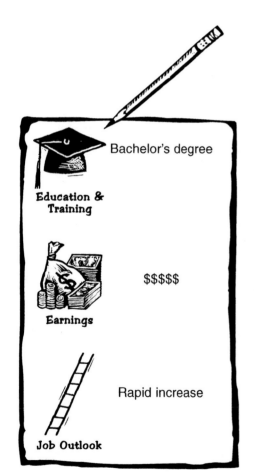

Bachelor's degree

Education & Training

$$$$$

Earnings

Rapid increase

Job Outlook

Computer Support Specialists & Systems Administrators

On the Job

What happens when a company's computers suddenly begin crashing? They call in the support specialist, the troubleshooters of the computer world. These workers find and fix problems for big businesses and individual computer owners. Systems administrators help companies decide what kind of system they need, then design, install, and support the organization's computer network. They may work overtime if problems arise.

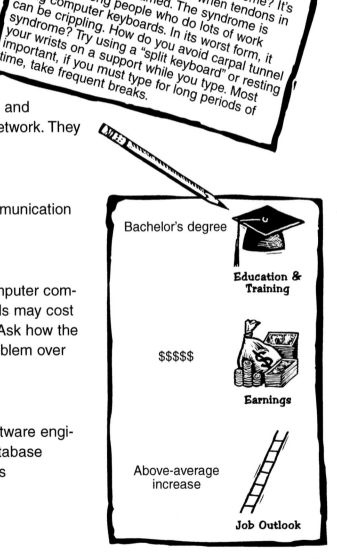

Something Extra

Have you heard of carpal tunnel syndrome? It's a painful condition that occurs when tendons in the wrist become inflamed. The syndrome is common among people who do lots of work using computer keyboards. In its worst form, it can be crippling. How do you avoid carpal tunnel syndrome? Try using a "split keyboard" or resting your wrists on a support while you type. Most important, if you must type for long periods of time, take frequent breaks.

Bachelor's degree

Education & Training

$$$$$

Earnings

Above-average increase

Job Outlook

Subjects to Study

Math, physics, computer science, communication skills, shop and technology courses

Discover More

Call the tech support hot line for a computer company. (Ask your parents first; these calls may cost money, and many are long-distance.) Ask how the support person can fix a computer problem over the phone.

Related Jobs

Computer programmers; computer software engineers; computer systems analysts, database administrators, and computer scientists

Mathematicians

On the Job

Mathematicians work in two areas: theory and applications. Theoretical mathematicians look for relationships between new math principles and old ones. This can help in science and engineering. Applied mathematicians use math to solve problems in business, government, and everyday life. Many mathematicians teach at colleges and universities.

Subjects to Study

Math, algebra, geometry, trigonometry, calculus, logic, computer science, physics, statistics

Discover More

To try your hand at some fun and challenging math activities, visit the MathCats at www.mathcats.com.

Related Jobs

Actuaries; statisticians; computer programmers; computer systems analysts, database administrators, and computer scientists; computer software engineers; operations research analysts; teachers—postsecondary; teachers—preschool, kindergarten, middle, elementary, and secondary; engineers; economists; market and survey researchers; financial analysts and personal financial advisors; physicists and astronomers

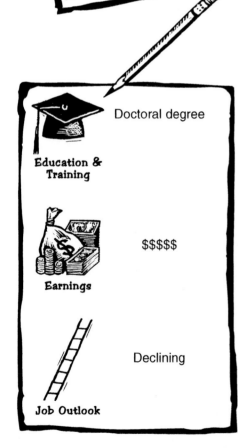

Education & Training
Doctoral degree

Earnings
$$$$$

Job Outlook
Declining

Operations Research Analysts

On the Job

Operations research analysts help businesses operate efficiently by applying mathematical principles to problems. First, analysts define and study the problem. Next, they gather information by talking with people and choosing which model they will use. Finally, they present their findings and recommendations to the company's management.

Subjects to Study

Math, statistics, computer skills, English, communication skills, logic

Discover More

Take a walk through your school building. Now, using graph paper, make a map of the building, including all the classrooms, offices, restrooms, cafeteria, and exits. Using your map, plot the most direct, effective way to deliver mail to each classroom and office. Then plot the most efficient exit route from each classroom.

Related Jobs

Computer systems analysts, database administrators, and computer scientists; computer programmers; engineers; mathematicians; statisticians; economists; market and survey researchers; computer and information systems managers; management analysts

Something Extra

Have you ever had to wait at an airport for a late flight? Airlines are famous for being late. To help them stay on time, operations research analysts set up schedules for flights and maintenance, estimate the number of passengers flying at different times, and decide how much fuel is needed for each flight. When you consider how many flights an airline runs each day, you can see what a big job that is. The wonder is that anyone ever gets anywhere on time!

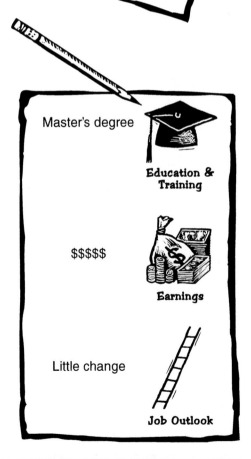

Master's degree

Education & Training

$$$$$

Earnings

Little change

Job Outlook

Statisticians

On the Job

Statisticians collect information from surveys and experiments. They decide where and how to gather the information, who to survey, and what questions to ask. They use the information they collect to make predictions about the economy or to assess various social problems. This helps business and government leaders make decisions.

Subjects to Study

Math, algebra, statistics, economics, business, sciences, computer skills, communication skills

Discover More

Telemarketing—calling people on the phone—is one way to conduct a survey. Check the want ads of your local newspaper for telemarketing job openings. Can you tell which companies need people to sell products and which ones need workers to gather information?

Related Jobs

Actuaries; mathematicians; operations research analysts; computer systems analysts, database administrators, and computer scientists; computer programmers; computer software engineers; engineers; economists; market and survey researchers; financial analysts and personal financial advisors

Education & Training
Master's degree

Earnings
$$$$$

Job Outlook
Little change

Computer Systems Analysts, Database Administrators, & Computer Scientists

On the Job

Systems analysts solve computer problems and help companies decide what kinds of computer systems are best for them. Computer scientists work as researchers and inventors. Some work for universities, others for research companies. Database administrators find ways to organize and store data. They work with large companies, maintaining the computer networks.

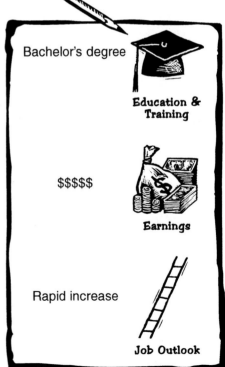

Something Extra

Just 30 years ago, there was no such job as database administrator. Today, this is one of the fastest-growing jobs in the U.S. And, because the technology is so new, the employment field is wide open for younger workers. In fact, many of today's high school seniors already know more than most of the U.S. workforce about computers—and that gap is likely to grow in the next several years.

Bachelor's degree

Education & Training

$$$$$

Earnings

Rapid increase

Job Outlook

Subjects to Study

Computer science, math, shop technology, library science, statistics

Discover More

What kinds of information backup systems does your school use? Ask your computer lab or media center specialist to show you the ways they store the information in the school's computers. Some back up the information onto other computers, but many simply use writable CDs or Zip disks to store material.

Related Jobs

Computer programmers, computer software engineers, computer and information systems managers, financial analysts and personal financial advisors, engineers, mathematicians

Architects, Except Landscape & Naval

On the Job

Architects design buildings and other structures. They make sure buildings are functional, safe, and economical. They draw plans of every part of a building, including the plumbing and electrical systems. They also help choose a building site and decide what materials to use. Most architects today use computers in their work, and many are self-employed.

Subjects to Study

Math, English, writing skills, communication skills, drawing courses, drafting, computer courses, shop and technology courses

Discover More

What does your dream house look like? Using graph paper, draw a room-by-room floor plan of your ideal home. Include all the elements you'd like—maybe a fireplace, an exercise room, a game room, or a spa. Don't forget the practical rooms—everyone needs a kitchen and a bath!

Related Jobs

Construction managers, landscape architects, civil engineers, urban and regional planners, designers

Education & Training
Professional degree

Earnings
$$$$$$

Job Outlook
Average increase

Landscape Architects

On the Job

Landscape architects make areas such as parks, malls, and golf courses beautiful and useful. They decide where the buildings, roads, and walkways will go, and how the flower gardens and trees should be arranged. They create designs, estimate costs, and check that the plans are being carried out correctly. Some work for major companies, but many are self-employed.

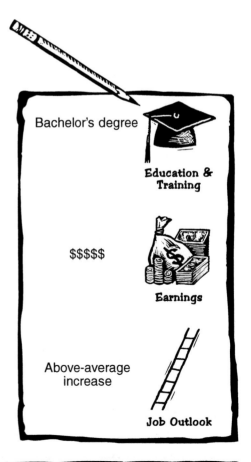

Something Extra

In the days before computers, architects had to draw their landscape designs by hand. Today, they use computer-aided design (CAD) systems and video simulations to let their clients see their ideas in full color. Then, if the client wants to make a change, the architect can do it with the click of a mouse—saving hours of time, work, and money.

Bachelor's degree

Education & Training

$$$$$

Earnings

Above-average increase

Job Outlook

Subjects to Study

Math, botany, ecology, drafting, art, geology, communications, computer skills

Discover More

Design a flower garden that will grow in your area's climate. What colors do you want? Should you use tall plants, short ones, or a combination? Do you want all spring-bloomers or plants that will bloom at various times? Check catalogs and local nurseries for prices. How much will your garden cost? How much maintenance will it need?

Related Jobs

Architects, except landscape and naval; surveyors, cartographers, photogrammetrists, and surveying technicians; civil engineers; urban and regional planners; conservation scientists and foresters; biological scientists, medical scientists; environmental scientists and geoscientists

Surveyors, Cartographers, Photogrammetrists & Surveying Technicians

Something Extra

Satellites are changing the way surveyors work today. A "Global Positioning System" uses radio signals from satellites to locate points on the earth. The surveyor places a radio receiver at the desired point. The receiver can collect information from several satellites at once. Such a receiver can also be placed in a car and used to trace a road system.

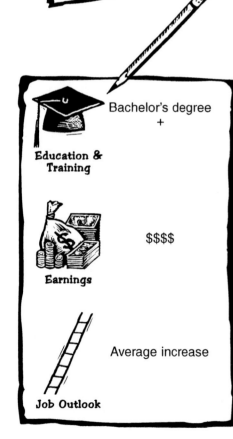

Bachelor's degree +

Education & Training

$$$$

Earnings

Average increase

Job Outlook

On the Job

These workers measure and map the earth's surface to set official land, air, and water boundaries. They may check old legal documents for information and write reports. They work outdoors in all kinds of weather and may travel long distances to work sites. Cartographers use the information surveyors gather to prepare maps and charts.

Subjects to Study

Algebra, geometry, trigonometry, drafting, mechanical drawing, computer science, English, writing skills, geography, geology

Discover More

Make a map of your neighborhood, showing how to get from your house to your school. Include all streets and important landmarks, bodies of water or forests, malls or business districts, parks and playgrounds—anything that acts as a landmark in your area. If you gave someone at school your map, could the person get to your house?

Related Jobs

Civil engineers; architects, except landscape and naval; landscape architects; environmental scientists and geoscientists; urban and regional planners

Engineers

On the Job

Engineers design machinery, buildings, and highways. They also develop new products and new ways of making them. Some engineers test the quality of products. Some supervise production in factories. They work in laboratories, factories, offices, and construction sites.

Something Extra

Can you imagine a world without engineers? It's nearly impossible in this day and age. Without engineers, we would have no bridges and dams, no interstate highways, no airliners or space shuttles, and no roller coasters or Tilt-a-Whirls at the amusement parks. Engineering affects almost every aspect of our lives today, from home to work to play.

Subjects to Study

Math, physics, chemistry, shop and technology courses, drafting, computer skills

Discover More

Using Hot Wheels® racetrack pieces, try building a raceway down a steep slope. How steep can you make the slope before the cars fly off? Now put a curve at the bottom of the slope. What happens to the cars? How much must you tilt the curve to keep the cars on the track? These are the kinds of questions engineers answer.

Related Jobs

Aerospace engineers; agricultural engineers; biomedical engineers; chemical engineers; civil engineers; computer hardware engineers; electrical and electronics engineers, except computer; environmental engineers; industrial engineers, including health and safety; materials engineers; mechanical engineers; mining and geological engineers, including mining safety; nuclear engineers; and petroleum engineers

Bachelor's degree

Education & Training

$$$$$

Earnings

Little change

Job Outlook

Aerospace Engineers

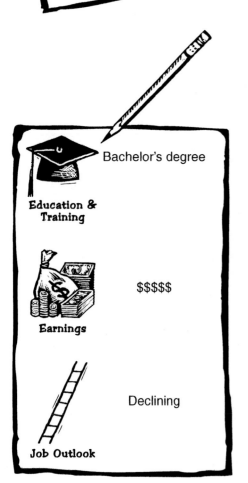

Education & Training — Bachelor's degree

Earnings — $$$$$

Job Outlook — Declining

On the Job

Aerospace engineers design and test aircraft, missiles, and spacecraft. They develop new technology in aviation, defense systems, and space exploration. Some specialize in certain types of craft, such as helicopters, spacecraft, or rockets. States such as Texas, California, and Washington have the most jobs for aerospace engineers. Many aerospace engineers work for the U.S. Department of Defense and NASA.

Subjects to Study

Math, physics, chemistry, computer technology, drafting, shop and technology courses

Discover More

You can learn more about aerospace engineering by building a model rocket with your teacher or another adult. What kind of fuel does the rocket use? Do different rocket kits use different kinds of fuel? Which fuel works better?

Related Jobs

Scientists, mathematicians, engineering technicians, science technicians, other types of engineers

Agricultural Engineers

On the Job

Agricultural engineers design the machinery and equipment used on farms, orchards, and ranches today. They find ways to conserve soil and water and to improve the way we process the nation's fruits, crops, and meats. Most work for engineering services, consulting with farmers and ranchers. Others work for local and state governments or in research labs.

Subjects to Study

Math, physics, chemistry, computer technology, drafting, shop and technology courses

Discover More

What kinds of equipment are used to maintain the grounds at your school? Ask your principal whether your school uses a lawn service or the school maintenance workers care for the grounds. Can you shadow them while they work? Look for ways to simplify the job. Is there a tool that might help? Can you design it?

Related Jobs

Biological scientists, agricultural and food scientists

Something Extra

Most of us don't think much about landslides, but they are responsible for many deaths every year. In 2001, thousands were killed in El Salvador alone; in 1997, Mexico sustained hundreds of deaths in one slide; in Southeast Asia, nearly every year brings many, many more. We can't control landslide triggers—earthquakes, hurricanes, and torrential rains will happen no matter what we do. But we can influence their impact through soil conservation. By simply planting trees and other ground covers, we can lessen the odds that people will be killed. Not a bad trade-off!

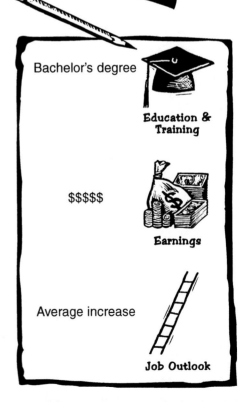

Bachelor's degree

Education & Training

$$$$$

Earnings

Average increase

Job Outlook

Biomedical Engineers

On the Job

If you've ever taken insulin or used an asthma inhaler, you've benefited from this field. Biomedical engineers develop tools and procedures that solve medical and other health problems. They develop artificial organs, replacement limbs, and new technologies, such as ultrasound or laser systems. Most work for manufacturing or health services, but some work for the government or as consultants.

Subjects to Study

Math, physics, chemistry, computer technology, health, shop and technology courses

Discover More

Say the words *animal research,* and many people get angry. They don't believe humans should exploit animals—even if it means saving human lives. Fortunately, there are organizations that promote the safe and responsible use of animals in medical research. To learn more, check out this Web site:www.kids4research.org

Related Jobs

Biological scientists, medical scientists, chemists and materials scientists

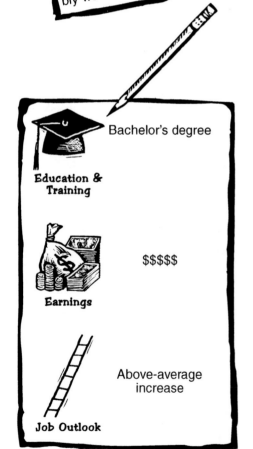

Education & Training
Bachelor's degree

Earnings
$$$$$

Job Outlook
Above-average increase

Chemical Engineers

On the Job

Chemical engineers help make new chemicals and chemical products. They design equipment, plan how to make the products, and supervise production. They usually work in laboratories or factories. Some may be hired to help companies control pollution.

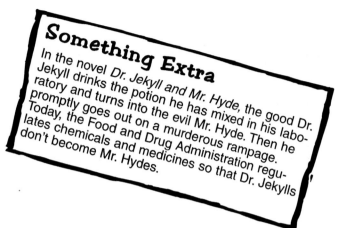

Something Extra

In the novel *Dr. Jekyll and Mr. Hyde*, the good Dr. Jekyll drinks the potion he has mixed in his laboratory and turns into the evil Mr. Hyde. Then he promptly goes out on a murderous rampage. Today, the Food and Drug Administration regulates chemicals and medicines so that Dr. Jekylls don't become Mr. Hydes.

Subjects to Study

Math, physics, chemistry, biology, environmental science, computer science, shop and technology courses

Discover More

Get three pieces of white chalk. Put one into a glass container of lemon juice, one into a glass container of vinegar, and the third into a glass of tap water. Leave them alone for three days, then check on them. The acidic lemon juice and vinegar will break down the chalk, in the same way that acid rain causes erosion.

Related Jobs

Chemists and materials scientists; physicists and astronomers; mechanical engineers; electrical and electronics engineers, except computer; mathematicians

Bachelor's degree

Education & Training

$$$$$

Earnings

Little change

Job Outlook

Civil Engineers

On the Job

Civil engineers design and supervise the building of roads, bridges, tunnels, airports, sewer systems, and buildings. Some civil engineers work in research or teach other engineers. Most work in large industrial cities, but some projects may be in isolated places or foreign countries. Civil engineers often move from place to place working on different projects.

Subjects to Study

Math, physics, drafting, computer science, shop and technology courses, environmental science, geology, foreign languages

Discover More

Using craft sticks, glue, paper clips, and rubber bands, build a bridge at least a foot long. Can you make it strong enough to support a one-pound weight? How many supports must you use? Does the glue hold, or do you need extra holding support? Now try a two-foot span.

Related Jobs

Mathematicians; engineering technicians; science technicians; architects, except landscape and naval; other engineers

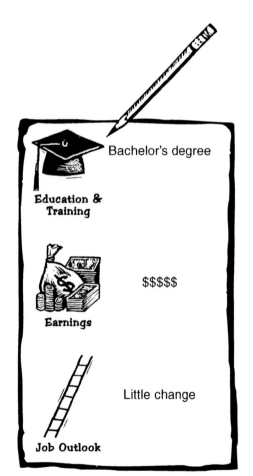

Education & Training — Bachelor's degree

Earnings — $$$$$

Job Outlook — Little change

Computer Hardware Engineers

On the Job

Computer hardware engineers design and test computer hardware—the nuts and bolts of the machine, including chips, circuit boards, keyboards, modems, and printers. They also may supervise other workers who make these components. Because computer systems are always being updated, these engineers must continually update their knowledge.

Something Extra

Just 40 years ago, the average person in the U.S. had never seen a real computer. Until the advent of PCs in the early 1980s, most people associated computers with HAL—the opinionated machine that took over the spacecraft in the movie *2001: A Space Odyssey*. Can you guess why the computer was named HAL? Here's a hint: Take each letter of the name forward one letter in the alphabet.

Subjects to Study

Math, physics, chemistry, computer technology, drafting, shop and technology courses

Discover More

Did you know that you can build your own computer? It's easier than you might think. Check out the directions at this Web site: www.webfreebees.net/howtobuildpc.html.

You'll have to buy the components, of course, but it's a lot less expensive than buying the finished product!

Related Jobs

Computer software engineers; electrical and electronics engineers, except computer

Bachelor's degree

Education & Training

$$$$$

Earnings

Little change

Job Outlook

Electrical & Electronics Engineers, Except Computer

On the Job

Electrical and electronics engineers design, test, and supervise the making of electrical equipment such as generators and motors, and wiring in cars, computers, and video equipment. They also solve problems involved with using this equipment. They determine how long a project will take to complete and how much it will cost.

Subjects to Study

Math, chemistry, physics, computer science, drafting, shop and technology courses

Discover More

Static electricity is all around us. Try this experiment on a cool, dry day. Fill a balloon with air. Rub it against your hair for about 15 seconds. What happens to your hair? Try moving the balloon nearer and then away from your head. Can you make your hair stand on end? That's static electricity.

Related Jobs

Computer hardware engineers

Bachelor's degree

Education & Training

$$$$$

Earnings

Little change

Job Outlook

Environmental Engineers

On the Job
Environmental engineers find ways to solve problems related to the environment. They work on water and air-pollution control, recycling, waste disposal, and public health issues. Some work with private companies and others work for federal, state, and local governments, making sure that we all have safe and healthy air to breathe and water to drink.

Something Extra
Have you ever been inside a greenhouse? It's an artificial environment gardeners use to grow plants year-round. The glass traps the heat of the sun and creates a warm climate, even in the middle of winter. Today, many scientists worry that Earth is becoming a giant greenhouse. The carbons emitted by our cars create an effect similar to the glass, trapping the Earth's heat. That might not seem so bad, until you realize that it means huge changes to our world—changes that include more severe hurricanes, tornadoes, and droughts. It's not nice to fool Mother Nature.

Subjects to Study
Math, physics, chemistry, computer technology, drafting, shop and technology courses

Discover More
To learn more about environmental hazards and how you can help solve them, check out the ideas at Kids Against Pollution:

www.kidsagainstpollution.org

Related Jobs
Mathematicians; engineering technicians; science technicians; other types of engineers

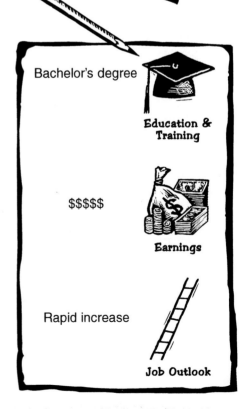

Bachelor's degree

Education & Training

$$$$$

Earnings

Rapid increase

Job Outlook

Industrial Engineers, Including Health & Safety

On the Job

Industrial engineers find the best ways to use people, machines, and materials to make a product. They help companies make the best products for the least amount of money. They may help a business owner decide where to build a new factory or how to set up an assembly line. They are the bridge between management and operations. Computers help them do faster work and save money.

Subjects to Study

Math, computer science, physics, shop and technology courses, drafting

Discover More

Set up an assembly-line operation to build a simple craft—for example, a gingerbread house. Where would you place the gingerbread pieces? How about the icing and decorations? Which workers will do which jobs? How quickly can they move a house through the line from start to finish?

Related Jobs

Mathematicians; engineering technicians; science technicians; architects, except landscape and naval; other engineers

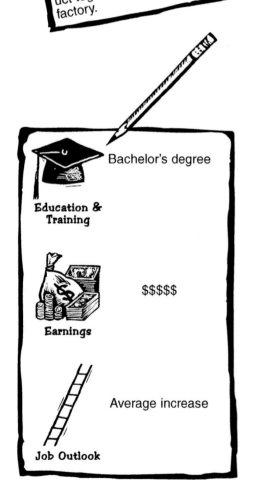

Bachelor's degree

Education & Training

$$$$$

Earnings

Average increase

Job Outlook

Materials Engineers

On the Job
These engineers develop new kinds of metals, ceramics, and other materials to do special jobs. They also study and test metals to make new products, such as the materials now being used in "stealth bombers." They might also look for ways to make a metal stronger without making it heavier. Most of these engineers work in private industry and must wear protective clothing and goggles on the job.

Something Extra
Materials engineers recently helped develop a new system for building ships and bridges that combines layers of steel and polyurethane. This new material makes the ships and bridges lighter, and helps them resist corrosion longer than if they were made of traditional materials.

Subjects to Study
Math, chemistry, physics, drafting, English, shop and technology courses

Discover More
Visit a pottery shop in your area, or arrange for a potter to visit your class. Try making a pot or vase using a pottery wheel. Does adjusting the speed of the wheel affect your work? Is it easier to make a small, rounded pot or a taller, slender one?

Related Jobs
Mathematicians; engineering technicians; science technicians; architects, except landscape and naval; other engineers

Bachelor's degree

Education & Training

$$$$–$$$$$

Earnings

Little change

Job Outlook

Mechanical Engineers

On the Job

Mechanical engineers design engines, machines, and other mechanical equipment. Some design rocket engines, robots, and refrigerators. They also design tools that other engineers use in their work. Most work for companies in the manufacturing industry. They use computers to help in their work.

Subjects to Study

Math, physics, drafting, computer science, shop and technology courses

Discover More

Hold a class "invention convention." Give everyone in your class the same set of objects. You might have some paper clips, wood pieces, rubber bands, strips of paper, glue, or other items. Now see what each of you can make from the items in half an hour. Whose invention is the most creative? The most useful? The most useless?

Related Jobs

Mathematicians; engineering technicians; science technicians; architects, except landscape and naval; and other engineers

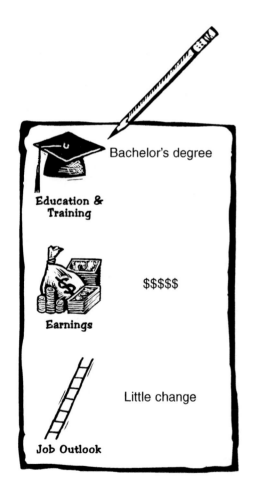

Education & Training
Bachelor's degree

Earnings
$$$$$

Job Outlook
Little change

Mining & Geological Engineers, Including Mining Safety Engineers

On the Job

These engineers find, remove, and prepare metals and minerals for industries. They make sure that mines, tunnels, and open pits are safe for workers and that mining operations don't damage the environment. Many specialize in mining one mineral, such as gold or coal. Some design new mining equipment. They may work in very dangerous conditions.

Something Extra

Mining is dirty, dangerous work. Sometimes gases underground make it downright deadly. In the 1800s, miners carried canaries in cages down into the mines with them. As long as the canary was alive and well, the miners knew the air was clean. If the bird died, they hurried back to the surface. Today, mining companies use sophisticated monitors to measure air quality. The monitors are more reliable and a lot easier on the bird population.

Subjects to Study

Math, physics, geology, chemistry, environmental science, drafting, shop and technology courses, computer skills

Discover More

Geology is the study of the earth. Try making a collection of rocks from your area. Can you identify them? What do they tell you about the ground under your feet?

Related Jobs

Mathematicians; engineering technicians; science technicians; architects, except landscape and naval; and other engineers

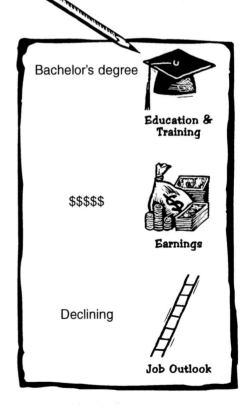

Bachelor's degree

Education & Training

$$$$$

Earnings

Declining

Job Outlook

Nuclear Engineers

On the Job

Nuclear engineers study nuclear energy and radiation. They design and operate nuclear power plants that provide electricity and power Navy ships. Other nuclear engineers develop nuclear weapons or study uses of radiation in industry and medicine. Many work for the federal government.

Subjects to Study

Math, chemistry, physics, drafting, biology, environmental studies, computer science, shop and technology courses

Discover More

Nuclear workers deal with properties of physics. Try this physics experiment. Take an empty soup can with the lid removed. Poke a hole in the side of the can near the bottom. Watching out for sharp edges, hold your finger over the hole and fill the can with water. Now turn out the lights and put a flashlight over the top of the can. Take your finger off the hole and watch the water pour out. Did you bend the light?

Related Jobs

Mathematicians; engineering technicians; science technicians; architects, except landscape and naval; and other engineers

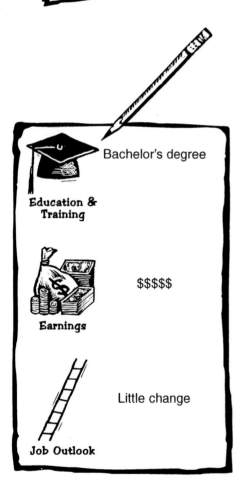

Education & Training
Bachelor's degree

Earnings
$$$$$

Job Outlook
Little change

Petroleum Engineers

On the Job

Petroleum engineers look for oil and natural gas and find the best ways to get it from the earth. Many work in states that have large deposits of fossil fuels, such as Texas, Oklahoma, Louisiana, and California. Some work at offshore oil-drilling sites. Others work in oil-producing countries such as Saudi Arabia.

Something Extra

In the 1980s, when Iraq invaded the tiny country of Kuwait, it made headlines around the world. Why? Many people believe it's because Kuwait is a major supplier of oil. A coalition of United Nations troops forced the Iraqis to retreat, but not before the invaders had set fire to several of Kuwait's oilfields. Those fires burned for years, creating an environmental mess that is still being removed.

Subjects to Study

Math, geology, chemistry, physics, environmental studies, biology, computer science, shop and technology courses

Discover More

Do you know why an oil spill is so bad for the environment? It's because oil floats on top of water instead of mixing in and dissolving. Try this experiment and see for yourself. Put food color in a bowl of water, then pour vegetable oil on top. Does the oil mix with the water?

Related Jobs

Mathematicians; engineering technicians; science technicians; architects, except landscape and naval; and other engineers

Bachelor's degree

Education & Training

$$$$$

Earnings

Declining

Job Outlook

Drafters

Something Extra

Drafters today use computer-aided drafting (CAD) systems to create drawings on a video screen. When CAD systems were first introduced, many people thought a new occupation (CAD operator) would result. But now it is obvious that people still need drafting skills to use the CAD system. Drafters today need both drawing and computer skills to do their jobs.

On the Job

Drafters prepare the drawings used to build everything from spacecraft to bridges. Using rough sketches done by others, they produce detailed technical drawings with specific information to create a finished product. Drafters use handbooks, tables, calculators, and computers to do their work. Many specialize in architecture, electronics, or aeronautics.

Education & Training

Voc/tech training

Earnings

$$$$

Job Outlook

Little change

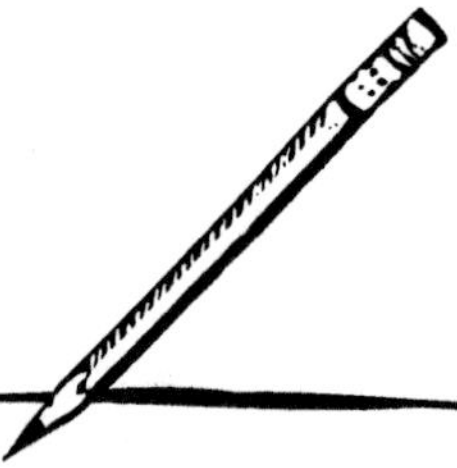

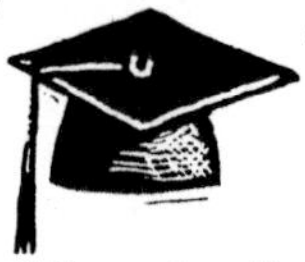

Subjects to Study

Math, physics, drafting, art and design courses, computer skills, English, shop and technology courses

Discover More

Try making your own drawing of a building or some kind of machine. You can use either paper and pencil or a computer drawing program. You can find books about drafting at the library.

Related Jobs

Architects, except landscape and naval; landscape architects; designers; engineers; engineering technicians; science technicians; surveyors, cartographers, photogrammetrists, and surveying technicians

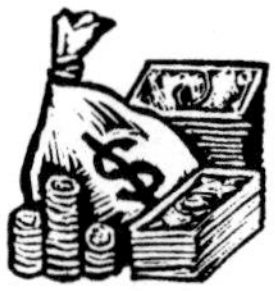

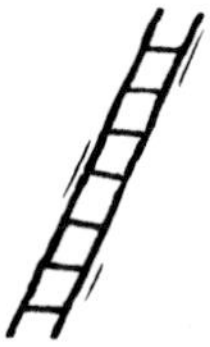

Engineering Technicians

On the Job

Engineering technicians use science, engineering, and math to solve problems for businesses. They help engineers and scientists with experiments and develop models of new equipment. Some supervise production workers or check the quality of products. Like engineers, they specialize in an area such as mechanics, electronics, or chemicals. Some may be exposed to hazards from equipment, chemicals, or toxic materials.

Something Extra

Manufacturing a product efficiently involves a lot of planning and testing. In 1895, King C. Gillette, a Boston bottle-cap salesman, came up with the idea of a disposable razor blade. He spent eight years developing the methods to mass-produce his product for sale to the public. Today, the company he founded is worth millions, and most Americans have used his invention at one time or another.

Subjects to Study

Math, physics, chemistry, electronics, shop and technology courses, drafting

Discover More

What's the simplest way to boil an egg? Easy, right? Just put the egg in a pan of boiling water and cook it. Now think about the reverse. How complicated can you make the job? On paper, draw an egg-boiling machine. Make it as complicated and ridiculous as you can.

Related Jobs

Science technicians; drafters; surveyors, cartographers, photogrammetrists, and surveying technicians; broadcast and sound engineering technicians and radio operators

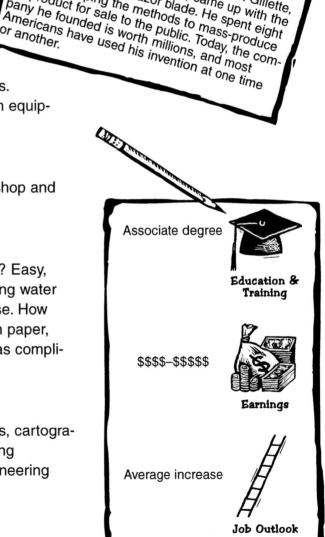

Associate degree

Education & Training

$$$$–$$$$$

Earnings

Average increase

Job Outlook

Agricultural & Food Scientists

On the Job

Agricultural scientists study farm crops and animals. They look for ways to control pests and weeds safely, increase crop yields with less labor, and save water and soil. They may specialize in plant, soil, or animal science. Many work outdoors in all kinds of weather. Food scientists work in the food processing industry, at universities, and for the government. They look for new food sources and preservatives and help ensure that our country's food supply is safe.

Subjects to Study

Biology, environmental science, physics, chemistry, communication skills, math, business, life sciences, nutrition, home economics

Discover More

Set up a growing experiment of your own. Choose a plant and get a package of seeds at a garden center. Now plant the seeds in four containers. Put two containers on a sunny windowsill and two in a shady spot. Water one in the window and one in the shade every day. Water the other two only once every four or five days. Which seeds grow best?

Related Jobs

Biological scientists; chemists and materials scientists; conservation scientists and foresters; farmers, ranchers, and agricultural managers; veterinarians; landscape architects

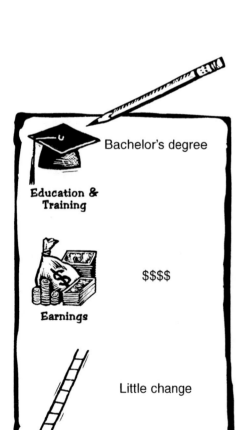

Education & Training
Bachelor's degree

Earnings
$$$$

Job Outlook
Little change

Biological Scientists

On the Job

Biological scientists study living things and their environment. They do research, develop new medicines, increase crop amounts, and improve the environment. Some study specialty areas such as viruses, ocean life, plant life, or animal life. They may work in company, college, or government labs, or as high school biology teachers.

Subjects to Study

Math, biology, botany, chemistry, physics, computer science, environmental studies

Discover More

Study the effects of acid rain on plant life. Get two small potted plants from a garden center. Keep them in the same place. Water one daily with regular tap water. Water the other with "acid rain" you make by adding a half teaspoon of white vinegar to two and a half teaspoons of tap water. Which plant grows better?

Related Jobs

Medical scientists, agricultural and food scientists, conservation scientists and foresters, physicians and surgeons, dentists, and veterinarians

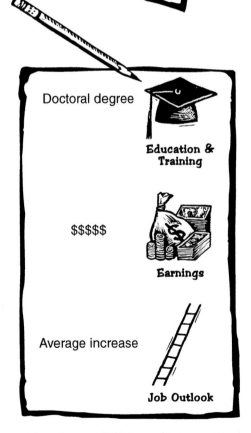

Doctoral degree

Education & Training

$$$$$

Earnings

Average increase

Job Outlook

Medical Scientists

On the Job

Medical scientists research human diseases in order to improve human health. Most medical scientists do basic research to learn more about viruses, bacteria, and other infectious diseases. Then this information is used to develop vaccines, medicines, and treatments for many diseases.

Subjects to Study

Chemistry, biology, math, physics, computer science

Discover More

Take a walk in the woods or the park and look for piles of leaves and fallen tree limbs and sticks. Notice that at the bottom of the piles, the leaves and sticks have started to crumble and fall apart. What causes this? Special microbes such as bacteria eat up dead material such as leaves and sticks and turn it into a powder called compost. Take some of the compost home and put it on your houseplants or in your garden. Does it help your plants grow bigger?

Related Jobs

Biological scientists, agricultural and food scientists, physicians and surgeons, dentists, veterinarians

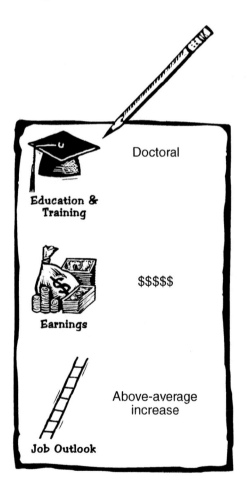

Education & Training
Doctoral

Earnings
$$$$$

Job Outlook
Above-average increase

Conservation Scientists & Foresters

On the Job

Foresters and conservation scientists manage, use, and protect natural resources such as water, wood, and wildlife. Foresters supervise the use of timber for lumber companies. Range managers oversee and protect range lands so that the environment is not damaged. Soil conservationists help farmers save the soil, water, and other natural resources. All of these workers spend time outdoors in all kinds of weather.

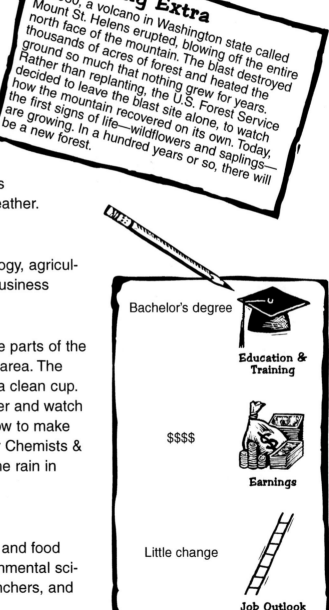

Something Extra

In 1980, a volcano in Washington state called Mount St. Helens erupted, blowing off the entire north face of the mountain. The blast destroyed thousands of acres of forest and heated the ground so much that nothing grew for years. Rather than replanting, the U.S. Forest Service decided to leave the blast site alone, to watch how the mountain recovered on its own. Today, the first signs of life—wildflowers and saplings— are growing. In a hundred years or so, there will be a new forest.

Subjects to Study

Math, chemistry, biology, botany, ecology, agriculture, computer science, economics, business

Discover More

Acid rain is a serious problem in some parts of the U.S. You can test for acid rain in your area. The next time it rains, collect rainwater in a clean cup. Put a strip of testing paper in the water and watch it change colors. (For directions on how to make testing paper, see "Discover More" for Chemists & Materials Scientists on page 71.) Is the rain in your area acidic?

Related Jobs

Environmental engineers; agricultural and food scientists; biological scientists; environmental scientists and geoscientists; farmers, ranchers, and agricultural managers

Bachelor's degree

Education & Training

$$$$

Earnings

Little change

Job Outlook

Atmospheric Scientists

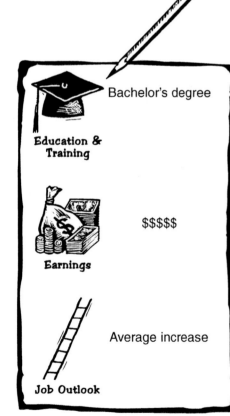

Education & Training

Bachelor's degree

Earnings

$$$$$

Job Outlook

Average increase

On the Job

Atmospheric scientists, commonly called meteorologists, study the atmosphere—the air that covers the earth—for its effects on our environment. The most well-known area of their work is weather forecasting. They also study trends in the earth's climate and apply their research to air-pollution control, air and sea transportation, and defense. Meteorologists often work nights, weekends, and holidays at weather stations.

Subjects to Study

Math, chemistry, physics, computer science, statistics, environmental science

Discover More

Contact a local TV station in your area and ask to become one of its "weather watchers." Hang a thermometer outside—a little way away from your home. Take daily readings. Place a large, rimmed dish on a flat surface outside to measure rain or snowfall. Call your reports in to the TV station and watch the weather report for your information.

Related Jobs

Environmental scientists and geoscientists; physicists and astronomers; mathematicians; civil engineers, chemical engineers, environmental engineers

Chemists & Materials Scientists

On the Job

Chemists and materials scientists look for and use new information about chemicals and other materials. They develop new paints, fibers, adhesives, drugs, and other products. They develop processes that save energy and reduce pollution. They make improvements in agriculture, medicine, and food processing. Most work in manufacturing firms or teach at colleges and universities. Their work can be dangerous.

Subjects to Study

Math, physics, chemistry, biology, computer science, English, business

Discover More

Make your own acid-testing paper. Boil red cabbage leaves for 15 minutes. Drain the leaves, saving the water. Cut a paper towel into strips and soak the strips in the cabbage water. Spread the strips out on newspaper to dry, then use them to test for acidity. Dip the strips into liquids. If they turn pink, the liquid is an acid. If they turn green, it is a base.

Related Jobs

Agricultural and food scientists, biological scientists, medical scientists, chemical engineers, materials engineers, physicists and astronomers, science technicians

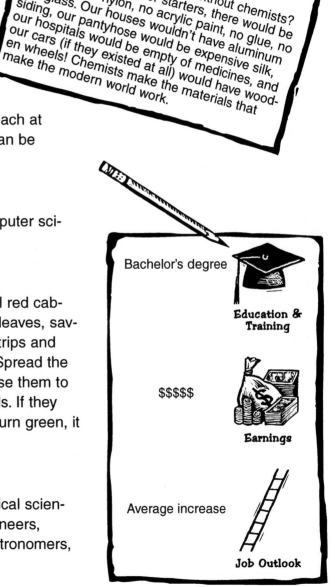

Something Extra

What would the world be like without chemists? It's hard to imagine. For starters, there would be no plastic, no nylon, no acrylic paint, no glue, no fiberglass. Our houses wouldn't have aluminum siding, our pantyhose would be expensive silk, our hospitals would be empty of medicines, and our cars (if they existed at all) would have wooden wheels! Chemists make the materials that make the modern world work.

Bachelor's degree

Education & Training

$$$$$

Earnings

Average increase

Job Outlook

Environmental Scientists & Geoscientists

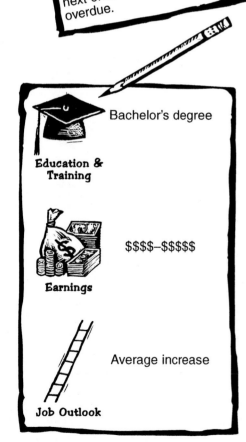

Education & Training
Bachelor's degree

Earnings
$$$$–$$$$$

Job Outlook
Average increase

On the Job

Environmental scientists and geoscientists study the earth and humans' impact on it. Some search for oil, natural gas, minerals, and underground water. Others, such as oceanographers, study the world's oceans and coastal waters. All of these scientists play an important role in cleaning up the earth's environment, designing waste-disposal sites, and cleaning up polluted land and water.

Subjects to Study

Math, computer science, chemistry, physics, geology

Discover More

Earthquakes happen when tectonic plates of the earth's surface move. You can see the same effect by cracking the shell of a hard-boiled egg. The thin shell represents the earth's crust, moving around on the slippery mantle. Move the pieces of shell around. What happens when they collide? Earthquake!

Related Jobs

Engineering technicians; science technicians; petroleum engineers; surveyors; cartographers, photogrammetrists, and surveying technicians; physicists and astronomers; chemists and materials scientists; atmospheric scientists

Physicists & Astronomers

On the Job

Physicists study the matter that makes up the universe. They also study forces of nature such as gravity and nuclear interaction. They use their studies to design medical equipment, electronic devices, and lasers. Astronomers study the moon, sun, planets, galaxies, and stars. Their knowledge is used in space flight and navigation. Many teach in colleges and universities.

Subjects to Study

Math, physics, chemistry, computer science, geology, astronomy

Discover More

Try this simple experiment: Set up a one-foot plate of plexiglass on wooden blocks on a table, so that the plate is 1 to 3 inches above the table. Now put a handful of Rice Krispies® cereal on the table. Rub the top of the plexiglass quickly with a piece of wool. The cereal will stand on end, then "jump" from the table to the plexiglass and back again.

Related Jobs

Engineers; chemists and materials scientists; atmospheric scientists; environmental scientists and geoscientists; computer systems analysts, computer scientists, and database administrators; computer programmers; mathematicians

Something Extra

In the early 1940s, physicists working at a secret U.S. defense lab in Los Alamos, New Mexico, made a scientific breakthrough. They split an atom, setting off a chain of events that led directly to the atomic bombs dropped by the U.S. during World War II on Hiroshima and Nagasaki, Japan. Several of those scientists later regretted their work on the bomb. For better or worse, they assured their place in the history books.

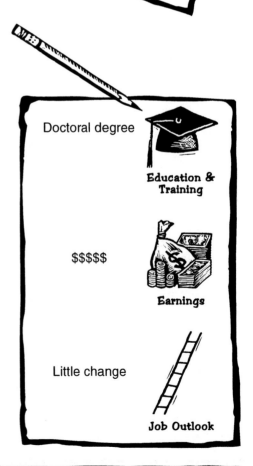

Doctoral degree

Education & Training

$$$$$

Earnings

Little change

Job Outlook

Economists

On the Job

Economists study how people use resources like land, labor, raw materials, and machinery to make products. They use their studies to advise businesses and government agencies.

Subjects to Study

Math, English, economics, business, computer science, accounting

Discover More

Do you ever hear your parents complain about the rising price of gasoline? Keep track of the price of premium gas at your local station each day over the course of several weeks. Plot the price changes on a graph. Are there days each week when the prices are the highest? On days when the prices are higher, are there any related events in the news that might have caused the price spike?

Related Jobs

Accountants and auditors; actuaries; financial analysts and personal financial advisors; financial managers; insurance underwriters; loan counselors and officers; purchasing managers, buyers, and purchasing agents; management analysts; market and survey researchers

Education & Training
Master's to Bachelor's degree to Doctoral degree

Earnings
$$–$$$$$

Job Outlook
Average increase

Market and Survey Researchers

On the Job

Market and survey researchers tell businesses about the best ways to sell a product based on information they gather through interviews and questionnaires. Market research analysts might also develop advertising brochures and commercials, sales plans, and product promotions such as rebates and giveaways. Some analysts are self-employed and travel to work for different clients.

Subjects to Study

Economics, psychology, English, sociology

Discover More

Take a survey in your class. Buy several different kinds of tortilla chips, then do a blind taste test. Blindfold several classmates, then have them taste the chips. Keep a tally of which ones they prefer. Ask why they prefer one brand over another. These are the kinds of market surveys that researchers perform.

Related Jobs

Economists, psychologists, sociologists, statisticians, urban and regional planners

Something Extra

A market researcher might spend her day on the telephone asking restaurants why they didn't buy more of a certain brand of crackers. Or she might invite groups of consumers to the office in the evening to test new products and give their opinions. Maybe you or your parents have been approached at the mall by someone with a clipboard wanting to ask your opinions. Market survey companies often have offices in malls because they can easily find lots of people to survey there.

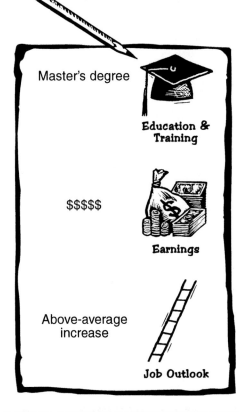

Master's degree

Education & Training

$$$$$

Earnings

Above-average increase

Job Outlook

Psychologists

On the Job

Psychologists study the way people think, feel, and act. They work to understand, explain, and change people's behavior. They may conduct training programs, do market research, or provide counseling. They may also work with mentally ill individuals. Psychologists work with schools, businesses, and health-care centers to help people deal with stress and changes in their lives, such as divorce and aging.

Subjects to Study

English, psychology, statistics, communication skills, biology, physical sciences, computer science, writing skills

Discover More

Try this experiment: Get a small fish in a bowl. Feed it at the same time every day. Each time you feed the fish, just before you put the food in the water, tap on the side of the bowl. Soon, when your fish sees you tap on the bowl, it will look for food on the water's surface. That's called *conditioning*.

Related Jobs

Clergy, counselors, physicians and surgeons, social workers, teachers—special education

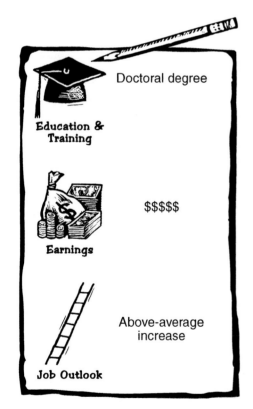

Education & Training
Doctoral degree

Earnings
$$$$$

Job Outlook
Above-average increase

Urban & Regional Planners

On the Job

Urban and regional planners develop programs that encourage growth in certain communities and regions. They make plans for the best use of land and study the area's schools, hospitals, parks, roads, and other facilities to see if they meet the needs of the community. They also deal with legal codes and environmental issues. They often travel to inspect the features of the land to help in their planning.

Something Extra

Have you heard the term *planned community*? Whereas most cities simply grow as more people move in and open businesses, planned communities are plotted in detail before the first house is built. The Disney Corporation built a planned community in Florida that's made to look like an old-fashioned town. It's called Celebration, and it's an easy day's drive from Disney World.

Subjects to Study

Math, English, public speaking, government, psychology, writing skills, computer science, sociology

Discover More

Plan a town on graph paper. Include all the roads, houses, schools, churches, and parks. Don't forget hospitals, police and fire stations, gas stations, a shopping district, and a town center.

Related Jobs

Architects, except landscape and naval; landscape architects; civil engineers; environmental engineers

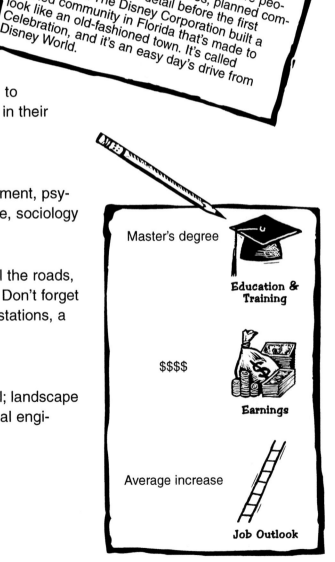

Master's degree

Education & Training

$$$$

Earnings

Average increase

Job Outlook

Social Scientists, Other

On the Job

There are many kinds of social scientists. Anthropologists study the origins and development of human society, ancient ways of life, language, tools, and archaeological remains around the world. Geographers study how physical geography affects politics and culture. Historians research and interpret the past. Political scientists study political systems and public policy. Sociologists study social behavior and groups as well as religious, political, and business organizations.

Subjects to Study

English, history, political science, sociology, statistics, mathematics

Discover More

Design a study to find out your classmates' favorite menu from your school cafeteria. Get a list of the school lunches served in the past month, then write a questionnaire asking students to rank their top three and their least-favorite menu. Ask your school newspaper to run the survey. Tally the results, then pass them along to the cafeteria staff!

Related Jobs

Economists; lawyers; statisticians; news analysts, reporters and correspondents; social workers; teachers; counselors

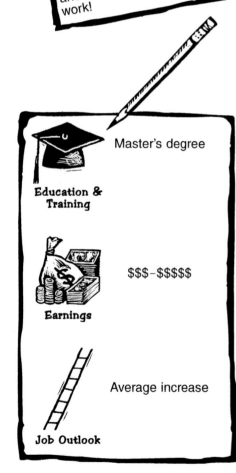

Master's degree

Education & Training

$$$-$$$$$

Earnings

Average increase

Job Outlook

Science Technicians

On the Job

Science technicians use science and math to solve research problems. They also investigate, invent, and help improve products. They set up, operate, and maintain lab equipment, monitor experiments, and record results. They may specialize in agriculture, biology, chemistry, or other sciences. Some work outdoors and may be exposed to chemicals or radiation.

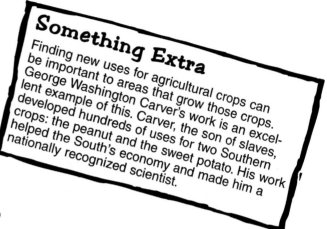

Something Extra

Finding new uses for agricultural crops can be important to areas that grow those crops. George Washington Carver's work is an excellent example of this. Carver, the son of slaves, developed hundreds of uses for two Southern crops: the peanut and the sweet potato. His work helped the South's economy and made him a nationally recognized scientist.

Subjects to Study

Math, physics, chemistry, biology, geology, shop and technology courses, computer science

Discover More

Science technicians need good eye-hand coordination and a good ability to follow written instructions. You can hone your skills by putting together model cars or model ships. Are the directions in the kit clear and easy to follow? How would you change them to make them clearer?

Related Jobs

Engineering technicians, broadcast and sound engineering technicians and radio operators, drafters, clinical laboratory technologists and technicians, diagnostic medical sonographers, radiologic technologists and technicians

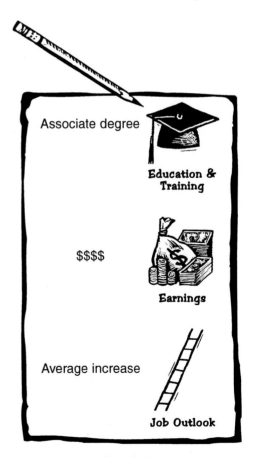

Associate degree

Education & Training

$$$$

Earnings

Average increase

Job Outlook

Clergy

On the Job

Clergy members help people in churches, synagogues, temples, and mosques. They might be Buddhist, Christian, Jewish, or Muslim, or belong to another faith. They may lead worshipers in prayer, deliver sermons, counsel people, work in hospitals, and perform weddings, baptisms, Bar/Bat Mitzvahs, and funerals. Some serve as missionaries far from home; others live and work in monasteries or schools.

Subjects to Study

English, writing skills, speech, social sciences, fine arts, music, foreign languages

Discover More

What kind of clergy work in your faith community? Volunteer to help out one afternoon a week. You might be surprised at the variety of jobs your pastor, priest, rabbi, or cleric must perform.

Related Jobs

Social workers, psychologists, teachers, counselors

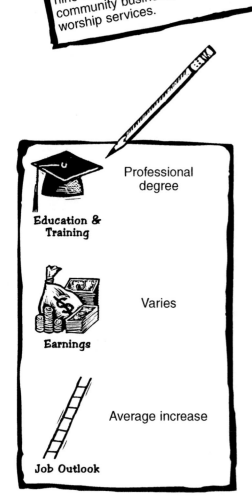

Education & Training
Professional degree

Earnings
Varies

Job Outlook
Average increase

Protestant Ministers

On the Job

Protestant ministers help people in churches and communities. They write and give sermons, counsel people, and perform ceremonies such as baptisms, marriages, and funerals. Ministers are on call for emergencies 24 hours a day, seven days a week. Most spend four weekdays each week in the church office, plus Sundays at church. Some ministers teach in seminaries and colleges. Some ministers must move every few years.

Subjects to Study

English, writing skills, speech, social sciences, fine arts, music, foreign languages

Discover More

Call your local church and ask if you can help out in the church office after school. You might answer the phone, make copies, or help type the church newsletter. Spend time watching the minister work, and don't forget to ask a lot of questions!

Related Jobs

Social workers, psychologists, teachers, counselors

Something Extra

Do you think ministers work only on Sundays? Think again! If a church member is sick or dying, the minister must visit at home or in the hospital. If a committee is meeting to plan a bake sale, the minister is expected to participate. If the church pipes freeze, it's often the minister who must call the plumber. Ministers are on call 24 hours a day, seven days a week. Their church and congregation are an important part of their lives.

Bachelor's degree +

Education & Training

$$$$

Earnings

Average increase

Job Outlook

Rabbis

On the Job

Rabbis work in Jewish congregations, teaching Jewish law and tradition, counseling people, and conducting services such as weddings and funerals. They give sermons on the Sabbath and on Jewish holidays. Rabbis may be on call 24 hours a day, seven days a week. Some teach in seminaries and colleges or write for religious publications. Many rabbis participate in community activities.

Subjects to Study

English, writing skills, speech, social sciences, fine arts, music, foreign languages

Discover More

You can practice your public-speaking skills by giving a talk to your class on something that interests you. Do some research to find information to back up your points. Can you hold your audience's attention?

Related Jobs

Social workers, psychologists, teachers, counselors

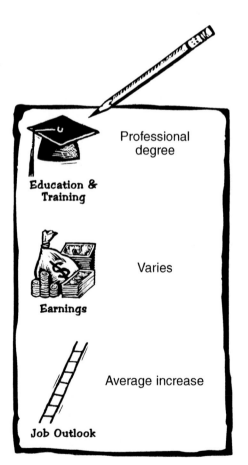

Education & Training
Professional degree

Earnings
Varies

Job Outlook
Average increase

Roman Catholic Priests

On the Job

Roman Catholic priests in local congregations write and give sermons,
counsel people, and perform baptisms, weddings, and funerals. They
may be on call 24 hours a day,
seven days a week, and many live
in parish rectories. All priests are
male; they must take a vow never
to marry. Priests also may be
missionaries in foreign countries,
live in monasteries, or teach in high schools,
colleges, or seminaries.

Something Extra

Being a priest means being part of an exclusive
order. In the Roman Catholic Church, only men
are allowed to be priests. Women may serve as
church leaders, deacons, or even as nuns, but
only men are priests. And not just any man can
serve: Priests must be unmarried. They do not
choose where they live, what churches they
serve, or even when they will retire. It takes a
special kind of devotion, and it's a lifelong commitment.

Subjects to Study

English, speech, social studies, Latin, foreign languages, psychology, sociology, history

Discover More

Spend a day with your parish priest. What kinds of
jobs does he do? Ask him about the hardest part
of the job and the most rewarding. He can tell you
about the training you need to be a priest.

Related Jobs

Social workers, psychologists, teachers, counselors

Master's degree

**Education &
Training**

$$$$

Earnings

Above Average
increase

Job Outlook

Counselors

On the Job

Counselors help people with their problems; the work they do depends on the people they serve. School counselors help students with personal, social, and behavioral problems. College placement counselors help students decide on careers and find jobs. Rehabilitation counselors help people with disabilities and addictions. Employment counselors help people decide what kinds of jobs they want and help them find work. Most counselors hold a Master's degree.

Subjects to Study

English, speech, psychology, social studies, computer science, writing and communication skills

Discover More

Talk to your school counselor about this job. Find out what professional organizations he or she belongs to. Write to one of those organizations or visit their Web sites to learn more about counseling.

Related Jobs

Teachers; social and human service assistants; social workers; psychologists; physicians and surgeons; registered nurses; clergy; occupational therapists; human resources, training and labor relations managers and specialists

Education & Training
Master's degree

Earnings
$$$–$$$$

Job Outlook
Above-average increase

Probational Officers & Correctional Treatment Specialists

On the Job

Many people who are convicted of crimes are placed on probation instead of being sent to jail. Probation officers supervise these people, making sure they stay out of trouble. Correctional treatment specialists work with people in jails and prisons, evaluating their progress, planning special programs, and counseling offenders. All of these specialists work with criminal offenders, some of whom are dangerous.

Something Extra

What happens when a man commits a crime in Ohio but is captured in Florida? Or a woman is convicted in Utah but will serve her sentence in Illinois? Sometimes, prisoners are simply handcuffed and put on a regular airplane—with a guard, of course. But what about prisoners who are too dangerous for commercial flights? They have their own airline! The U.S. Marshals Service operates a fleet of planes they use to transport prisoners from one place to another. The Justice Prisoner and Alien Transportation System (JPATS) operates regular flights to 40 cities around the country. They probably don't show in-flight movies (and certainly not *Con Air*)!

Subjects to Study

English, speech, psychology, social studies, criminal justice, sociology

Discover More

Call your state's Department of Corrections, explain your interest in the job, and ask to interview a probation officer. What are the best parts of the job? What are the worst? Does the officer work from 9 to 5, or is he or she on call 24 hours a day? You can get more information on this job from the American Probation and Parole Association at www.appa-net.org.

Related Jobs

Social workers, social and human service assistants, counselors, police and detectives

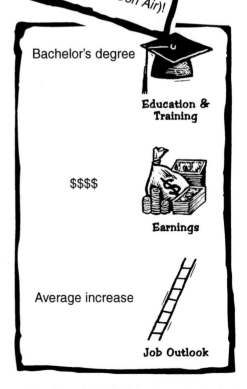

Bachelor's degree

Education & Training

$$$$

Earnings

Average increase

Job Outlook

Social & Human Service Assistants

On the Job

Social and human service assistants are in the business of helping people. They might work in a food bank, train mentally handicapped adults to do a job, or supervise teenagers in a group in a day program. They evaluate clients' needs, help them fill out the paperwork to get benefits, keep records, and file reports with social service agencies. They work in offices, hospitals, group homes, and private agencies.

Subjects to Study

English, speech, psychology, sociology, writing skills

Discover More

You can check out the social service field by volunteering at a food bank, an adult day-care center, a mental-health institution, or a community center in your neighborhood.

Related Jobs

Social workers; clergy; counselors; childcare workers; occupational therapist assistants and aides; physical therapy assistants and aides; nursing, psychiatric and home health aides

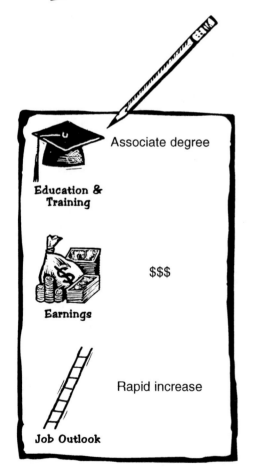

Associate degree

Education & Training

$$$

Earnings

Rapid increase

Job Outlook

Social Workers

On the Job

Social workers work with people to help them find solutions to their problems. They might help a client find housing, a job, or health care. They deal with issues like child abuse, unplanned pregnancy, alcohol or drug abuse, and criminal behavior. They help people cope with serious illnesses and crisis situations. They may work in hospitals, social service agencies, group homes, government agencies, or schools.

Something Extra

Do people tell you you're a good listener? Do you enjoy helping your friends figure out solutions to their problems? Are you patient and good at puzzles? If so, social work might be a good field for you. A social worker's job is never the same from day to day. On Monday, you might help an elderly client find affordable housing, on Tuesday counsel a pregnant teenager, and on Wednesday visit an abused child in a foster home.

Subjects to Study

English, communication skills, psychology, biology, sociology, history, foreign languages

Discover More

Talk to the counselor at your school about this job. Ask about the training and the kinds of situations he or she deals with on a daily basis. Ask if he or she can help you set up a peer-counseling service.

Related Jobs

Clergy, counselors, probation officers and correctional treatment specialists, psychologists, social and human services assistants

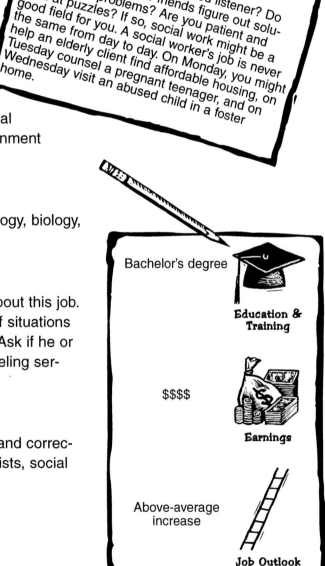

Bachelor's degree

Education & Training

$$$$

Earnings

Above-average increase

Job Outlook

Court Reporters

On the Job

These workers put spoken words into written form. They make notes using shorthand or a stenotype machine, which prints shorthand. Then they type up the notes so that other people can read them. This is how court reporters record all statements made during court or government proceedings. Sometimes they type as fast as 200 words per minute. Because they are the only ones recording what is being said, they must be accurate.

Subjects to Study

English, stenographic skills, word processing, spelling, foreign languages, typing, computer skills, communication skills, listening skills

Discover More

Watch an actual court case on TV. Find the court reporter in the courtroom and watch what he or she does. Listen to all the statements made by the lawyers, witnesses, and judge. Try to imagine correctly recording every word they say.

Related Jobs

Secretaries and administrative assistants; medical transcriptionists; receptionists and information clerks; human resources assistants, except payroll and timekeeping; paralegals and legal assistants

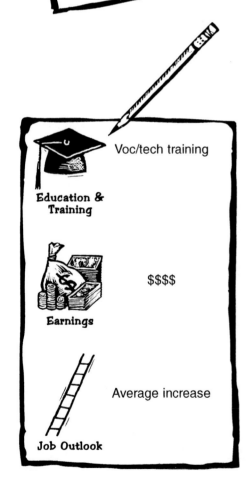

Voc/tech training

Education & Training

$$$$

Earnings

Average increase

Job Outlook

Judges, Magistrates & Other Judicial Workers

On the Job

Judges, magistrates, and other judicial workers oversee trials and make sure that everyone follows the court rules. They preside over all types of cases, from traffic tickets to murder trials. In court cases without a jury, the judge decides the verdict. All judges work for the government, either local, state, or federal. Nearly all judges have law degrees.

Something Extra

The U.S. Supreme Court is the highest court in the U.S. Its nine members decide on the cases that set the laws for the rest of the country, and their word is the final ruling. Rulings from the Supreme Court have established the rights of criminal suspects to obtain a lawyer, a woman's right to seek an abortion, and the rights of all students to attend desegregated schools. In 2000, the Supreme Court even helped decide the election of President George W. Bush, halting the recount of votes requested by Bush's opponent, Al Gore.

Subjects to Study

English, writing skills, public speaking, government, history, foreign languages, psychology, computer science, logic

Discover More

Have a mock trial in your social studies class. Different students can be lawyers for the prosecution and the defense, the defendant, the witnesses, the jury, and the judge. The judge has the final say about what can and cannot be presented.

Related Jobs

Counselors; lawyers; paralegals and legal assistants; private detectives and investigators

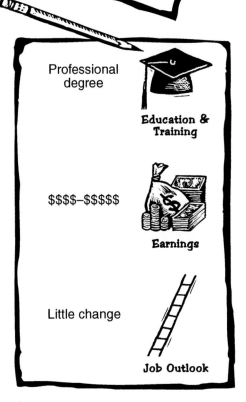

Professional degree

Education & Training

$$$$–$$$$$

Earnings

Little change

Job Outlook

Lawyers

On the Job

Lawyers give people advice about the law and their rights. They represent people in court, presenting evidence that supports a client's position, asking questions, and arguing their case. Lawyers must do research to find the information they need to support their cases. They must have good reading, writing, and speaking skills.

Subjects to Study

English, writing skills, public speaking, government, history, foreign languages, psychology, computer science, logic

Discover More

Organize a class debate. Pick a topic you feel strongly about, take a position, and argue your side. Be sure you do some research first—read articles and books on the topic and find out what other people think of it. Can you change your opponent's mind?

Related Jobs

Paralegals and legal assistants; judges, magistrates, and other judicial workers

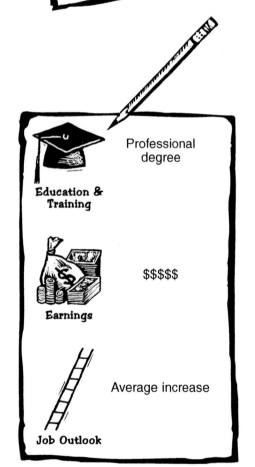

Education & Training
Professional degree

Earnings
$$$$$

Job Outlook
Average increase

Paralegals and Legal Assistants

On the Job

Paralegals help lawyers prepare their cases. They do research and write reports that lawyers use to present their arguments in court. They may meet with clients to get information about a case, but they do not argue cases in court or set fees. Some paralegals have a wide variety of tasks, while others specialize in one area of the law, such as tax law or publishing law.

Something Extra

Paralegals today use computers to do their research. Special software packages and the Internet put a world of information at their fingertips. They simply enter a topic and receive a list of all documents on that subject. They also use computers to organize the volumes of paper needed to support cases. These programs help today's paralegals do in one day work that used to take weeks!

Subjects to Study

English, business courses, keyboarding, computer and writing skills, foreign languages, logic

Discover More

Contact a law firm or a legal-aid society in your area. Ask to talk to a paralegal. Find out what his or her duties involve. Ask how he or she became interested in the occupation and what kind of training the job requires.

Related Jobs

Claims adjusters, appraisers, examiners, and investigators; occupational health and safety specialists and technicians

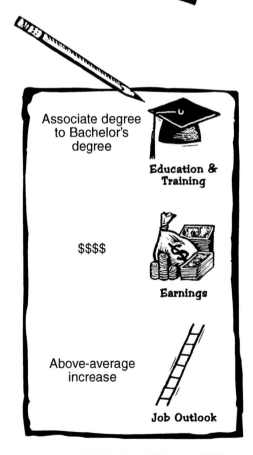

Associate degree to Bachelor's degree

Education & Training

$$$$

Earnings

Above-average increase

Job Outlook

Archivists, Curators & Museum Technicians

On the Job

These workers choose, buy, and care for collections of books, records, art, and other items for libraries and museums. The items might be coins, stamps, plants, paintings, sculptures, or even animals. They may also work with records on paper, film, or computers. They plan exhibits, education programs, and tours. Most work with the public and may travel to add to their collections.

Subjects to Study

English, speech, history, art, chemistry, physics, business, accounting

Discover More

Visit a museum or zoo in your area. Ask the tour guide about the collection. Who decides what to buy for the collection? Where do the exhibits come from? What would you like to see in the exhibit that's not already there?

Related Jobs

Artists and related workers; librarians; social scientists, other

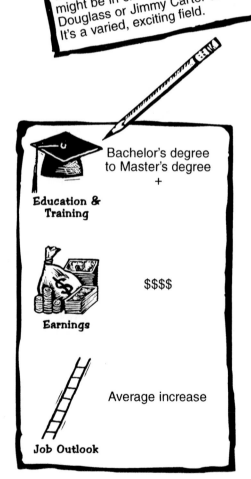

Education & Training
Bachelor's degree to Master's degree +

Earnings
$$$$

Job Outlook
Average increase

Instructional Coordinators

On the Job

Instructional coordinators develop teaching materials, train teachers, and assess school programs. They often specialize in a specific subject, such as language arts, math, or gifted and talented programs. Most work for school districts or independent consulting firms, and they spend time traveling between schools. The work can be stressful and involve long hours. Many instructional coordinators are former teachers and school administrators.

Subjects to Study

English, literature, social sciences, business, psychology, computer science, foreign languages

Discover More

Call your school district's main offices and ask to interview the instructional coordinator or curriculum specialist. Does that person work only during the school year, or year-round? What are the best and worst parts of the job?

Related Jobs

Teachers; education administrators; counselors; human resources, training and labor relations managers and specialists

Something Extra

What happens when a school district's students aren't passing standardized tests? Most often, the district calls in a specialist to help find and solve the problem. As schools across the country place more and more emphasis on these tests, this job field is expected to grow rapidly. But the specialist is employed only as long as the district sees good results!

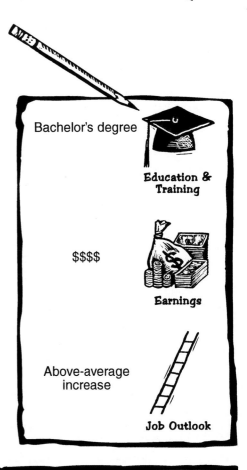

Bachelor's degree

Education & Training

$$$$

Earnings

Above-average increase

Job Outlook

Librarians

On the Job

Librarians help people use the library and its materials. They help people find the books they need and fill out applications for library cards. They may give talks on how to use the library or read to children during special programs. Some manage other workers, prepare budgets, and order materials for their libraries. They may shelve books, update files, and design special displays.

Subjects to Study

English, literature, accounting, social sciences, business, psychology, computer science

Discover More

Take a tour of your school's library. Does your librarian order the books for your library? How does he or she decide which books to order? What guidelines does your school district provide? Ask if you can look through the publishers' catalogs and circle some titles that look interesting to you.

Related Jobs

Archivists, curators, and museum technicians; teachers; computer systems analysts, database administrators, and computer scientists

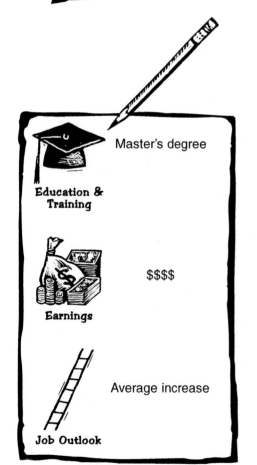

Education & Training
Master's degree

Earnings
$$$$

Job Outlook
Average increase

Library Technicians

On the Job

Library technicians help librarians order, code, shelve, and organize library materials. They help people find materials and information. Some help maintain audiovisual equipment, prepare displays, and supervise other support staff. They answer questions, help patrons check out materials, and may send out notices to people with overdue books. Some work in school libraries, helping students find information they need for reports.

Subjects to Study

English, literature, accounting, computer skills, business courses

Discover More

Check your local library for volunteer opportunities. You might be put to work shelving books, helping at the checkout counter, supervising small children during reading programs, or straightening up at the end of the day.

Related Jobs

Library assistants, clerical; information and record clerks; medical records and health information technicians

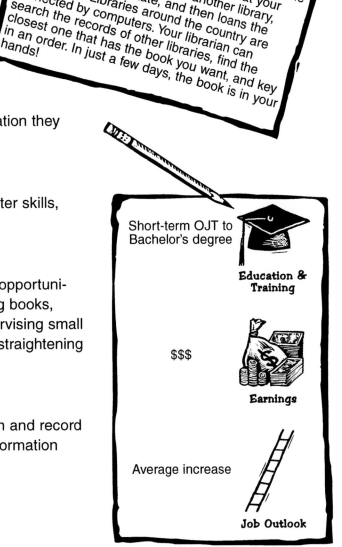

Something Extra

What happens when you want a book your library doesn't have? You can order it through the interlibrary loan system. This means that your library borrows the book from another library, usually one in your state, and then loans the book to you. Libraries around the country are connected by computers. Your librarian can search the records of other libraries, find the closest one that has the book you want, and key in an order. In just a few days, the book is in your hands!

Short-term OJT to Bachelor's degree

Education & Training

$$$

Earnings

Average increase

Job Outlook

Teacher Assistants

On the Job

Teacher assistants help children in the classroom and school cafeteria or on the playground and field trips. Sometimes they pay special attention to individual students or small groups who need more help with a subject. They help teachers by grading papers, keeping attendance records, typing, filing, ordering supplies, helping out in the computer lab, or preparing class lessons.

Subjects to Study

English, communication skills, office skills, computer skills, math, foreign languages, speech

Discover More

Volunteer to help care for younger children at your school, church, or a local day-care center or youth organization. You might help them with schoolwork, play games, or teach a craft.

Related Jobs

Teachers—preschool, kindergarten, elementary, middle, and secondary; teachers–special education; librarians; childcare workers; library technicians; library assistants, clerical; occupational therapist assistants and aides

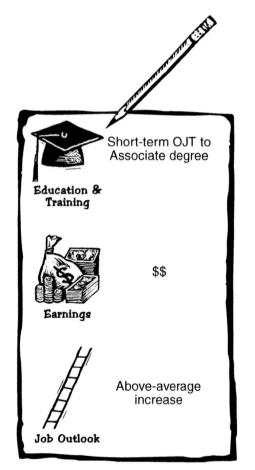

Education & Training
Short-term OJT to Associate degree

Earnings
$$

Job Outlook
Above-average increase

Teachers—Adult Literacy & Remedial & Self-Enrichment Education

On the Job

Adult education teachers work with people who want to update their job skills or prepare for the GED exam. They also teach writing, reading, and math—often in evening or weekend classes. Some work with adults who do not speak English. They may teach classes in job-related skills such as welding, health technology, and cosmetology. Some teach classes "just for fun," like yoga and meditation.

Something Extra

Did you know that a significant portion of the adult population in the U.S. cannot read? Even people who graduate from high school sometimes have trouble reading. This makes it very hard to get and hold a job, to pay bills, or even to get a driver's license. Without reading skills, it's nearly impossible to get ahead in today's society.

Subjects to Study

English, communication and writing skills, math, psychology, biology, physics, chemistry, history, social sciences, physical education, home economics or shop courses, computer science, foreign languages

Discover More

Call a local community college or high school and ask for the catalog of continuing-education courses. Find a class that interests you, then call the school and ask whether you can sit in on a session of that class.

Related Jobs

Teachers—preschool, kindergarten, elementary, middle, and secondary; teachers—special education; counselors; social workers; dancers and choreographers; artists and related workers; musicians, singers, and related workers

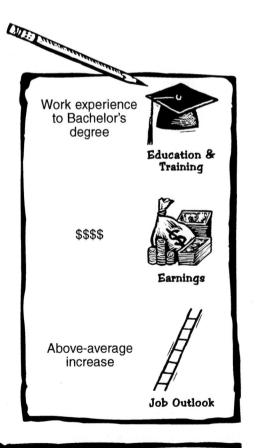

Work experience to Bachelor's degree

Education & Training

$$$$

Earnings

Above-average increase

Job Outlook

Teachers—Postsecondary

On the Job

Postsecondary teachers work at colleges, community colleges, universities, and research facilities. They specialize in one field, such as history, physics, or journalism. They do research and write articles and books about their findings. Most professors hold advanced degrees. While many schools do not hold classes during the summer months, faculty work year-round, preparing lectures, attending seminars, and conducting research.

Subjects to Study

English, math, communication and writing skills, speech, sciences, social sciences, foreign languages, computer science

Discover More

Visit a college campus and sit in on a class or two. Watch the professor and think about how the class resembles or differs from your classes at school. Talk to the professor after class and ask about the job.

Related Jobs

Teachers—preschool, kindergarten, elementary, middle, and secondary; education administrators; librarians; counselors; writers and editors; public relations specialists; management analysts

Education & Training
Bachelor's degree to Doctoral degree

Earnings
$$$$

Job Outlook
Rapid increase

Teachers—Preschool, Kindergarten, Elementary, Middle & Secondary

On the Job

Teachers help students learn in school. They plan lessons, prepare tests, grade papers, and write reports of students' progress. They meet with parents and school staff to talk about grades and problems. Some teach a specific grade; others teach one subject to students in many grades. Most work more than 40 hours a week. Some work second jobs during the summer months. Many supervise school activities such as clubs and sports teams.

Something Extra

Think about the challenges of being a working parent. You have to find someone to watch your kids while you are at work. This is hard enough during the school year, but in the summers and on Christmas break, it's especially tough. One of the things many teachers like about teaching is that they get the same days off as their kids. This cuts down on child-care costs and lets them plan vacations and activities with their kids.

Subjects to Study

English, social studies, math, sciences, psychology, foreign languages, computer science

Discover More

Talk with your school counselor about programs such as peer tutoring or cadet teaching in your school. You can help younger students who are having trouble with a subject or grade papers for a teacher.

Related Jobs

Teachers—postsecondary; counselors; teacher assistants; education administrators; librarians; child care workers; public relations specialists; social workers; athletes, coaches, umpires, and related workers

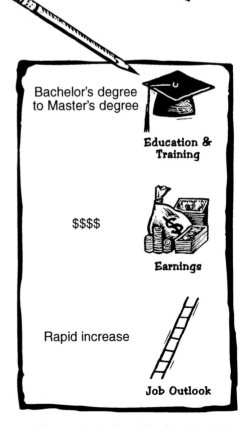

Bachelor's degree to Master's degree

Education & Training

$$$$

Earnings

Rapid increase

Job Outlook

Teachers–Special Education

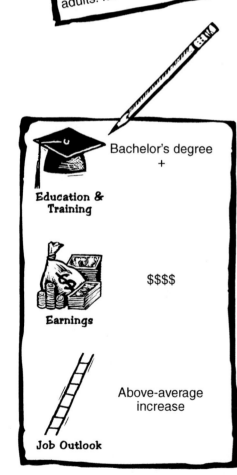

Education & Training — Bachelor's degree +

Earnings — $$$$

Job Outlook — Above-average increase

On the Job

Special education teachers work with students who have disabilities. Most work in elementary, middle, or high schools, but some work with toddlers and preschoolers. They prepare classes to meet their students' needs, grade papers, and write reports. They may teach academic studies or life skills. They meet with parents, counselors, school psychologists, and occupational or physical therapists to come up with the best school plan for each student.

Subjects to Study

English, social studies, math, sciences, psychology, foreign languages, computer science

Discover More

Arrange with your teacher to spend a day observing a special education class at your school. Watch how the teacher interacts with the students. You might be able to help out by reading to younger children or tutoring them.

Related Jobs

Psychologists; social workers; speech-language pathologists; audiologists; counselors; teacher assistants; occupational therapists; recreational therapists; teachers—preschool, kindergarten, elementary, middle, and secondary

Artists & Related Workers

On the Job

Artists use a variety of methods and materials to communicate through art. They might use oil paints, watercolors, pencils, clay, chalk, or even scrap metal to create artworks. Visual artists are usually called graphic artists or fine artists. Graphic artists use art to meet the needs of business clients, such as stores, ad agencies, and publishing firms. Fine artists create artwork to sell and display in museums or galleries. More than half are self-employed and must use good business skills to be successful.

Something Extra

When she was in her late 70s, a time when most other people are thinking of retirement, Grandma Moses decided to try her hand at a completely new job: She became an artist. This famous American painter recorded scenes of life on the farm. Her style, which resembles the way a child might paint, is known as *primitivism*.

Subjects to Study

Art, drawing, drafting, computer skills, English, communication skills, anatomy, business math

Discover More

The best way to prepare for this career is to take art classes, visit museums, study the styles of other artists, and practice, practice, practice.

Related Jobs

Architects, except landscape and naval; archivists, curators, and museum technicians; designers; landscape architects; photographers; computer software engineers; desktop publishers

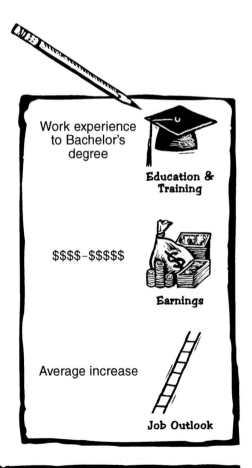

Work experience to Bachelor's degree

Education & Training

$$$$-$$$$$

Earnings

Average increase

Job Outlook

Designers

On the Job

Designers create things that are attractive and useful. They may design clothing, furniture, homes, cars, flowers, or new products for the home or office. They must decide what materials to use and consider fashion trends, safety, and cost. Designers work in all kinds of companies—auto manufacturers, furniture companies, publishing houses, ad agencies, design firms, flower shops—in several different industries. Many designers are self-employed.

Subjects to Study

Art, drawing, drafting, business, communication skills, English, computer skills

Discover More

On paper, redesign a room of your home. Check out magazines for ideas. Get paint and wallpaper samples from the hardware store. Will you recover the furniture in new fabric? Hang new drapes? Replace the flooring? Decide on a color scheme and draw the room.

Related Jobs

Artists and related workers; architects, except landscape and naval; engineers; landscape architects; photographers; computer software engineers; desktop publishers

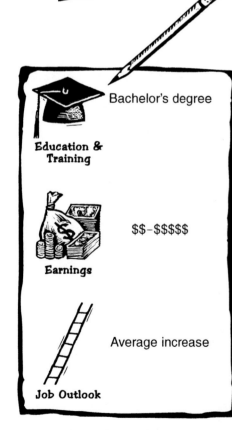

Education & Training
Bachelor's degree

Earnings
$$-$$$$$

Job Outlook
Average increase

Actors, Producers & Directors

On the Job

Actors, producers, and directors make words come alive through plays, TV shows, and films. Actors play characters, speaking the lines written in the script and adding their own movements. Directors choose plays and scripts, select the actors, and conduct rehearsals for productions. Producers arrange the financing and decide the size of the production and the budget. Directors and producers often work under tight deadlines and stressful conditions.

Subjects to Study

English, public speaking, drama, music, dance, art, photography, communication skills

Discover More

You can learn more about the theater by auditioning for a role in a school or community play. If being on stage is not for you, try working backstage, making props, working the lights or sound system, or helping with costumes and makeup.

Related Jobs

Announcers; dancers and choreographers; musicians, singers, and related workers; designers; writers and editors; top executives

Something Extra

Making it as an actor is tough. That's why most actors work at least part-time at another job while they wait for their big breaks. For example, movie hunk Brad Pitt donned a chicken suit for a fast-food restaurant in California. TV's Calista Flockhart worked as an aerobics instructor. And comedienne Whoopi Goldberg worked as a funeral parlor cosmetician, observing, "I'd rather work on dead people. They don't move."

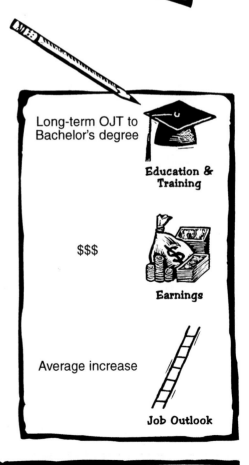

Long-term OJT to Bachelor's degree

Education & Training

$$$

Earnings

Average increase

Job Outlook

Athletes, Coaches, Umpires & Related Workers

On the Job

From football to ice skating, professional athletes train every day to stay in top physical condition for competition. Coaches organize, lead, teach, and referee indoor and outdoor games such as volleyball and soccer. Some also teach specific skills, such as weight training, tennis, and gymnastics. Umpires make sure everyone follows the rules and sometimes have to make tough decisions. All of these jobs are very competitive.

Subjects to Study

Physical education, nutrition, biology, anatomy, sports education

Discover More

Participate in sports or physical-fitness activities at your school or local gym or YMCA. Take classes in an activity that interests you, then ask if you can be a team member, team manager, or coach's assistant.

Related Jobs

Dietitians and nutritionists; physical therapists; recreation and fitness workers; recreational therapists; teachers—preschool, kindergarten, elementary, middle, and secondary

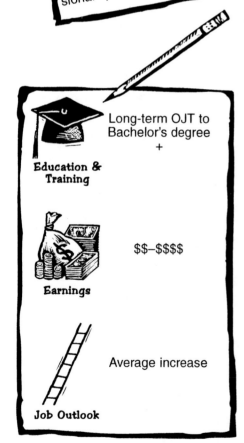

Education & Training
Long-term OJT to Bachelor's degree +

Earnings
$$–$$$$

Job Outlook
Average increase

Dancers & Choreographers

On the Job

Dancers express ideas and stories through the movement of their bodies. Dance styles include classical ballet, modern dance, tap, jazz, and different folk dances. Dancers perform in musicals, operas, TV shows, movies, music videos, and commercials. Dancers must be strong, coordinated, and dedicated. Choreographers create dances and teach dancers. They may work for one company or on a freelance basis. Those who operate their own studios must have good business skills. Most performances are in the evening and on weekends.

Something Extra

Pointe ballet training traditionally starts at the age of 12, although regular ballet classes usually start much earlier. Most dancers have their first professional auditions by the time they are 17 or 18. But the training and practice for professional ballet dancers never ends. Most professional dancers work out for several hours every day. By the time they are 30, most are done with their performing days and move into teaching and choreography.

Subjects to Study

Music, dance, physical education, drama, English, history, literature

Discover More

Sign up for dance classes at a local studio. Try several styles, from ballet to tap to swing. Ask the teacher about the job. Does he or she work at another job in addition to teaching? Does he or she perform with a dance company?

Related Jobs

Actors, producers, and directors; musicians, singers, and related workers; designers; barbers, cosmetologists, and other personal appearance workers; athletes, coaches, umpires, and related workers

Voc/tech training +

Education & Training

$$–$$$$

Earnings

Average increase

Job Outlook

Musicians, Singers & Related Workers

On the Job

Musicians and singers play instruments and perform vocal music. They may perform alone or in groups, before live audiences or in recording studios. Composers write original songs for bands, orchestras, or singers. Conductors lead musical groups such as orchestras, dance bands, and ensembles. Most musicians work nights and weekends and must travel to perform. Because it's so hard to support themselves with music, many take other jobs as well. Many musicians work in cities with recording studios, such as New York, Los Angeles, and Nashville.

Subjects to Study

Vocal music, instrumental music, English, creative writing, business math

Discover More

Participate in your school band, orchestra, or choir. Audition for a role in a school or community musical. Take lessons to learn a musical instrument.

Related Jobs

Precision instrument and equipment repairers; actors, producers, and directors; announcers; dancers and choreographers

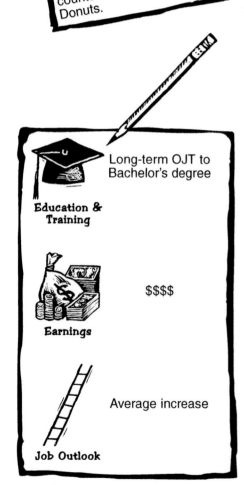

Education & Training
Long-term OJT to Bachelor's degree

Earnings
$$$$

Job Outlook
Average increase

Announcers

On the Job

Radio announcers (or disc jockeys) plan and perform radio programs. They may choose and play music, interview guests, and write program material. Television announcers and newscasters prepare and present the news, weather, and sports, although most specialize in one of these areas. They may work unusual hours, including very early in the morning and very late at night. When emergency situations arise, they must be there to cover them for the news.

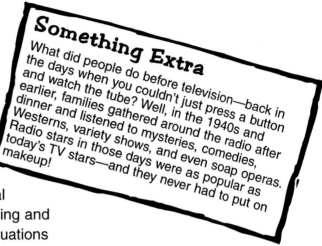

Something Extra

What did people do before television—back in the days when you couldn't just press a button and watch the tube? Well, in the 1940s and earlier, families gathered around the radio after dinner and listened to mysteries, comedies, Westerns, variety shows, and even soap operas. Radio stars in those days were as popular as today's TV stars—and they never had to put on makeup!

Subjects to Study

English, public speaking, drama, foreign languages, electronics, computer skills

Discover More

Ask the principal at your school if you can make the morning announcements one day. Write out your "intro" and try to make it humorous or catchy. Can you entertain your audience members while you keep them informed? That's the job of a news anchor.

Related Jobs

News analysts, reporters, and correspondents; interpreters and translators; actors, producers, and directors; musicians, singers, and related workers; broadcast and sound engineering technicians and radio operators

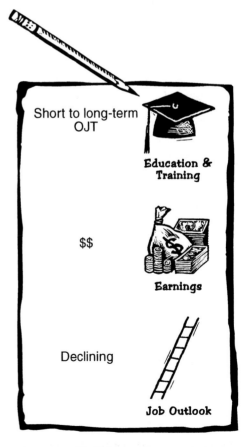

Short to long-term OJT

Education & Training

$$

Earnings

Declining

Job Outlook

Broadcast & Sound Engineering Technicians & Radio Operators

On the Job

Broadcast and sound engineering technicians work with electronic equipment to record and transmit radio and television programs. They operate, install, and repair microphones, TV cameras, tape recorders, and antennas. They often work holidays, weekends, and evenings for news programs. When disasters happen, they must be on the scene to record the news. Setting up equipment sometimes requires heavy lifting and climbing.

Subjects to Study

Math, shop courses, physics, electronics, English, computer skills

Discover More

Build your own electronic equipment using a hobby kit. Check a toy or hobby store to see what kind of equipment is available. Operating a "ham" or amateur radio is great experience for this occupation.

Related Jobs

Engineering technicians; science technicians; electrical and electronics installers and repairers; computer support specialists and systems administrators; communications equipment operators

Education & Training
Voc/tech training

Earnings
$$$–$$$$

Job Outlook
Average increase

Interpreters and Translators

On the Job

Interpreters and translators convert spoken and written words from one language into another. These language specialists also relay concepts and ideas between languages. They must thoroughly understand the subject about which they are translating. They also need to be sensitive to other cultures.

Subjects to Study

English writing and comprehension, foreign languages, computers

Discover More

The United Nations is an assembly of representatives from countries all over the world. The UN's job is to maintain international peace and security, to develop friendly relations among nations, to help solve international problems, and to promote human rights and freedoms. Its headquarters in New York employs many translators. Learn more about the UN at www.un.org/Pubs/CyberSchoolBus/untour/

Related Jobs

Teachers, announcers, writers and editors, computer software engineers, court reporters, medical transcriptionists

Something Extra

Did you know that one out of every five Americans speaks a language other than English at home? That's 47 million people who speak Spanish, Chinese, French, German, Tagalog, Russian, or another language. So imagine how much the need is growing for people who can translate and interpret between English and these languages. Many businesses and government agencies have an urgent need for translators to help them communicate with their customers.

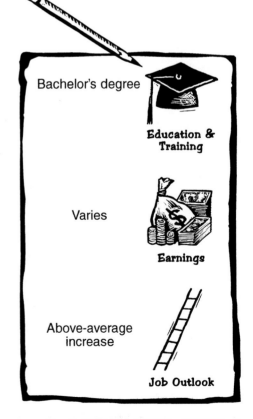

Bachelor's degree

Education & Training

Varies

Earnings

Above-average increase

Job Outlook

News Analysts, Reporters & Correspondents

On the Job

News analysts, reporters, and correspondents gather information and write articles about events around the world. Some take photographs or shoot videos. Radio and television reporters often report "live" from the scene of crimes or disasters. The work is usually hectic and stressful and the deadlines are tight. Reporting can be dangerous work and requires long hours, irregular schedules, and travel.

Subjects to Study

English, journalism, social studies, history, creative writing, speech, computer science, foreign languages

Discover More

Collect three or more newspapers that are all reporting on the same story. Read the reports and then make notes about how each newspaper's story differs from the others. The facts may be the same, but one paper may choose to play up sensational aspects while another pushes a different viewpoint.

Related Jobs

Writers and editors, public relations specialists, announcers, interpreters and translators

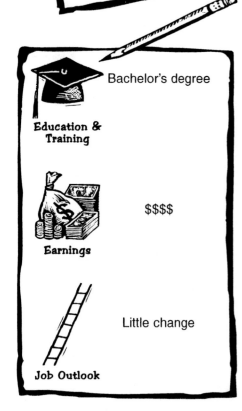

Bachelor's degree

Education & Training

$$$$

Earnings

Little change

Job Outlook

Photographers

On the Job

Photographers use cameras to record people, places, and events on film. Most specialize in commercial, portrait, or journalistic photography. Commercial photographers may take school or wedding pictures or photos for ads. Portrait photographers work in studios, taking pictures of people for special occasions. Journalistic photographers work for newspapers and magazines.

Subjects to Study

English, journalism, photography, art, creative writing, business, accounting

Discover More

Take photos of special people and places in your life. Try using different kinds of film and different lenses. For example, use black-and-white film to photograph your neighborhood. Use a telephoto lens to take pictures of small flowers and insects.

Related Jobs

Architects, except landscape and naval; artists and related workers; designers; news analysts, reporters, and correspondents; television, video, and motion picture camera operators and editors

Something Extra

Photojournalists use their cameras to record history and news events for magazines and newspapers. It can be dangerous work. In 1992, Dan Eldon, a photographer from the *Philadelphia Inquirer*, went to Somalia to document the famine there. Because of his work, the U.S. began delivering food supplies to the war-ravaged country—a move that was not popular with some of the Somalian leaders. Less than a year later, Eldon was stoned to death by a mob in Somalia. He was 22 years old.

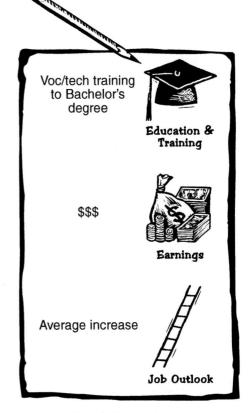

Education & Training
Voc/tech training to Bachelor's degree

Earnings
$$$

Job Outlook
Average increase

Public Relations Specialists

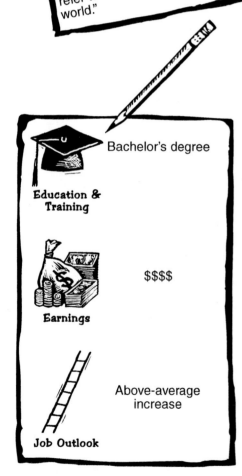

Bachelor's degree

Education & Training

$$$$

Earnings

Above-average increase

Job Outlook

On the Job

Public relations specialists work to present a good image of their clients to the public. Their job is to make sure the clients' good news is spread far and wide and to put a positive "spin" on bad news. They write press releases and speeches and set up "photo opportunities" of their clients doing good things. Many work more than 40 hours a week. In an emergency, they may be on call around the clock.

Subjects to Study

English, creative writing, journalism, psychology, sociology, computer skills, public speaking, foreign languages

Discover More

Write a press release for your class, announcing some good news or interesting event. Be sure the release is honest but puts forth the best possible image. Keep it short and snappy, to be sure it gets attention!

Related Jobs

Advertising, marketing, promotions, public relations, and sales managers; demonstrators, product promoters, and models; news analysts, reporters, and correspondents; lawyers; market and survey researchers; sales representatives, wholesale and manufacturing; police and detectives

Television, Video & Motion Picture Camera Operators & Editors

On the Job

Camera operators work behind the scenes on TV shows, documentaries, motion pictures, and industrial films. They shoot the film you see on screen, sometimes from high up on scaffolding or flat on their bellies on the ground. They may work long, irregular hours in places all over the world. Film editors look at the hundreds of hours worth of film shot for a project and decide which scenes to include and which to cut.

Something Extra

For a good view of what's possible in filmmaking today, rent the movie *Forrest Gump*. Among other tricks, the filmmakers spliced and altered vintage film to show their hero, Tom Hanks, shaking hands with John F. Kennedy, more than 30 years after Kennedy's death.

Subjects to Study

English, journalism, photography, art, creative writing, business, accounting

Discover More

Use a digital camcorder to make your own movie. These cameras let you load your movie onto a computer and then alter the images in countless ways. Give your leading lady green hair, drop in a few aliens, and you've got the ultimate in science fiction!

Related Jobs

Artists and related workers, broadcast and sound engineering technicians and radio operators, designers, photographers

Short-term OJT to Voc/tech training

Education & Training

$$$$

Earnings

Average increase

Job Outlook

Writers & Editors

On the Job

Writers write novels and nonfiction books, articles, movies, plays, poems, and ads. They must also be able to sell what they have written. Editors choose the stories and books that publishing houses will print. Magazine editors choose articles for publication and assign stories to writers. Many of them also write stories and articles. Editors also review, rewrite, and correct the work of writers. Technical writers write training manuals, catalogs, assembly instructions, and project proposals.

Subjects to Study

English, creative writing, journalism, computer skills, history, psychology, business math

Discover More

Submit a story to a local newspaper or magazine. Check out *The Writer's Market* for those that encourage young writers, such as *Stone Soup.* You could also enter a writing contest.

Related Jobs

News analysts, reporters, and correspondents; interpreters and translators; announcers; public relations specialists

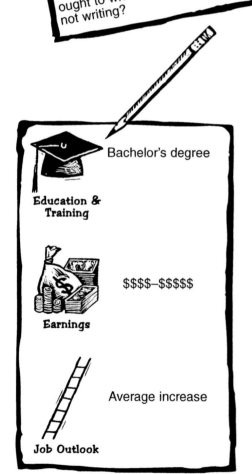

Bachelor's degree

Education & Training

$$$$–$$$$$

Earnings

Average increase

Job Outlook

Audiologists

On the Job
Audiologists work with people who cannot hear as well as they should. They recommend treatments such as hearing aids, implants, or surgery. They work in hospitals, nursing homes, and schools.

Subjects to Study
English, math, physics, chemistry, biology, psychology, communications

Discover More
You have probably had a hearing test at school. The next time hearing tests are being done at your school, ask the nurse or other person giving the test to tell you more about it. How does it measure hearing loss? What happens next if a student is found to have a hearing loss?

Related Jobs
Occupational therapists, optometrists, physical therapists, psychologists, recreational therapists, counselors, speech-language pathologists

Something Extra
It used to be that deaf people were consigned to lives on the sidelines, but not today. Heather Whitestone McCallum, Miss America 1995, was deaf most of her life until doctors restored her hearing in 2002. She communicated through speaking and dancing and lived quite successfully in a hearing world. Deaf actress Marlee Matlin won an Academy Award® for her role in the movie Children of a Lesser God and has had several TV roles, including a stint on Seinfeld and a recurring role as a political aide on The West Wing.

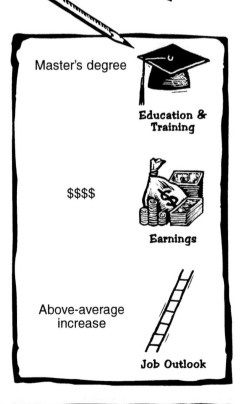

Master's degree

Education & Training

$$$$

Earnings

Above-average increase

Job Outlook

Chiropractors

Something Extra

What does a chiropractor have to do with treating headaches? As it turns out, quite a lot. Headaches can result from poor posture, tension, or a misalignment of the spinal cord. Using massage, heat therapy, and realignment exercises and techniques, chiropractors can help people who suffer from persistent or chronic headaches. They also teach people how to prevent headaches in the first place, which might be the best treatment of all.

On the Job

Chiropractors help people who have problems with their muscles, nerves, or skeleton, especially the spine. They examine patients, order tests, and take X rays. They treat patients by massaging or adjusting the spinal column. They also use water and heat therapy. They stress nutrition, exercise, and reducing stress in treatment. They do not prescribe drugs or perform surgery. Many are self-employed.

Subjects to Study

Health, biology, anatomy, nutrition, chemistry, physics, psychology, math, social sciences

Discover More

Aromatherapy is the practice of using different smells to relax, calm, or energize yourself. Try an experiment at home. Buy several different scented candles. Each evening at dinner, light a different candle. (Get your parents' permission first!) How do the different scents affect your mood?

Related Jobs

Dentists, occupational therapists, optometrists, physical therapists, physicians and surgeons, podiatrists, veterinarians

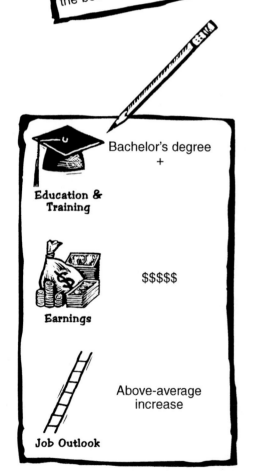

Education & Training
Bachelor's degree +

Earnings
$$$$$

Job Outlook
Above-average increase

Dentists

On the Job

Dentists help people take care of their teeth. They remove teeth and straighten them with braces, repair broken teeth, and fill cavities. They may replace a patient's original teeth with a "bridge" of false teeth. They may also perform surgery to treat gum disease. They teach people how to brush, floss, and care for their teeth to prevent problems. They wear masks, gloves, and safety glasses to protect themselves from infectious diseases. Many are self-employed.

Something Extra

Dentists have been practicing for nearly 7,000 years, although you might not recognize some of the treatments used back then as dentistry. In ancient Babylon, for example, "dentists" used worms, prayers, and herbs to treat tooth decay. In the Middle Ages, dentists were considered the first surgeons—although about all they could do was remove teeth, which they did to treat nearly every condition you can think of.

Subjects to Study

Biology, anatomy, chemistry, physics, health, business math, communication skills

Discover More

Visit your dentist and ask him or her about the job. What kind of training is available in your area? What is the best part of the job? What's the worst? Is your dentist bothered that so many people are afraid of dentists?

Related Jobs

Chiropractors, optometrists, physicians and surgeons, podiatrists, psychologists, veterinarians

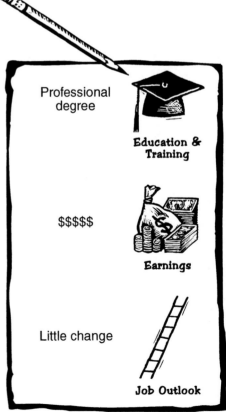

Professional degree

Education & Training

$$$$$

Earnings

Little change

Job Outlook

Dietitians & Nutritionists

On the Job

Dietitians and nutritionists plan, prepare, and serve meals in clinics, schools, nursing homes, and hospitals. They help prevent and treat illnesses by teaching clients to eat properly. Some specialize in helping overweight or critically ill patients, or in caring for kidney or diabetic patients. Those supervising kitchen workers may be on their feet most of the day in a hot, steamy kitchen. Some are self-employed and act as consultants.

Subjects to Study

Health, nutrition, home economics, biology, chemistry, English, accounting

Discover More

Plan and prepare a healthy, low-fat meal for your family. Be sure to include grains, fruits, vegetables, dairy products, and protein.

Related Jobs

Food service managers, registered nurses

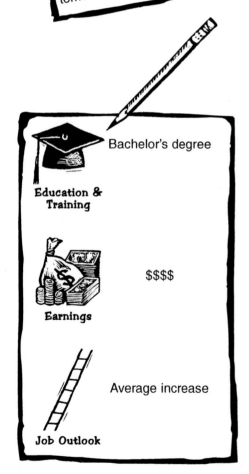

Bachelor's degree

Education & Training

$$$$

Earnings

Average increase

Job Outlook

Occupational Therapists

On the Job

Occupational therapists help people with disabilities become independent and productive. They may help a patient learn to use a wheelchair or work on a new skill. They also help patients find jobs and develop job skills. They usually work in hospitals, schools, or rehab centers. Some provide home health care. Most spend a lot of time on their feet. The job can be tiring, because therapists must sometimes lift patients and move equipment.

Something Extra

Occupational therapists work in all kinds of settings, from nursing homes to hospitals. But did you know that they also work in preschools? Many work with developmentally delayed children, helping kids make up lost time and opportunities to get them ready for school. This work might involve helping children play games that challenge their abilities, work puzzles, and learn to use crayons and scissors.

Subjects to Study

Biology, chemistry, physics, health, art, psychology, English, foreign languages

Discover More

Volunteer at a local nursing home to help with activities. You might teach a stroke victim to knit, read to a person whose sight is fading, or simply visit someone whose family is far away.

Related Jobs

Audiologists, chiropractors, physical therapists, recreational therapists, counselors, respiratory therapists, speech-language pathologists

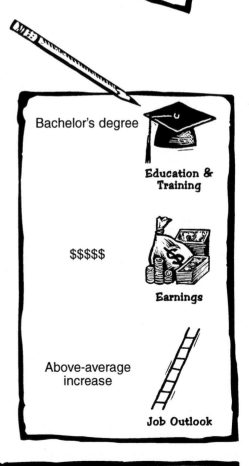

Bachelor's degree

Education & Training

$$$$$

Earnings

Above-average increase

Job Outlook

Optometrists

On the Job

Optometrists examine people's eyes to diagnose vision problems and eye diseases. They prescribe glasses and contact lenses and treat certain eye diseases. Some optometrists work especially with the elderly or children. Others develop ways to protect workers' eyes from on-the-job strain or injury. Many are self-employed and work Saturdays and evenings to meet their patients' schedules.

Subjects to Study

Physics, chemistry, biology, anatomy, psychology, speech, business math

Discover More

Arrange for your class to have a vision screening. With your teacher, contact a local optometrist and ask him or her to visit your school, talk about the job, and do a basic vision screening.

Related Jobs

Chiropractors, dentists, physicians and surgeons, podiatrists, veterinarians, audiologists

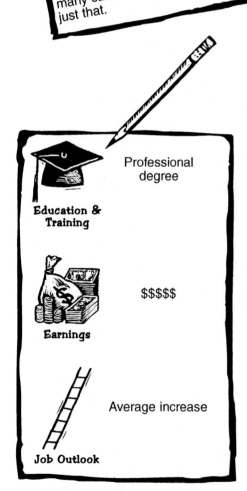

Education & Training — Professional degree

Earnings — $$$$$

Job Outlook — Average increase

Pharmacists

On the Job

Pharmacists measure and sell medication to people who are sick when a doctor says they need it. They must know about the correct use, make-up, and effects of drugs. They tell patients about medicines, including reactions and possible side effects, and answer questions. Those in hospitals and clinics advise doctors and nurses on drugs and their effects. Most pharmacists spend much of the workday on their feet. They may wear gloves and safety masks when working with drugs. Many work nights and weekends.

Something Extra

A big part of a pharmacist's job is answering questions. Because pharmacists work with the public, these might range from "Can I take this cold remedy with this pain reliever?" to "Where's the bathroom?" Their special knowledge makes them the expert for patients and doctors alike. In fact, several cases have been reported of pharmacists catching doctors' errors, especially in hospitals, often with life-saving effects.

Subjects to Study

Math, biology, chemistry, physics, social sciences, English, foreign languages

Discover More

Talk to a pharmacist and ask about the training needed for this job. Ask how he or she keeps up with new drugs that hit the market every day. Then, just for fun, ask about the most ridiculous question he or she has been asked on the job.

Related Jobs

Pharmacy technicians, pharmacy aides, biological scientists, medical scientists, chemists and materials scientists, physicians and surgeons

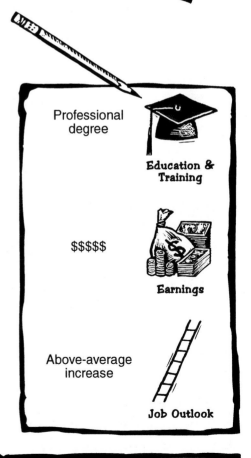

Professional degree

Education & Training

$$$$$

Earnings

Above-average increase

Job Outlook

Physical Therapists

On the Job

Physical therapists work with accident victims, stroke patients, and people with disabilities. They evaluate patients and make plans to help them recover their physical abilities and relieve pain. They may use electricity, heat, or cold to relieve pain, reduce swelling, or increase flexibility. They work in hospitals, clinics, and private offices with special equipment. Physical therapists must be strong enough to move patients and equipment.

Subjects to Study

Biology, chemistry, physics, psychology, anatomy, English, foreign languages

Discover More

Talk to the gym teacher at your school about this kind of work. Ask him or her to help you put together an exercise plan to help you build your own strength and endurance.

Related Jobs

Audiologists, chiropractors, occupational therapists, recreational therapists, counselors, respiratory therapists, speech-language pathologists

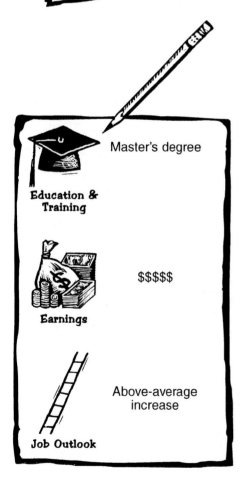

Education & Training
Master's degree

Earnings
$$$$$

Job Outlook
Above-average increase

Physician Assistants

On the Job

Physician assistants always work under the supervision of a physician. They handle many of the routine but time-consuming tasks physicians do, such as taking medical records, examining patients, and ordering X rays and tests. They also treat minor injuries. They often work weekends and evenings.

Physician assistants may be on their feet for long periods of time.

Something Extra

In many small, rural communities in the United States, medical doctors are in short supply. Some communities have no resident doctors at all. In such communities, physician assistants (PAs) are the primary health care providers. They see patients on a day-to-day basis, handling routine office visits. A doctor visits the clinic one or two days a week. The PA can call the doctor for advice or in emergencies.

Subjects to Study

Biology, chemistry, math, psychology, English, foreign languages, anatomy, nutrition

Discover More

To learn more about this job, check out the Web site of the American Academy of Physician Assistants: www.aapa.org/geninfo1.html

Related Jobs

Audiologists, occupational therapists, physical therapists, speech-language pathologists

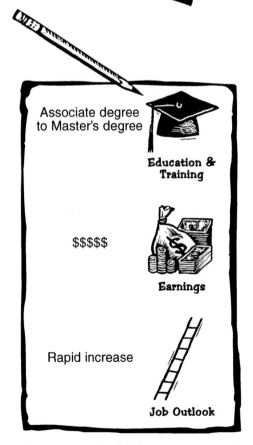

Associate degree to Master's degree

Education & Training

$$$$$

Earnings

Rapid increase

Job Outlook

Physicians & Surgeons

On the Job

Physicians help people who are sick or have been hurt. They examine patients, perform tests, prescribe treatments, and teach people about health care. Surgeons perform operations on patients with life-threatening illness and injuries. Physicians work in hospitals, clinics, and private practice. Many work 60 hours a week or more. They may be on call for emergency visits to the hospital. Most doctors must travel frequently from their offices to hospitals to care for patients.

Subjects to Study

Physics, chemistry, biology, psychology, health, nutrition, English, math

Discover More

Call your local hospital and ask about volunteer opportunities. Many have programs that let young people visit with or read to patients, deliver things, greet visitors, and help with the library cart.

Related Jobs

Chiropractors, dentists, optometrists, physician assistants, podiatrists, registered nurses, veterinarians

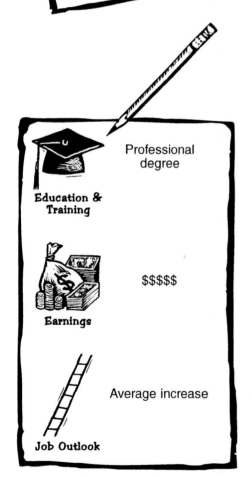

Education & Training
Professional degree

Earnings
$$$$$

Job Outlook
Average increase

Podiatrists

On the Job

Podiatrists diagnose and treat diseases and injuries of the foot and lower leg. They may treat corns, calluses, ingrown toenails, bunions, heel spurs, and arch problems. They also treat ankle and foot injuries, deformities, and infections. They take care of foot problems caused by diseases such as diabetes. They prescribe medications and order physical therapy. They set broken bones and perform surgery. Podiatrists usually run their own small businesses, but they may also visit patients in nursing homes and perform surgeries at hospitals.

Subjects to Study

Biology, chemistry, physics, anatomy, health, English, business math

Discover More

For more information on this job, see the careers section of the Web site for the American Podiatric Medical Association: www.apma.org/careers.htm

Related Jobs

Chiropractors, dentists, optometrists, physicians and surgeons, veterinarians

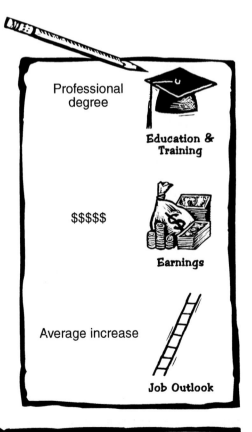

Professional degree

Education & Training

$$$$$

Earnings

Average increase

Job Outlook

Recreational Therapists

On the Job

Recreational therapists help people with medical problems improve their health and well-being. They teach patients games, arts and crafts, dance, music, and sports activities. These activities help patients regain skills they've lost because of illness or injury and improve their state of mind. They work closely with medical staff in hospitals and nursing homes. They must be strong enough to move patients and equipment and to participate in activities.

Subjects to Study

English, speech, communication skills, anatomy, psychology, health, art, music, dance, physical education

Discover More

Volunteer some time each week at a nursing home in your neighborhood. Ask the activities director if you can help him or her plan and carry out activities for the residents. You might help with an art project, read to a patient, or just play along in a game.

Related Jobs

Occupational therapists, physical therapists, recreation and fitness workers, counselors

Bachelor's degree

Education & Training

$$$$

Earnings

Little change

Job Outlook

Registered Nurses

On the Job

Registered nurses care for the sick and injured and help people stay well. In clinics, hospitals, and nursing homes, they provide much of the day-to-day care for patients, under a doctor's supervision. They take patient histories, give shots and medicines, and teach patients about helping with their own care. Some assist in surgeries. Nurses often work nights, weekends, and holidays. They must be able to cope with emergencies and high stress.

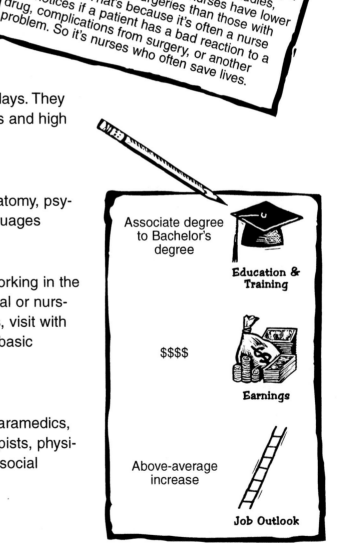

Something Extra

You might know that nurses help doctors, but did you know that if you have surgery, your life might depend on one? According to several studies, hospitals with more registered nurses have lower death rates following surgeries than those with fewer nurses. That's because it's often a nurse who notices if a patient has a bad reaction to a drug, complications from surgery, or another problem. So it's nurses who often save lives.

Subjects to Study

Health, biology, chemistry, physics, anatomy, psychology, nutrition, English, foreign languages

Discover More

One of the best ways to learn about working in the medical field is to volunteer at a hospital or nursing home. You might organize activities, visit with patients, deliver supplies, or help with basic patient care.

Related Jobs

Emergency medical technicians and paramedics, occupational therapists, physical therapists, physician assistants, respiratory therapists, social workers

Associate degree to Bachelor's degree

Education & Training

$$$$

Earnings

Above-average increase

Job Outlook

Respiratory Therapists

On the Job

Respiratory therapists care for patients with breathing problems, from premature babies to heart attack victims. They perform tests, connect patients to machines that help in breathing, and teach patients how to use these machines at home. Therapists may also help in surgery by removing mucus from a patient's lungs so that he or she can breathe more easily. Those in hospitals spend most of their time on their feet. They must be able to work calmly in emergencies.

Subjects to Study

Health, biology, chemistry, physics, English

Discover More

Asthma is on the rise in the United States, especially among children. Talk to someone who has asthma and find out what type of medicine or therapy he or she uses to prevent or treat asthma attacks.

Related Jobs

Registered nurses, occupational therapists, physical therapists

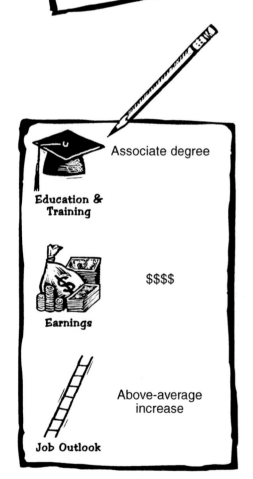

Education & Training
Associate degree

Earnings
$$$$

Job Outlook
Above-average increase

Speech-Language Pathologists

On the Job

Speech-language pathologists work with people who cannot speak well. They teach patients how to improve their language skills. They may teach sign language to nonspeaking patients.

Subjects to Study

English, foreign languages, speech, biology, chemistry, physics, psychology

Discover More

Speech therapists help clients learn to speak clearly. Practice your speaking skills by recording yourself while reading. Play back the recording and listen to your speaking skills. Are you clear and understandable? If not, practice speaking in front of a mirror and watch how you make the sounds.

Related Jobs

Audiologists, occupational therapists, optometrists, physical therapists, psychologists, recreational therapists, counselors

Something Extra

People who stutter often can speak and sing more smoothly when they speak as part of a group, as in a choir or when reciting the Pledge of Allegiance. Scientists used this fact to invent a device that helps people who stutter. It looks like a small hearing aid that is worn in the ear. The aid makes it sound to the person like he or she is speaking in a group, and so he or she can speak more fluently.

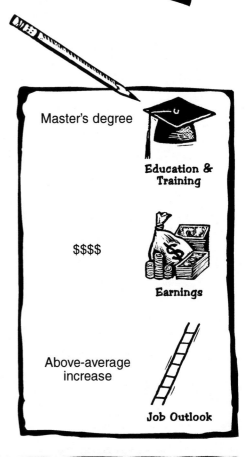

Master's degree

Education & Training

$$$$

Earnings

Above-average increase

Job Outlook

Veterinarians

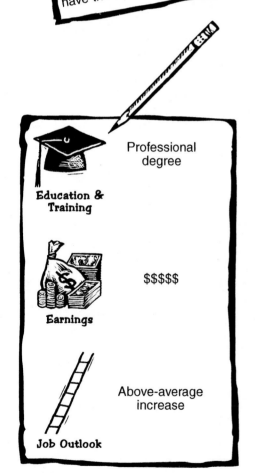

Education & Training
Professional degree

Earnings
$$$$$

Job Outlook
Above-average increase

On the Job

Veterinarians care for pets, farm animals, zoo residents, and laboratory animals. They set broken bones, treat injuries, prescribe medicine, perform surgery, and vaccinate animals against diseases. They teach people how to care for animals. Most veterinarians treat animals in private clinics or hospitals and work 50 hours or more a week. They may work nights and weekends. Those treating large animals travel to farms or ranches to see their patients. A number of veterinarians engage in research.

Subjects to Study

Biology, chemistry, physics, business math, English

Discover More

Visit an animal shelter and talk to the workers about volunteer opportunities. Some shelters let volunteers come in to feed, bathe, play with, and pet the animals.

Related Jobs

Chiropractors, dentists, optometrists, physicians and surgeons, podiatrists, biological scientists, medical scientists, animal care and service workers, veterinary technologists and technicians

Cardiovascular Technologists & Technicians

On the Job

Cardiovascular technologists and technicians help doctors treat heart and blood vessel diseases. They use a variety of tests, monitor the results, and prepare patients for tests. They may schedule patient appointments, type doctors' reports, keep patient files, and care for the testing equipment. They usually work in hospitals and clinics and may work evenings and weekends.

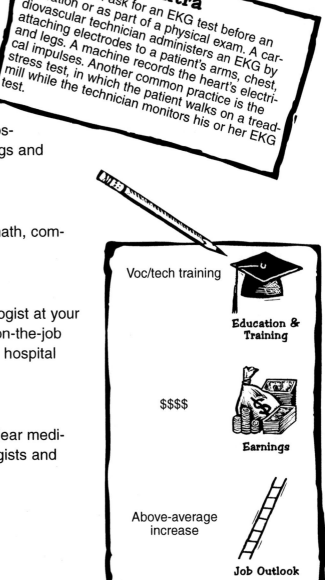

Something Extra

Doctors often ask for an EKG test before an operation or as part of a physical exam. A cardiovascular technician administers an EKG by attaching electrodes to a patient's arms, chest, and legs. A machine records the heart's electrical impulses. Another common practice is the stress test, in which the patient walks on a treadmill while the technician monitors his or her EKG test.

Subjects to Study

Shop courses, communication skills, math, computer skills, health

Discover More

Talk to an EKG supervisor or a cardiologist at your local hospital. Ask a technician about on-the-job training opportunities in your area. The hospital staff can tell you more about this job.

Related Jobs

Diagnostic medical sonographers, nuclear medicine technologists, radiologic technologists and technicians, respiratory therapists

Voc/tech training

Education & Training

$$$$

Earnings

Above-average increase

Job Outlook

Clinical Laboratory Technologists & Technicians

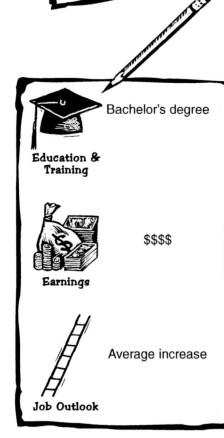

Bachelor's degree

Education & Training

$$$$

Earnings

Average increase

Job Outlook

On the Job

These workers do medical tests to help detect, diagnose, and treat diseases. They match blood types, test for drug levels, and look for abnormal cells. They analyze test results and send them back to doctors. Special equipment allows them to do more than one test at a time. They may work nights and weekends. They wear gloves and masks to protect themselves from infections and diseases.

Subjects to Study

Biology, chemistry, physics, computer skills, math

Discover More

Rub slices of white bread against different surfaces: a trash can, your hair, the inside of your desk, the floor, dirt, whatever. Seal each piece in a plastic bag with a label telling what it touched. Let the bags sit for a week, then look at them through a magnifying glass. Which surface generated the most mold? (Important: When finished, throw the bags away without opening them. Mold can make you sick!)

Related Jobs

Chemists and materials scientists, science technicians, veterinary technologists and technicians

Dental Hygienists

On the Job

Dental hygienists examine patients' teeth and gums to find disease. They help dentists by cleaning patients' teeth, taking and developing X rays, and applying fluoride to the teeth. They teach patients how to brush and floss their teeth correctly. Many work part-time for more than one dentist, and they often work on weekends and evenings. They wear gloves and masks to protect themselves from diseases.

Something Extra

Many people are afraid to visit the dentist, either because of a bad experience they had or because of horror stories they've heard from others. Part of a dental hygienist's duties is talking to patients to put them at ease. Being a good communicator and having a good "chair-side manner" is important in this occupation. The more relaxed the patient is, the easier the exam will be.

Subjects to Study

Biology, chemistry, health, nutrition, anatomy, English, foreign languages

Discover More

Do a simple experiment in your class. Have half the students brush their teeth three times a day and floss every day. Ask the other half to continue with a regular teeth-cleaning routine. At the end of the school year, invite a dentist to check the class's teeth. Which group has better checkups?

Related Jobs

Dental assistants, medical assistants, occupational therapist assistants and aides, physical therapist assistants and aides, physician assistants, registered nurses

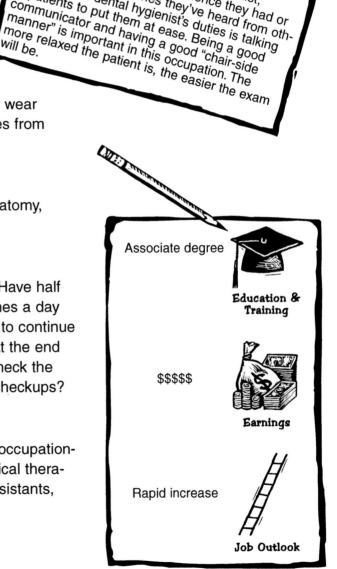

Associate degree

Education & Training

$$$$$

Earnings

Rapid increase

Job Outlook

Diagnostic Medical Sonographers

On the Job

Sonographers use special machines that send sound waves through the body to diagnose illness. Doctors use the results of these tests to find tumors, check growing fetuses, and make medical decisions. Sonographers are on their feet for long periods and may have to lift patients. Most work normal hours, although they may be on call for emergencies.

Subjects to Study

Health, biology, math, shop courses, computer science, English

Discover More

To learn more about sonography, visit an obstetrician's office and ask to watch an ultrasound. The sonographer uses the machine to actually "see" inside a womb and show images of a growing baby.

Related Jobs

Cardiovascular technologists and technicians, clinical laboratory technologists and technicians, nuclear medicine technologists, radiologic technologists and technicians, respiratory therapists

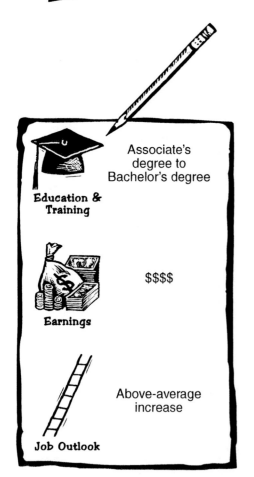

Education & Training
Associate's degree to Bachelor's degree

Earnings
$$$$

Job Outlook
Above-average increase

Emergency Medical Technicians & Paramedics

On the Job

Emergency medical technicians (EMTs) and paramedics drive ambulances and give emergency medical care. They determine a patient's medical condition at the scene, stabilize the patient, then drive him or her to the hospital. They work outdoors in all kinds of weather, and the work can be very stressful. Some patients may become violent, and EMTs may be exposed to diseases. They work for fire departments, hospitals, and private ambulance services.

Something Extra

What's a typical day like for an EMT? There is no such thing! Because EMTs respond to emergencies, their jobs are never the same from day to day. They might be the first on the scene of a car accident in the morning, revive a heart attack victim at lunch, and deliver a baby in a taxicab by dinner. EMTs must be able to remain calm in any situation—because they never know what's around the next corner.

Subjects to Study

Driver education, health, biology, chemistry, anatomy, English, foreign languages

Discover More

Check with the Red Cross in your area to register for a first-aid or CPR course. You can learn how to save another person's life and be helpful in different kinds of emergencies.

Related Jobs

Air traffic controllers, firefighting occupations, physician assistants, police and detectives, registered nurses

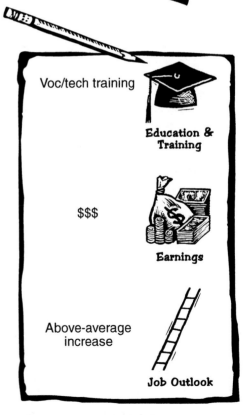

Voc/tech training

Education & Training

$$$

Earnings

Above-average increase

Job Outlook

Licensed Practical & Licensed Vocational Nurses

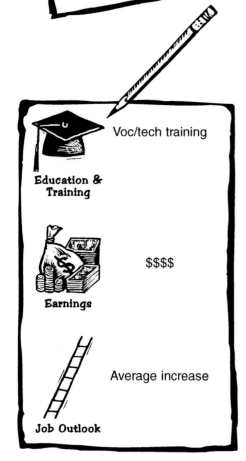

Voc/tech training

Education & Training

$$$$

Earnings

Average increase

Job Outlook

On the Job

Licensed practical nurses (LPNs) take care of sick and injured people. They are supervised by doctors or registered nurses. They help patients with bathing, dressing, and personal hygiene, feed them, and care for their emotional needs. They keep their patients as comfortable as possible. Licensed vocational nurses (LVNs) work with people who have been disabled and need rehabilitation services. Nurses must be strong enough to lift patients and able to deal with stress. They can be exposed to infectious diseases.

Subjects to Study

Health, anatomy, psychology, first aid, nutrition, home economics courses, English, foreign languages

Discover More

Licensed practical nursing courses are offered in some high school vocational programs. Talk to your school counselor about these programs and find out whether any are available through high schools in your area.

Related Jobs

Emergency medical technicians and paramedics, social and human service assistants, surgical technologists, teacher assistants

Medical Records & Health Information Technicians

On the Job

These workers organize and keep track of patients' medical records. First, they make sure all the right forms have been signed. Then they put the information into a computer file. Finally, they code the information so that it can be pulled up easily. They may work day, evening, or night shifts. Health information technicians must be computer literate and pay attention to details.

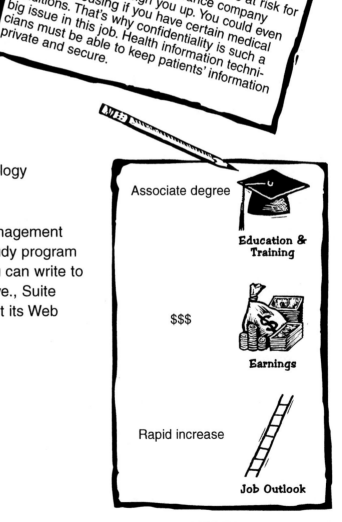

Something Extra

What happens if someone gets a hold of your medical records? Well, if your family has a history of cancer, for example, a business might decide not to hire you because you are at risk for high medical bills. Or an insurance company might decide not to sign you up. You could even be denied housing if you have certain medical conditions. That's why confidentiality is such a big issue in this job. Health information technicians must be able to keep patients' information private and secure.

Associate degree

Education & Training

$$$

Earnings

Rapid increase

Job Outlook

Subjects to Study

English, computer skills, anatomy, biology

Discover More

The American Health Information Management Association offers an independent-study program for health information technicians. You can write to the association at 919 N. Michigan Ave., Suite 1400, Chicago, IL 60611, or check out its Web site: www.ahima.org.

Related Jobs

Medical transcriptionists

Nuclear Medicine Technologists

On the Job

Nuclear medicine technologists give radioactive drugs to patients. These drugs help doctors diagnose and treat diseases. Using a camera, the technologist follows the drug as it enters the patient's body and records the drug's effects.

Technologists must keep accurate, detailed patient records. Technologists must be careful to keep from being exposed to too much radiation. They wear badges that measure radiation levels.

Subjects to Study

Biology, chemistry, physics, math, computer science

Discover More

You can get more information about this job by writing to the Joint Review Committee on Educational Programs in Nuclear Medicine Technology, #1 2nd Avenue East, Suite C, Polson, MT 59860-2320.

Related Jobs

Cardiovascular technologists and technicians, clinical laboratory technologists and technicians, diagnostic medical sonographers, radiologic technologists and technicians, respiratory therapists

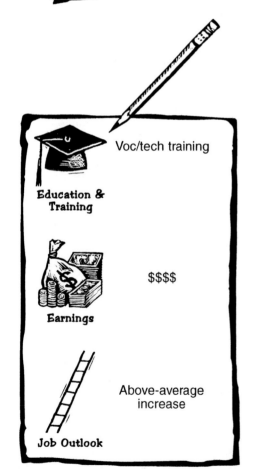

Education & Training — Voc/tech training

Earnings — $$$$

Job Outlook — Above-average increase

Occupational Health & Safety Specialists & Technicians

On the Job

These workers help keep workplaces safe and workers healthy. Almost half work for federal, state, or local government agencies to enforce rules on health and safety. The rest work for companies to ensure that their workplaces are operating safely. They identify hazardous conditions and practices and make recommendations for fixing them. They also check that dangerous materials, such as chemicals, are stored and used properly.

Something Extra

On September 11, 2001, the U.S. suffered the most devastating terrorist attack in history. Months later, New York occupational health and safety inspectors were still working at the scene of the World Trade Center collapse, testing air and soil samples and collecting blood samples from rescue and cleanup workers. Their findings were grim. Firefighters, paramedics, construction workers, and others who spent much time at Ground Zero showed definite signs of asbestos poisoning—which means that the 9/11 attacks might be claiming more victims for years to come.

Subjects to Study

Biology, chemistry, physics, geology, English, computer science

Discover More

Government health and safety specialists use rules established by the Occupational Safety and Health Administration (OSHA), part of the U.S. Department of Labor. You can learn more about OSHA from its Web site: www.osha.gov.

Related Jobs

Construction and building inspectors, correctional officers, police and detectives

Bachelor's degree +

Education & Training

$$$$

Earnings

Average increase

Job Outlook

Opticians, Dispensing

On the Job

Dispensing opticians work for eye doctors, making glasses and contact lenses according to the doctors' orders. They also keep customer records, track inventory, and help customers find frames that fit them well. Many work evenings and weekends or part-time. They must be careful with the glass-cutting machinery and chemicals they use to make lenses.

Subjects to Study

Physics, anatomy, algebra, geometry, mechanical drawing, business math

Discover More

Visit an optical store in your community. Look through the wide selection of eyewear and decide which frames best fit your face. Talk to one of the dispensing opticians about this job.

Related Jobs

Jewelers and precious stone and metal workers, precision instrument and equipment repairers

Education & Training — Voc/tech training

Earnings — $$$

Job Outlook — increase / Average

Pharmacy Technicians

On the Job

Pharmacy technicians help licensed pharmacists provide medicines and other health-care products to patients. They help measure and prepare medications, handle telephone calls, work the cash register, stock shelves, and perform other clerical duties. They do most of their work standing, and they may work nights and weekends, since many pharmacies are open 24 hours a day.

Something Extra

"Can I take this medicine along with the herbal supplement I'm taking?" "Does this diet drug work?" "My baby is running a fever. What should I give her?" "Where is the shampoo?" These are the kinds of questions pharmacy workers are asked every day. Since they deal with people who are sick or in pain, pharmacy workers must be patient and helpful. Since they often work in stores, they also must be able to answer questions about other merchandise. In short, these workers need good people skills!

Subjects to Study

Math, computer skills, chemistry, health education, English

Discover More

Visit your local pharmacy and ask the pharmacist if you can "apprentice." He or she might let you help out with stocking or cleaning shelves. While you work, watch the pharmacist on the job and ask about training opportunities in your area.

Related Jobs

Pharmacists, pharmacy aides, dental assistants, licensed practical and licensed vocational nurses, medical transcriptionists, medical records and health information technicians, occupational therapist assistants and aides, physical therapist assistants and aides, surgical technologists

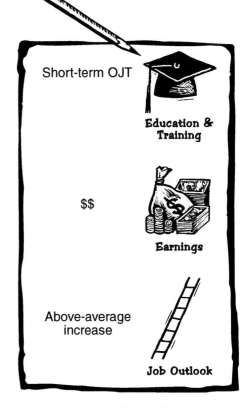

Short-term OJT

Education & Training

$$

Earnings

Above-average increase

Job Outlook

Radiologic Technologists & Technicians

On the Job

Radiologic technologists and technicians work in hospitals and clinics. They operate the machines that take X-ray pictures or magnetic resolution pictures of people's bones and internal organs. They must wear badges that measure the amount of radiation they are exposed to on the job. These workers might work nights or weekends and might be on call during odd hours. They are on their feet most of the day and must be strong enough to lift patients.

Subjects to Study

Biology, chemistry, physics, math, computer science

Discover More

You can get more information about this job by writing to the Joint Review Committee on Educational Programs in Nuclear Medicine Technology, #1 2nd Avenue East, Suite C, Polson, MT 59860-2320.

Related Jobs

Cardiovascular technologists and technicians, clinical laboratory technologists and technicians, diagnostic medical sonographers, nuclear medicine technologists, respiratory therapists

Education & Training
Associate's degree to Bachelor's degree

Earnings
$$$$

Job Outlook
Above-average increase

Surgical Technologists

On the Job

Surgical technologists set up equipment in the operating room, prepare patients for surgery, and take patients to and from the operating room. They help the surgical team "scrub" and put on gloves, masks, and surgical clothing. During an operation, they help with supplies and instruments and operate lights and equipment. After the operation, they restock the operating room. Surgical technicians must be able to stay calm and steady in stressful circumstances.

Something Extra

Most doctors use anesthesia to prevent a patient from feeling pain during surgery. Today, however, some patients are undergoing major surgery without anesthesia. Instead, doctors are using acupuncture, an ancient Chinese practice of inserting needles into various parts of the body that control feelings. Once the needles are in place, the patient feels no pain.

Subjects to Study

Health, biology, chemistry, math, anatomy, English, foreign languages

Discover More

Surgical technicians must be comfortable dealing with operations of all kinds. One way to test your tolerance for this is to take a biology course in which you dissect an animal.

Related Jobs

Dental assistants, licensed practical and licensed vocational nurses, clinical laboratory technologists and technicians, medical assistants

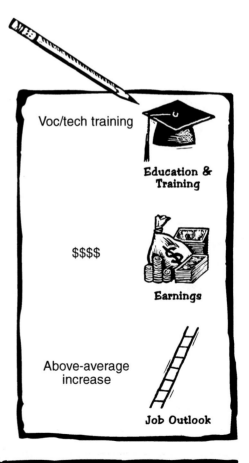

Voc/tech training

Education & Training

$$$$

Earnings

Above-average increase

Job Outlook

Veterinary Technologists and Technicians

On the Job

Veterinary Technologists and Technicians perform many of the same duties for a veterinarian that a nurse would for a physician, including laboratory and clinical work such as urine and blood tests. They may work in private vets' offices, zoos, research facilities, and other places where veterinarians work.

Subjects to Study

Biology, math, chemistry, communications

Discover More

Volunteer to help out at your local Humane Society or vet's office. Watch the veterinary technicians at work and see the kinds of things they do to help the vet and the animals. It's often unpleasant work, but you do get to be around animals!

Related Jobs

Animal care and service workers, veterinarians

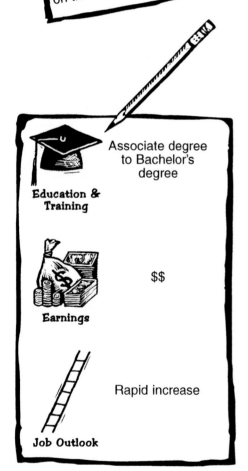

Education & Training
Associate degree to Bachelor's degree

Earnings
$$

Job Outlook
Rapid increase

Service Occupations

Dental Assistants

On the Job

Dental assistants help dentists during patient exams and treatments. They schedule appointments, keep patient records, handle billing, and order supplies. Those with lab duties clean removable dentures and make temporary crowns for teeth. They wear gloves and masks to protect themselves from diseases and germs.

Many work evenings and Saturdays, and they spend a good part of their time on their feet.

Subjects to Study

Biology, chemistry, health, business, math, computer skills, psychology

Discover More

Visit your dentist's office and ask about careers in this field. Does your dentist employ an assistant? What does he or she do? Ask the assistant about training and the job.

Related Jobs

Medical assistants, occupational therapist assistants and aides, pharmacy aides, pharmacy technicians, physical therapist assistants and aides

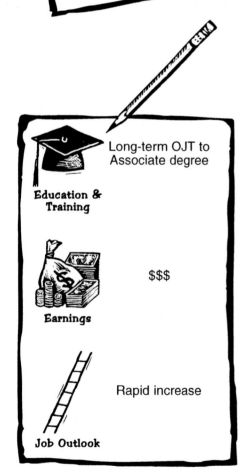

Education & Training
Long-term OJT to Associate degree

Earnings
$$$

Job Outlook
Rapid increase

Medical Assistants

On the Job

Medical assistants help keep your doctor's office running smoothly. They answer phones, greet patients, schedule appointments, arrange for hospital admissions and tests, handle billing, and file records. They may take medical histories, explain treatments to patients, and help doctors with exams. They must have good people skills. Many work evenings and weekends.

Something Extra

Do you like small children? Does holding a baby make your day? Do people tell you that you have "a way" with kids? If so, being a medical assistant in a pediatrician's office might be just the job for you. Pediatric medical assistants must enjoy children, have a high tolerance for noise and chaos, and love helping people.

Subjects to Study

Math, health, biology, typing, bookkeeping, computer skills, office skills, English, foreign languages

Discover More

Ask your own doctor if you can spend a day in the office, watching what the medical assistants do. Maybe you can help file papers, answer phones, or make copies.

Related Jobs

Dental assistants, medical records and health information technicians, occupational therapist assistants and aides, pharmacy aides, physical therapist assistants and aides

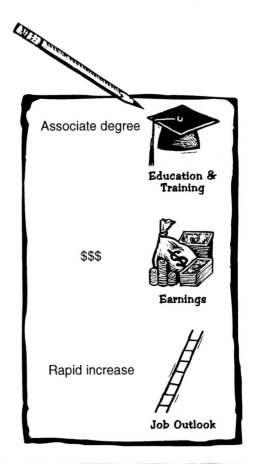

Associate degree

Education & Training

$$$

Earnings

Rapid increase

Job Outlook

Medical Transcriptionists

On the Job

Medical transcriptionists listen to dictated recordings made by doctors and transcribe them into medical reports, letters, and other written materials. They use a special headset, using a foot pedal to pause the tape when necessary, and type the materials into a computer, editing it for grammar and clarity. Some transcriptionists work in doctor's offices or hospitals, but many work as freelancers from home.

Subjects to Study

Typing, English, anatomy, medical terminology, foreign languages

Discover More

Make a recording of yourself or a friend reading material out loud from a book or magazine. Then try typing the material from the recording. Even if the person on the recording reads slowly, you'll have to type fast to keep up!

Related Jobs

Court reporters; human resources assistants, except payroll and timekeeping; receptionists and information clerks; secretaries and administrative assistants; medical assistants; medical records and health information technicians

Education & Training — Associate degree

Earnings — $$$

Job Outlook — Above-average increase

Nursing, Psychiatric & Home Health Aides

On the Job

Nursing and psychiatric aides care for patients in hospitals, nursing homes, and mental health clinics. Home health aides care for patients in the home. All of these workers feed, bathe, and dress patients, help them get in and out of bed, take temperatures and blood pressures, and set up equipment. They report any signs or changes to doctors or nurses. Most work some weekends and evening hours. They must be strong enough to lift and move patients.

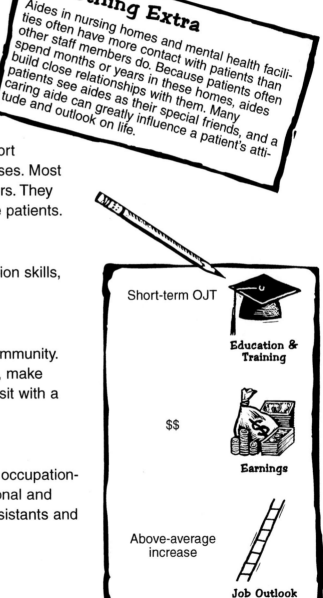

Something Extra

Aides in nursing homes and mental health facilities often have more contact with patients than other staff members do. Because patients often spend months or years in these homes, aides build close relationships with them. Many patients see aides as their special friends, and a caring aide can greatly influence a patient's attitude and outlook on life.

Subjects to Study

Health, nutrition, anatomy, communication skills, English, psychology

Discover More

Volunteer at a nursing home in your community. You might be asked to read to patients, make deliveries, help with activities, or just visit with a patient who is lonely.

Related Jobs

Childcare workers, medical assistants, occupational therapist assistants and aides, personal and home care aides, physical therapist assistants and aides

Short-term OJT

Education & Training

$$

Earnings

Above-average increase

Job Outlook

Occupational Therapist Assistants & Aides

On the Job

Occupational therapist assistants help therapists in clinics, rehab centers, nursing homes, and home health care programs. They help injured patients regain use of damaged muscles. They might also help patients learn to use wheelchairs or other devices. They also help mentally disabled patients learn living skills like cooking and keeping a checkbook. Occupational therapy aides keep patient records and set up equipment. These workers must be strong enough to lift and move patients and equipment.

Subjects to Study

Health, anatomy, physical education, communication skills, English, psychology

Discover More

Try teaching younger children an activity or game. Plan out the activity, decide whether it's appropriate for their age group, then teach the children how to play. Watch to make sure they play fairly and safely.

Related Jobs

Occupational therapists, dental assistants, medical assistants, pharmacy aides, pharmacy technicians, physical therapist assistants and aides

Education & Training

Short-term OJT to Associate degree

Earnings

$$–$$$$

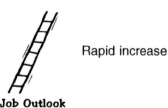

Job Outlook

Rapid increase

Pharmacy Aides

On the Job

Pharmacy aides help licensed pharmacists by answering phones, stocking shelves, and running the cash register. They also maintain patient files, prepare insurance papers, and take inventory of medicines and supplies. Some also clean pharmacy equipment. They may work evenings or weekends; some even work overnight shifts in 24-hour pharmacies.

Subjects to Study

English, foreign languages, biology, typing, business

Discover More

Talk with the pharmacist at your local drug store. What opportunities are available for students wanting to work part-time? Maybe you'll land a job!

Related Jobs

Pharmacy technicians, cashiers, stock clerks and order fillers, dental assistants, licensed practical and licensed vocational nurses, medical transcriptionists, medical records and health information technicians, occupational therapist assistants and aides, physical therapist assistants and aides, surgical technologists

Something Extra

Pharmacy aides play a critical role in helping the pharmacy maintain good patient records. This has become more important than ever in recent years, with so many older Americans taking more than one prescription drug at a time. For example, it's not uncommon for a single person to take medication for high blood pressure, heart problems, and arthritis. The pharmacist must keep track of those medications to ensure that the patient doesn't have a bad drug interaction, which could be serious or even fatal.

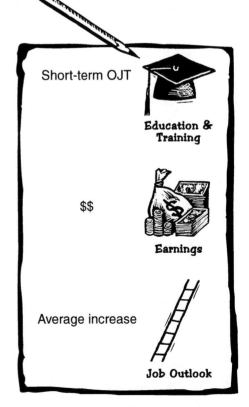

Short-term OJT

Education & Training

$$

Earnings

Average increase

Job Outlook

Physical Therapist Assistants & Aides

Something Extra

When LeBron James pulls a muscle, who does he turn to for help? A sports medicine specialist is a physical therapist specializing in sports-related injuries. These workers help athletes prepare their bodies for competition, and they are on hand during sporting events to help in emergencies. After an injury or illness, they work with an athlete to help him or her rebuild muscle tone and agility.

On the Job

Physical therapist assistants help physical therapists care for patients in hospitals, nursing homes, and home health care programs. They help patients recovering from injuries or disease improve their mobility, relieve pain, and regain muscle use. They may help with exercises, give massages, and apply hot/cold packs. Physical therapy aides keep equipment in good order, move patients to and from the treatment area, and help with record keeping.

Subjects to Study

Health, anatomy, physical education, communication skills, English, psychology

Discover More

Ask your gym teacher to show you some exercises you can use to strengthen your own muscles. Then teach these exercises to family members or friends. Set up a regular exercise schedule for yourself.

Related Jobs

Physical therapists, dental assistants, medical assistants, occupational therapist assistants and aides, pharmacy aides, pharmacy technicians

Education & Training
Short-term OJT to Associate degree

Earnings
$$–$$$$

Job Outlook
Rapid increase

Correctional Officers

On the Job

Correctional officers guard people who are awaiting trial and those who have been convicted of crimes. They keep order and enforce rules in jails or prisons and assign and supervise inmates' work. They help inmates with personal problems and report any bad behavior. To prevent escapes, they stand guard in towers and at gates. They work indoors and outdoors under very stressful conditions. Many work nights and weekends. These workers must be strong and able to use firearms.

Something Extra

In the late 1700s, England used the colony of Australia as a huge prison. Convicted thieves and murderers boarded ships in England and sailed to Australia, 12,000 miles from home. Some prisoners mistakenly believed that the island country was connected to China and died trying to walk to freedom. Others tried to escape by sea and were never heard from again. Much of Australia's population today is descended from these exiles.

Subjects to Study

Physical education, driver's education, psychology, sociology

Discover More

Some state prisons give tours to the public or to school groups. Check to see whether you can visit one to learn more about this job.

Related Jobs

Security guards and gaming surveillance officers, police and detectives, probational officers and correctional treatment specialists

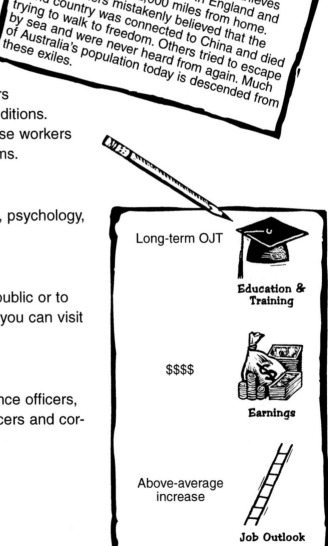

Long-term OJT

Education & Training

$$$$

Earnings

Above-average increase

Job Outlook

Firefighting Occupations

On the Job

Firefighters protect people from the dangers of fires. They must stay physically fit and strong. At the scene of a fire, they rescue victims, perform emergency medical aid, and operate and maintain equipment. During their shifts, firefighters live at the fire station. Most work 50 hours a week or more. Forest firefighters may parachute into a fire area to put out fires and dig a fire line. Firefighting is one of the most dangerous jobs in the U.S. economy.

Subjects to Study

Physical science, chemistry, driver's education, physical education

Discover More

Tour the fire station in your neighborhood or at your local airport. Ask the firefighters about their jobs, the training they receive, and the risks of the job.

Related Jobs

Emergency medical technicians and paramedics, police and detectives

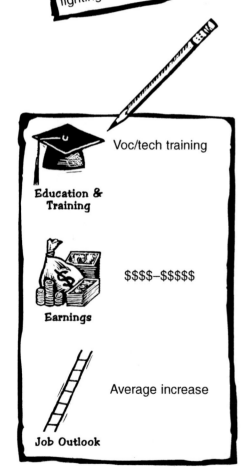

Education & Training
Voc/tech training

Earnings
$$$$–$$$$$

Job Outlook
Average increase

Police & Detectives

On the Job

Police, detectives, and special agents protect people from crime and violence. They patrol highways, issue traffic tickets, and help accident victims. They also collect evidence and investigate crimes. Police detectives often testify in court about their cases. Most work some evenings and weekends. Police work is dangerous and stressful.

Something Extra

The top law enforcement officers in the United States are the special agents of the Federal Bureau of Investigation. These top cops investigate crimes such as bank robberies, terrorism, kidnapping, drug smuggling, and spying. Special agents train at the FBI Academy in Virginia and are then assigned to a field office, usually not anywhere near their hometowns.

Subjects to Study

English, psychology, sociology, chemistry, physics, driver's education, physical education, foreign languages

Discover More

Police officers often check for fingerprints at the scene of a crime. Make your own fingerprinting kit with talcum powder, a paintbrush, and a magnifying glass. Dust the powder lightly on a solid, shiny surface such as a doorknob. Blow gently. The powder will blow away, except where the greasy marks are. Brush the powdered spots lightly with the paintbrush and examine the prints with the glass.

Related Jobs

Correctional officers, private detectives and investigators, security guards and gaming surveillance officers

Long-term OJT to Bachelor's degree

Education & Training

$$$$–$$$$$

Earnings

Above-average increase

Job Outlook

Private Detectives & Investigators

On the Job

Private detectives and investigators work for lawyers, insurance companies, and other kinds of businesses. They gather information for trials, track down people who owe companies money, and conduct background checks. Some are self-employed and specialize in searching for missing persons or finding information for divorce cases.

They may spend long hours watching a person or place, hunting for clues, and interviewing people. They often work irregular hours and travel, and the work may be dangerous.

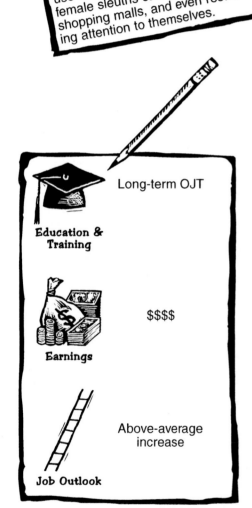

Education & Training
Long-term OJT

Earnings
$$$$

Job Outlook
Above-average increase

Subjects to Study

English, psychology, sociology, chemistry, physics, driver's education, physical education, foreign languages

Discover More

An investigator's main job is collecting information. Use your investigative skills to find interesting information about this job. What can you find at the library or on the Internet that you didn't know before?

Related Jobs

Bill and account collectors; claims adjusters, appraisers, examiners, and investigators; police and detectives; security guards and gaming surveillance officers; accountants and auditors; financial analysts and personal finance advisors

Security Guards & Gaming Surveillance Officers

On the Job

Guards protect property from fire, theft, vandalism, and break-ins. They patrol the area by walking, driving a car or motor scooter, or checking people entering and leaving the area. Guards may carry a nightstick or gun. Most work some nights and weekends, and the work can be dangerous. Gaming surveillance officers work in casinos and gaming parlors, watching for people who are trying to cheat the system.

Something Extra

Do people call you independent? Do you think of yourself as a loner? Security guards often work alone for hours at a time—especially those who work as night watchmen. To provide them with some protection, businesses sometimes give their night guards transmitters. The guards use these to maintain contact with a central station. If the guard does not check in at the expected times, or if he or she doesn't respond to a call, the station sends someone to check on him or her.

Subjects to Study

English, driver's education, physical education, communication skills, computer skills

Discover More

Call a security company in your area and ask if you can speak with someone who hires security guards. Ask that person about the skills you would need to be a guard. Does the company provide training?

Related Jobs

Correctional officers, police and detectives, private detectives and investigators

Short-term OJT

Education & Training

$$–$$$

Earnings

Above-average increase

Job Outlook

Chefs, Cooks & Food Preparation Workers

On the Job
Chefs and cooks plan and make meals in restaurants, schools, cafeterias, and hospitals. They supervise other workers, order supplies, and plan menus. Kitchen workers help chefs and cooks by chopping vegetables, measuring ingredients, and stirring soups and sauces. They also keep the kitchen clean and wash dishes.

These workers are on their feet all day in crowded, hot kitchens. Most work evenings and weekends, and many work part-time.

Subjects to Study
Home economics, nutrition, vocational education, math, health

Discover More
Plan your family's dinner menus for a week. Make a grocery list for your meals, then go with a parent to the store and get your ingredients. Help out in the kitchen to make your meals.

Related Jobs
Food processing occupations, food service managers

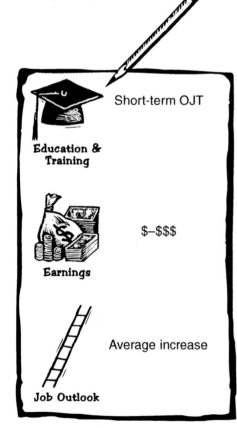

Education & Training — Short-term OJT

Earnings — $–$$$

Job Outlook — Average increase

Food & Beverage Serving & Related Workers

On the Job

Food and beverage service workers deal with customers in restaurants. They take food orders, fill drink orders, serve food, prepare the bill, and may accept payment. Other workers clean dirty tables and reset them with silverware and napkins. These workers spend hours on their feet. They carry heavy trays and must serve customers quickly and courteously. Most work evenings and weekends, and many work part-time.

Subjects to Study

English, foreign languages, math, accounting, speech

Discover More

The best way to learn about the restaurant industry is to work in it. Look for a part-time job at a fast-food restaurant. Or talk to friends who have worked in one. Find out what they liked and disliked about the job. What hours and days did they work?

Related Jobs

Flight attendants, gaming services occupations, retail salespersons

Something Extra

Working in a restaurant is a time-honored first job for many people. And, because the hours are flexible, many aspiring actors and actresses take restaurant jobs while they wait for their big breaks. Movie actors Brad Pitt and Kevin Bacon and *Friends* star Jennifer Aniston all waited tables while they auditioned in Hollywood. Comedian Drew Carey worked in a Denny's restaurant. And Sandra Bullock worked as a bartender while waiting for her first big role.

Short-term OJT

Education & Training

$–$$

Earnings

Average increase

Job Outlook

Building Cleaning Workers

On the Job

Building cleaning workers keep offices, schools, hospitals, hotels, and other public buildings clean and in good condition. They clean, repair, empty trash cans, paint, and mow lawns. Cleaning supervisors assign jobs, supervise workers, and order supplies. These people often work evenings and weekends. The work can be dirty and strenuous.

Subjects to Study

Shop courses, home economics, physical education, accounting

Discover More

Talk to the janitor at your school. Make a list of all the chores and different tasks he or she does. Ask about the best part of the job. What is the worst part of the job?

Related Jobs

Pest control workers; industrial machinery installation, repair, and maintenance workers except millrights; grounds maintenance workers

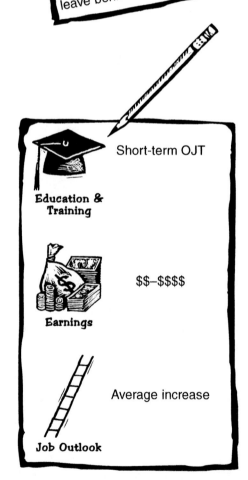

Education & Training — Short-term OJT

Earnings — $$–$$$$

Job Outlook — Average increase

Grounds Maintenance Workers

On the Job

Grounds maintenance workers care for lawns, trees, gardens, and other plants and keep the grounds free of litter. They may prune, feed, and water gardens and mow and water lawns at private homes and public places. They also maintain athletic fields, golf courses, cemeteries, and parks. They work outside in all kinds of weather. Many are self-employed and work seasonally.

Something Extra

Are you happiest when you're outside? Does your perfect day involve sunshine, fresh air, and hard work? Do you like using your muscles and your mind together? If so, landscaping work might be just what you're looking for. These workers plant, prune, weed, and mow to make public areas beautiful. If your green thumb is your pride and joy, this could be the job for you.

Subjects to Study

Biology, zoology, botany, driver's education, business math

Discover More

Plant some flowers around your home or in a pot inside. Start with some easy annuals like snapdragons, petunias, or marigolds. Next, try something trickier, like orchids or roses. Can you make your flowers grow?

Related Jobs

Agricultural workers; farmers, ranchers, and agricultural managers; forest, conservation, and logging workers; landscape architects; biological scientists

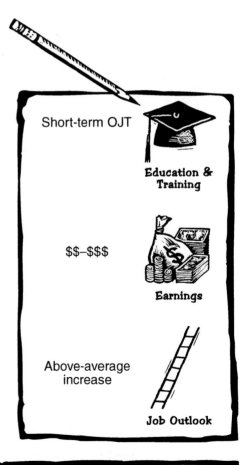

Short-term OJT

Education & Training

$$–$$$

Earnings

Above-average increase

Job Outlook

Pest Control Workers

On the Job

Pest control workers find and kill roaches, rats, mice, spiders, termites, ants, bees—all kinds of pests that invade people's homes and offices. They use chemicals, poisonous fumes, traps, and electrical equipment to eliminate pests. They travel to homes and offices to perform their work, often crawling and climbing into tight places. They wear protective gear, including respirators, gloves, and goggles, when working with pesticides. Some work evenings and weekends, but most work regular 40-hour-a-week shifts. Some pest controllers are self-employed.

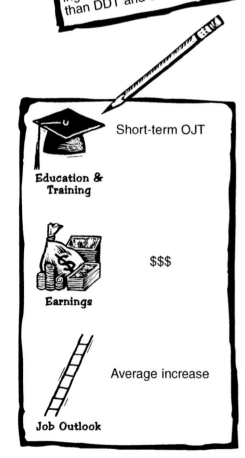

Education & Training
Short-term OJT

Earnings
$$$

Job Outlook
Average increase

Subjects to Study

Biology, chemistry, physical education, computer skills, business math, driver's education

Discover More

Learn more about the kinds of bugs that inhabit your state by starting a bug collection. Find as many different kinds of insects as possible, then mount them on heavy-duty white cardboard using straight pins. Identify them using a field guide from the library, then label each specimen you find and learn about its habitat, food, and natural prey.

Related Jobs

Building cleaning workers; carpenters; electricians; heating, air-conditioning, and refrigeration mechanics and installers

Animal Care & Service Workers

On the Job

Animal care and service workers feed, water, bathe, and exercise animals in clinics, kennels, and zoos. They play with the animals, watch them for illness or injury, and clean and repair their cages. Kennel staff care for cats and dogs; stable workers groom, exercise, and care for horses; and zookeepers care for wild and exotic animals. They may work outdoors in all kinds of weather. The work can be dirty and dangerous. Many work weekends and nights, and some travel with animals to sports events or shows.

Something Extra

Feeding the animals in a zoo can be a real challenge. Zookeepers must know what kind of food the animals need, how much they need, and when to feed them. They must be very careful feeding animals such as lions, tigers, and alligators. Exotic animals might need special foods that must be specially ordered or grown. Zookeepers must plan menus for hundreds of picky eaters on a daily basis—just like preschool workers!

Subjects to Study

Life sciences, zoology, biology, chemistry, physical education

Discover More

You can learn more about this occupation by volunteering at a zoo or animal shelter. You might play with or cuddle small animals, clean cages, put out food and water, or take animals for walks.

Related Jobs

Farmers, ranchers, and agricultural managers; agricultural workers; veterinarians; veterinary technologists and technicians; biological scientists; medical scientists

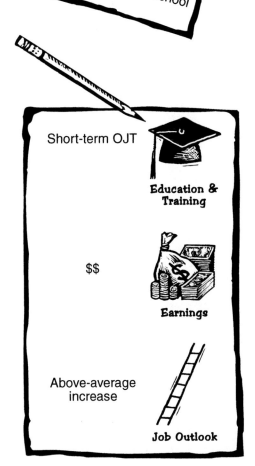

Short-term OJT

Education & Training

$$

Earnings

Above-average increase

Job Outlook

Barbers, Cosmetologists & Other Personal Appearance Workers

On the Job

These workers help people look their best. They cut, shampoo, style, color, and perm hair. They may fit customers for hairpieces, shave male customers, and give facial massages and advice on makeup. Many cosmetologists are trained to give manicures. They also keep customer records and order supplies. These workers spend a lot of time on their feet. Many work part time, and many are self-employed.

Subjects to Study

Communication skills, business, accounting, speech, health

Discover More

Set up a beauty salon at home and practice on yourself or a friend. Look through magazines for the latest styles, then wash and style your friend's hair and give him or her a facial.

Related Jobs

Recreation and fitness workers

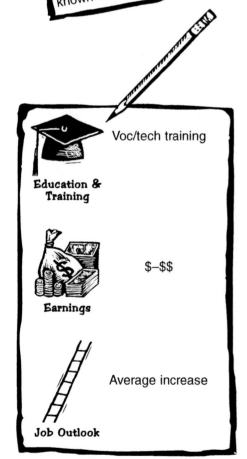

Voc/tech training

Education & Training

$–$$

Earnings

Average increase

Job Outlook

Childcare Workers

On the Job

Childcare workers care for children under the age of five. Those caring for infants and toddlers may change diapers, heat bottles, and rock children to sleep. Those caring for preschoolers serve meals, play games, read stories, and organize activities to help the children socialize and learn new skills.
The work can be tiring, and workers must be strong enough to lift and move children.

Subjects to Study

English, child development, psychology, home economics, art, music, drama, health, speech

Discover More

Visit a day-care center and talk with the workers and children. What type of training do the workers have? The easiest way to learn about this job is to baby-sit or help someone else take care of young children.

Related Jobs

Teacher assistants; teachers—preschool, kindergarten, elementary, middle, and secondary; and teachers—special education

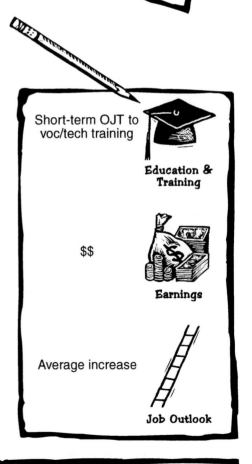

Short-term OJT to voc/tech training

Education & Training

$$

Earnings

Average increase

Job Outlook

Flight Attendants

Education & Training
Long-term OJT to voc/tech training

Earnings
$$$$

Job Outlook
Average increase

On the Job

Flight attendants help keep airline passengers safe and comfortable. In an emergency, they help passengers react calmly and quickly. They also stock the plane with food, drinks, blankets, first-aid kits, and other supplies. During the flight, they serve food and drinks and answer questions. They may administer first aid to passengers who become ill. They work long, irregular hours, travel extensively, and spend hours on their feet. They must remain calm in emergencies.

Subjects to Study

English, communication skills, foreign languages, speech, first aid, health, physical education, self-defense courses

Discover More

For more information on becoming a flight attendant, visit the Web site for the Association of Flight Attendants: www.afanet.org.

Related Jobs

Emergency medical technicians and paramedics, firefighting occupations

Gaming Services Occupations

On the Job

Most gaming services workers are employed by casinos—places where people play games of chance for money. Supervisors oversee the gaming tables and workers. Slot attendants watch over the slot machines, making sure everything is working smoothly. Gaming dealers operate games such as blackjack, craps, and roulette. All gaming workers must be licensed and have good customer-relations skills.

Something Extra

Say the word casino, and most people immediately think of Las Vegas, Nevada—gaming capital of the world. But today, there are casinos in states all across the U.S., from Mississippi to Illinois to Washington State. Some operate on riverboats, others on Native American reservation lands. But all are in the business of selling dreams.

Subjects to Study

English, foreign languages, math, business, psychology

Discover More

You can learn the rules for different card and table games used in casinos, and about casino careers, by checking out www.americangaming.org.

Related Jobs

Security guards and gaming surveillance officers, recreation and fitness workers, sales worker supervisors, cashiers, retail salespersons, gaming cage workers, tellers

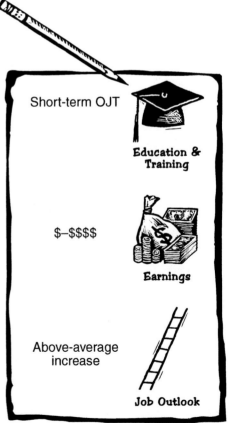

Short-term OJT

Education & Training

$–$$$$

Earnings

Above-average increase

Job Outlook

Personal & Home Care Aides

On the Job

Home health and personal care aides help elderly, disabled, and seriously ill patients to live at home instead of in a nursing home. They clean, do laundry, prepare meals, and help with personal hygiene. They also check the patient's pulse and blood pressure and give medication. Aides keep records of each patient's condition and progress. They often work part-time and weekend hours.

Subjects to Study

Home economics, nutrition, health, first aid, English, foreign languages

Discover More

Set up your own "rent-a-kid" service in your neighborhood. Can you help out in your neighbors' homes by cleaning, ironing clothes, running errands, or doing yard work to earn extra money?

Related Jobs

Nursing, psychiatric and home health aides; occupational therapist assistants and aides; physical therapist assistants and aides

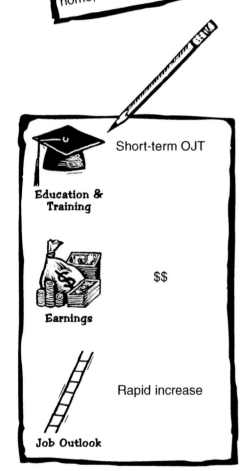

Education & Training
Short-term OJT

Earnings
$$

Job Outlook
Rapid increase

Recreation & Fitness Workers

On the Job

Recreation and fitness workers often work as camp counselors or coaches, organizing leisure activities at parks, health clubs, camps, tourist sites, and other places. They teach people how to use recreation equipment properly and safely. They often work nights and weekends. Recreation workers may work in state and national parks, health clubs, or even cruise ships. Many work part time.

Something Extra

People from all walks of life can get a taste of the wilderness with Outward Bound expeditions. Teenagers, senior citizens, school groups, and business groups can take two-week treks into the mountains. There, they go hiking, white-water rafting, rock climbing, and backcountry skiing. Outward Bound trainers help the adventurers build their self-confidence and their teamwork, while making sure they are safe.

Subjects to Study

English, communication skills, business, accounting, physical education, swimming, art, music, drama, sports

Discover More

Call your local YMCA, YWCA, Boys' or Girls' Club, or community center and volunteer to help out. You might be asked to watch younger children, teach them games, or help maintain equipment.

Related Jobs

Counselors; probational officers and correctional treatment specialists; psychologists; recreational therapists; social workers; athletes, coaches, umpires, and related workers

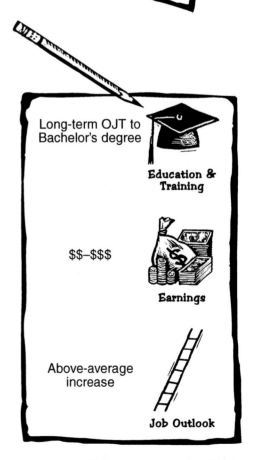

Long-term OJT to Bachelor's degree

Education & Training

$$–$$$

Earnings

Above-average increase

Job Outlook

Sales & Related Occupations

Cashiers

On the Job

Cashiers add up customers' bills, take their money, and give change. They also fill out charge forms for credit cards and give receipts. Cashiers are responsible for the money they collect during their shifts. They cannot leave their cash drawers without permission from their supervisor. Cashiers use cash registers, scanners, and computers regularly.

Subjects to Study

Math, English, communication skills, computer skills, typing, business

Discover More

Volunteer to work as a cashier at a church, club, or family rummage sale. Make sure you have enough money in the cash drawer to make change for the customers. Save the tags from the items paid for at your cash drawer. Add the total sales to the amount that was in your cash drawer before the sale. Then count the money in your drawer. Does it balance?

Related Jobs

Tellers, counter and rental clerks, food and beverage serving and related workers, gaming cage workers, Postal Service workers, retail salespersons

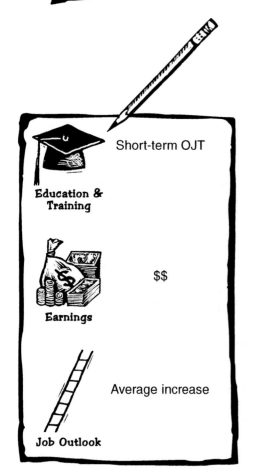

Short-term OJT

Education & Training

$$

Earnings

Average increase

Job Outlook

Counter & Rental Clerks

On the Job
Counter and rental clerks take orders, figure out fees, receive payment, and accept returns. They answer questions about what kinds of items are in stock and how much they cost. They must know about the company's services and policies. Some fill out forms and tickets by hand, but most use computers and scanners.

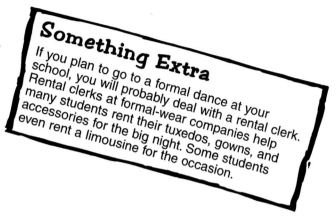

Something Extra
If you plan to go to a formal dance at your school, you will probably deal with a rental clerk. Rental clerks at formal-wear companies help many students rent their tuxedos, gowns, and accessories for the big night. Some students even rent a limousine for the occasion.

Subjects to Study
Math, English, communication skills, computer skills, typing

Discover More
Go to a video store and rent a video or DVD. Watch what the rental clerk does to rent the item to you and to make sure that you will return it. Ask questions about the job.

Related Jobs
Tellers, cashiers, food and beverage serving and related workers, gaming cage workers, Postal Service workers, retail salespersons

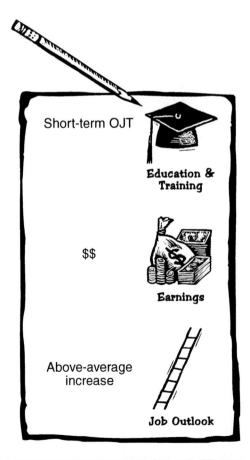

Short-term OJT

Education & Training

$$

Earnings

Above-average increase

Job Outlook

Demonstrators, Product Promoters & Models

On the Job

Demonstrators show products to customers, either in retail stores or in private homes. Product promoters try to convince stores to carry new products. They may set up displays in stores or host special activities to show off their products. Models pose for photographs to display clothing, makeup, and other accessories. They also wear designer clothes during fashion shows and work in television commercials. All of these workers travel as part of their jobs.

Subjects to Study

Communication, marketing, mathematics, photography, public speaking, sociology, foreign languages

Discover More

Do a product demonstration for your class. Design a catchy poster and slogan, write a script, and come up with a gimmick to draw people's attention. Try to convince your classmates that your product is one they definitely want to have.

Related Jobs

Actors, producers, and directors; insurance sales agents; real estate brokers and sales agents; retail salespersons; sales representatives, wholesale and manufacturing; reservation and transportation ticket agents and travel clerks

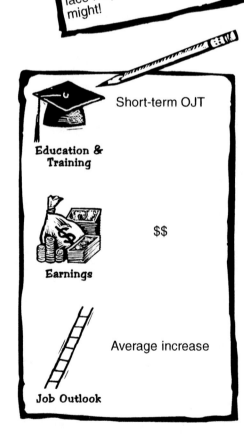

Education & Training
Short-term OJT

Earnings
$$

Job Outlook
Average increase

Insurance Sales Agents

On the Job

Insurance agents sell insurance policies to people and businesses. Insurance policies protect the people and companies who buy them against different kinds of losses. Common policies include health, life, and car insurance. Insurance agents and brokers help people choose the policies that best meet their needs. Agents work for a single insurance company. Insurance brokers are independent and sell insurance for several different companies. Agents and brokers often must schedule meetings in the evenings or on weekends.

Something Extra

People buy insurance to protect their assets. But not all assets are cars or houses. The famous insurance group Lloyd's of London has issued some odd insurance policies in recent years. Some of these policies include accident insurance for Russian cosmonauts traveling to the MIR space station; coverage in case of a crocodile attack; and insuring a famous model's legs, a singer's vocal chords, and a food critic's taste buds.

Subjects to Study

Math, accounting, economics, government, psychology, sociology, speech, computer skills

Discover More

Ask your parents what kinds of insurance they have. How did they choose their insurance plans? Do they receive insurance through their employers?

Related Jobs

Real estate brokers and sales agents; securities, commodities, and financial services sales agents; financial analysts and personal financial advisors; financial managers; insurance underwriters; claims adjusters, appraisers, examiners, and investigators

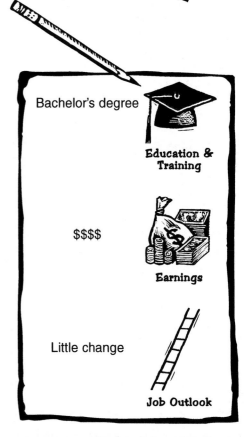

Bachelor's degree

Education & Training

$$$$

Earnings

Little change

Job Outlook

Real Estate Brokers & Sales Agents

Something Extra

Most people shopping for a new home look at a lot of different houses. After a while, it's easy to forget which home had which feature. Did the house on Elm Street have a fireplace? Did the house on Parker have the covered porch, or was that the one on Fifth? That's why some people videotape the houses they visit. This helps them remember what they liked and didn't like about each house. Some agents use videos to show homes to clients who are moving from one area to another.

On the Job

Real estate agents and brokers help people buy and sell homes and rental properties. Real estate agents show homes, help buyers get financing, and make sure the contract conditions are met. Brokers may sell houses and rent and manage properties. These workers must know and understand their local housing market.

Subjects to Study

Math, English, accounting, economics, business, communication skills, computer skills, psychology

Discover More

You can usually find free real estate and rental magazines at grocery stores or drugstores. Look through one to find out what homes and properties are available in your community. How much do homes and apartments in your area cost?

Related Jobs

Insurance sales agents; retail salespersons; sales representatives, wholesale and manufacturing; securities, commodities, and financial services sales agents; property, real estate, and community association managers

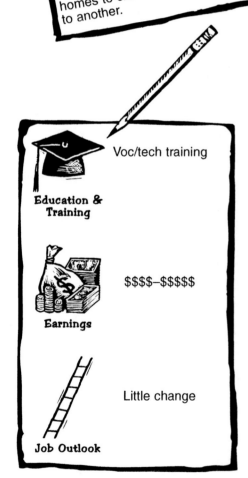

Voc/tech training

Education & Training

$$$$–$$$$$

Earnings

Little change

Job Outlook

Retail Salespersons

On the Job

Retail salespersons help customers choose and buy all kinds of items, from sweaters and makeup to lumber and plumbing. Their primary job is to interest customers in whatever products they are selling. They also fill out sales checks, take payment, bag purchases, and give change and receipts. Most sales workers are responsible for keeping track of the money in their cash registers.

Subjects to Study

Math, English, communication skills, computer skills

Discover More

Watch the sales workers the next time you go shopping. What jobs do they do? How do they approach customers? How do they help you?

Related Jobs

Sales representatives, wholesale and manufacturing; securities, commodities, and financial services sales agents; counter and rental clerks; real estate brokers and sales agents; purchasing managers, buyers, and purchasing agents; insurance sales agents; sales engineers; cashiers

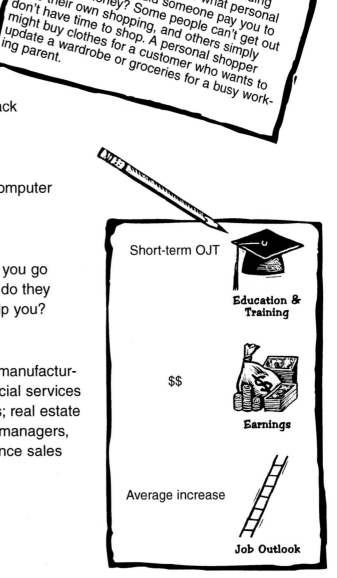

Something Extra

How would you like to get paid for spending someone else's money? That's what personal shoppers do. Why would someone pay you to spend their money? Some people can't get out to do their own shopping, and others simply don't have time to shop. A personal shopper might buy clothes for a customer who wants to update a wardrobe or groceries for a busy working parent.

Short-term OJT

Education & Training

$$

Earnings

Average increase

Job Outlook

Sales Engineers

Something Extra

We've all heard the jokes about traveling sales-men. Sales engineers are a far cry from the people peddling vacuum cleaners and encyclo-pedias door-to-door. Their customers are large and small businesses that need specialized ser-vices and products—everything from production machinery to dry-cleaning chemicals, and from huge database systems to tiny electrical compo-nents. They don't go door-to-door, but they do travel a lot. Some spend months at a time on the road, racking up frequent-flyer miles!

On the Job

Sales engineers work for companies that produce complex products—such as chemicals or technical tools. They help customers decide which prod-ucts or services will work best for them. Selling is an important part of the job, but sales engineers also help their customers learn to use the products they buy. They also may help companies produce bet-ter materials based on customer feedback.

Subjects to Study

Math, chemistry, biology, physics, English, foreign languages, psychology

Discover More

For more information on becoming a sales engi-neer, contact the Manufacturers' Agents National Association at www.manaonline.org, or the Manufacturers Representatives Educational Research Foundation at www.mrerf.org.

Related Jobs

Advertising, marketing, promotions, public rela-tions, and sales managers; engineers; insurance sales agents; purchasing managers, buyers, and purchasing agents; real estate brokers and sales agents; sales representatives, wholesale and manufacturing; securities, commodities, and finan-cial services sales agents

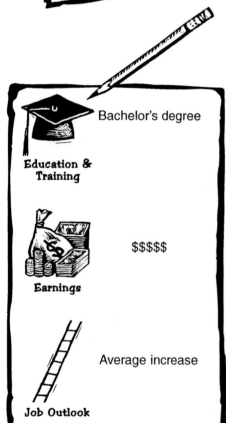

Education & Training
Bachelor's degree

Earnings
$$$$$

Job Outlook
Average increase

Sales Representatives, Wholesale & Manufacturing

On the Job

Manufacturing and wholesale sales representatives sell products to businesses, government agencies, and other institutions, often traveling for several days or weeks at a time. They answer questions about their products and show clients how the products can meet their needs and save them money. They also take orders and resolve problems or complaints about their merchandise.

Something Extra

Most sales representatives are paid on commission. Instead of receiving a regular paycheck, they get paid based on their sales: The more they sell, the more money they make. Few or no sales means little or no money. Many sales means big paychecks. Salespeople must learn to budget and pay their bills knowing that their income is unpredictable.

Subjects to Study

Math, English, speech, communication skills, accounting, business, psychology, foreign languages, computer skills

Discover More

Think of some businesses in your community (such as hospitals, grocery stores, and restaurants) that might order products from manufacturers' sales representatives. What kind of products would each of these businesses buy?

Related Jobs

Advertising, marketing, promotions, public relations, and sales managers; insurance sales agents; purchasing managers, buyers, and purchasing agents; real estate brokers and sales agents; retail salespersons; sales engineers; securities, commodities, and financial services sales agents

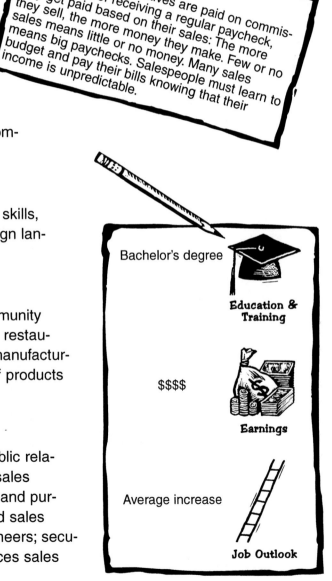

Bachelor's degree

Education & Training

$$$$

Earnings

Average increase

Job Outlook

Sales Worker Supervisors

On the Job

Sales worker supervisors work in all kinds of stores—dress shops, toy stores, convenience stores, and bakeries. They hire, train, and supervise workers. They also make the schedule of who will work what hours. They order supplies, keep the books, make bank deposits, and often wait on customers. Most work evenings and weekends.

Subjects to Study

Math, English, psychology, business, communication skills, computer skills

Discover More

Visit a shop in your neighborhood and ask the manager if you can help out after school one or two days a week. You might help stock shelves or clean up. Watch the manager at work and ask about the best and worst parts of the job.

Related Jobs

Financial managers, food service managers, lodging managers, medical and health services managers

Education & Training
Work experience to long-term OJT

Earnings
$$$$–$$$$$

Job Outlook
Little change

Securities, Commodities & Financial Services Sales Agents

On the Job

Securities and commodities sales agents buy and sell stocks, bonds, and other financial products for clients who want to invest in the stock market. They explain terms and the advantages and disadvantages of different investments. Financial service sales agents usually work for banks. They contact potential customers to sell their bank's services, which might include retirement planning and other investment services.

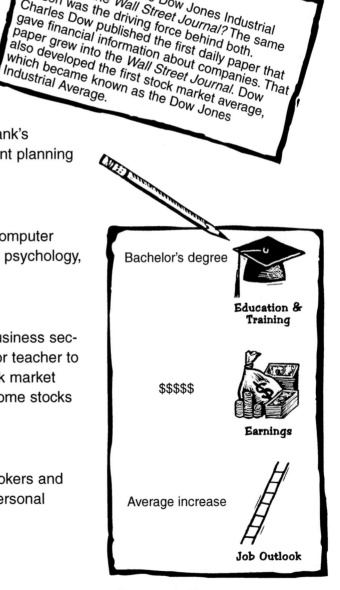

Something Extra

Have you heard of the Dow Jones Industrial Average or the *Wall Street Journal?* The same person was the driving force behind both. Charles Dow published the first daily paper that gave financial information about companies. That paper grew into the *Wall Street Journal.* Dow also developed the first stock market average, which became known as the Dow Jones Industrial Average.

Bachelor's degree

Education & Training

$$$$$

Earnings

Average increase

Job Outlook

Subjects to Study

Math, English, communication skills, computer skills, speech, accounting, economics, psychology, government, business

Discover More

Find the stock market listings in the business section of your newspaper. Ask a parent or teacher to explain them to you. Listen to the stock market report on news programs or look up some stocks on the Internet.

Related Jobs

Insurance sales agents, real estate brokers and sales agents, financial analysts and personal financial advisors

Travel Agents

On the Job

Travel agents make hotel, airline, car-rental, and cruise reservations for people and businesses. They plan group tours and conferences. They tell clients what papers they need to travel in foreign countries. They must be up-to-date on cultural and political issues, restaurants, and tourist attractions.

Subjects to Study

Communication skills, computer skills, typing, geography, English, foreign languages, history, math, business, accounting

Discover More

What foreign country are you curious about? Read about that country and find it on a map. Then find an Internet site where you can learn more about life in that country.

Related Jobs

Reservation and transportation ticket agents and travel clerks

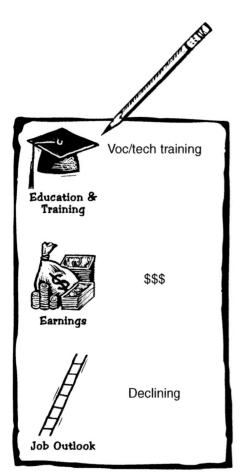

Voc/tech training

Education & Training

$$$

Earnings

Declining

Job Outlook

Office & Administrative Support Occupations

Communications Equipment Operators

On the Job

Most communications equipment operators are telephone operators, helping customers find the phone numbers they need, place collect calls, or make overseas calls. These operators are employed by large telephone companies. Switchboard operators work in offices, hospitals, and hotels helping to route incoming and outgoing phone calls.

Communications equipment operators work in offices, usually wearing portable headgear that frees their hands for typing. They may work nights and weekends.

Subjects to Study

Communication, public speaking, computer skills, typing, foreign languages, spelling skills

Discover More

For more information about a career as a communications equipment operator, contact the Communications Workers of America, 2725 El Camino Ave., Sacramento, CA 95821; (916) 484-9421. Or check out their Web site: www.cwa-union.org.

Related Jobs

Dispatchers; hotel, motel, and resort desk clerks; information and record clerks; customer service representatives; receptionists and information clerks; reservation and transportation ticket agents and travel clerks

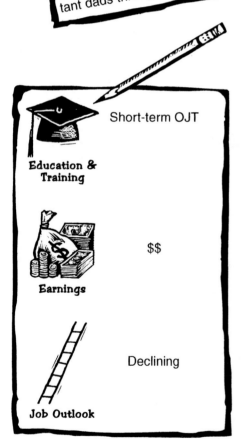

Short-term OJT

Education & Training

$$

Earnings

Declining

Job Outlook

Computer Operators

On the Job

Computer operators supervise computer hardware systems and keep them working smoothly. They watch for and try to prevent computer problems. On a daily basis, they might check the computer's controls and load tapes, paper, and disks as needed. When there is a computer error, they must locate and solve the problem.

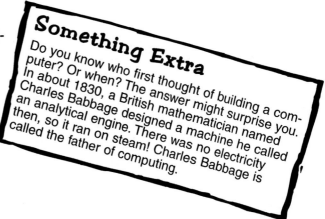

Something Extra

Do you know who first thought of building a computer? Or when? The answer might surprise you. In about 1830, a British mathematician named Charles Babbage designed a machine he called an analytical engine. There was no electricity then, so it ran on steam! Charles Babbage is called the father of computing.

Subjects to Study

Math, English, communication skills, computer science, computer skills, typing

Discover More

How do blind people use computers? Visit your local library and ask whether it has any talking or Braille computers. (Braille is a special kind of raised writing that blind people "read" with their fingertips.) Sit in front of the computer, close your eyes, and try to use it.

Related Jobs

Computer software engineers; computer programmers; computer support specialists and systems administrators; computer systems analysts, database administrators, and computer scientists; data entry and information processing workers; secretaries and administrative assistants

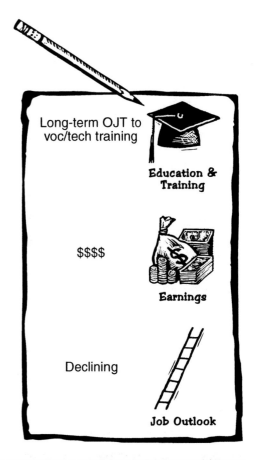

Long-term OJT to voc/tech training

Education & Training

$$$$

Earnings

Declining

Job Outlook

Customer Service Representatives

On the Job

Customer service representatives work directly with customers, answering questions, taking orders, and solving problems when things go wrong.

Many work for utilities, such as electric or gas companies or cable TV companies. They may handle billing mistakes, arrange for customers to have services switched on or off, and listen to lots of complaints.

These workers spend a lot of time on the phone.

Subjects to Study

English, foreign languages, psychology, office skills, typing, computer skills

Discover More

The next time you have a problem with a product or service, pay special attention to how the customer service representative handles it. He or she must stay calm under pressure, be polite and helpful, and work quickly and efficiently.

Related Jobs

Information and record clerks; financial clerks; tellers; insurance sales agents; securities, commodities, and financial services sales agents; retail salespersons; computer support specialists and system administrators; gaming services occupations

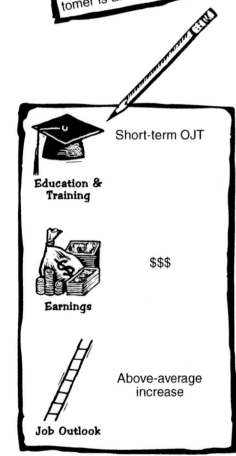

Education & Training
Short-term OJT

Earnings
$$$

Job Outlook
Above-average increase

Data Entry & Information Processing Workers

On the Job

Information processing workers set up and type reports, letters, manuscripts, and mailing labels. They may have other office duties as well, such as filing, answering telephones, and sorting mail. Data entry workers fill out forms that appear on computer screens or enter lists of items or numbers. Sometimes they also proofread and edit documents.

Subjects to Study

English, office skills, computer skills, typing, spelling, punctuation, grammar

Discover More

Before you begin a career in this field, you must type at least 50 words per minute accurately. One way to learn to type faster is by typing to music. Start with something moderately slow, then work up to faster and faster beats. The more you practice, the easier it becomes!

Related Jobs

Dispatchers, communications equipment operators, court reporters, medical records and health information technicians, secretaries and administrative assistants, computer operators

Something Extra

You have a lot of choices if you can type, word process, and do data entry. You might work for a large insurance company or type manuscripts for a book author. You can work for a service that does data entry for many different companies or work in a hospital, a doctor's office, a fashion-design firm, or a lawyer's office. You can even start your own business and work from home.

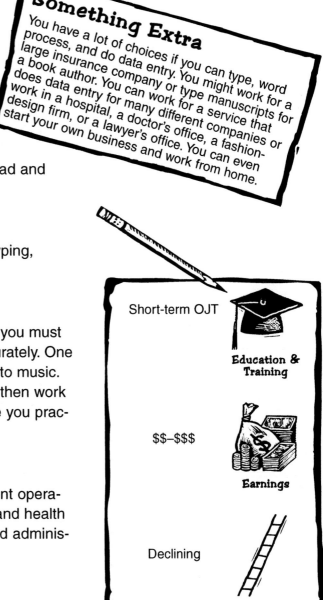

Short-term OJT

Education & Training

$$–$$$

Earnings

Declining

Job Outlook

Desktop Publishers

On the Job

Desktop publishers use computers to format text, photos, charts, and other graphic elements to produce newsletters, magazines, calendars, business cards, newspapers, books, and other publications. Most work in firms that handle commercial printing and in newspaper plants, but many are self-employed. This is one of the 10 fastest growing jobs in the U.S.

Subjects to Study

Computer studies, art, graphic design, photography, English, business, typing

Discover More

Use a personal computer at home or school to design your own newsletter, or volunteer to work on your school newspaper or yearbook. Look through several magazines and newsletters—what catches your eye? What would you change? Can you think of a more attractive way to present the material?

Related Jobs

Medical records and health information technicians, pharmacy aides, dental assistants, occupational therapist assistants and aides, physical therapist assistants and aides

Education & Training
Short- to long-term OJT

Earnings
$$$$

Job Outlook
Above-average increase

Financial Clerks

On the Job

Financial clerks keep track of money. They record all amounts coming into or leaving a business. Most work in offices maintaining records, but some work directly with customers, taking in and paying out money. When bills are not paid on time, financial clerks contact customers to find out why and try to resolve the problem. Some also keep track of a store's inventory and order replacement stock when supplies are low.

Something Extra

Do you know what embezzlement is? It means stealing money from your workplace, often by "doctoring" the books. It's a common problem in the U.S., costing businesses millions of dollars annually. So what's the solution? Financial clerks! These workers are on the front lines in the war against embezzlement, double-checking their company records for accuracy and completeness. In several recent court cases, it was the financial clerk who brought in defining evidence against company bigwigs who were embezzling.

Subjects to Study

Math, business, computer studies, English, foreign languages

Discover More

Volunteer to be the treasurer for a school, church, or social club. Your job is to keep track of all the money coming in and being spent by your organization, and to keep good records so that the club knows where its money is coming from and going.

Related Jobs

Brokerage clerks; cashiers; credit authorizers, checkers, and clerks; interviewers; order clerks; secretaries and administrative assistants

Associate degree

Education & Training

$$–$$$$

Earnings

Little change

Job Outlook

Bill & Account Collectors

On the Job

Bill and account collectors keep track of accounts that are overdue and try to collect payment on them. Some are employed by third-party collection agencies; others work directly for companies such as stores, hospitals, or banks. They locate and notify customers who owe money. They use computers and special software to keep track of clients, and they spend a lot of time on the phone.

Subjects to Study

Math, English, computer skills, business, accounting, foreign languages, psychology

Discover More

Spend a day in the collection office of your local hospital. Talk to the collectors and ask for their most interesting cases; many have wild stories about people going to great lengths to escape paying their bills.

Related Jobs

Bookkeeping, accounting, and auditing clerks; gaming cage workers; payroll and timekeeping clerks; procurement clerks; tellers

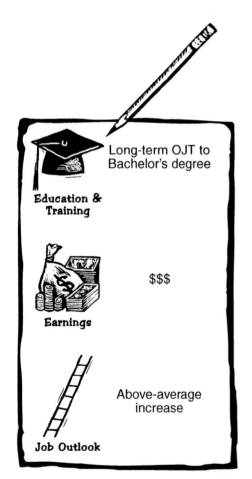

Education & Training
Long-term OJT to Bachelor's degree

Earnings
$$$

Job Outlook
Above-average increase

Billing & Posting Clerks & Machine Operators

On the Job

Billing and posting clerks keep records of customers' charges and payments. They calculate the total amount due from a customer and prepare a detailed bill showing any new charges and payments. Billing machine operators print out bills and invoices, which are sent to customers.

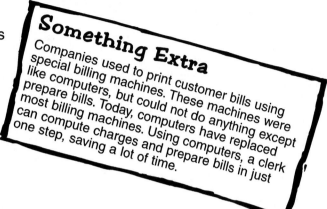

Something Extra

Companies used to print customer bills using special billing machines. These machines were like computers, but could not do anything except prepare bills. Today, computers have replaced most billing machines. Using computers, a clerk can compute charges and prepare bills in just one step, saving a lot of time.

Subjects to Study

Math, computer skills, office skills, English, typing, accounting, bookkeeping, business

Discover More

Ask your parents to show you some of the bills they receive. What information is included on each bill? Ask what the terms "transaction date" and "closing date" mean.

Related Jobs

Bill and account collectors; bookkeeping, accounting, and auditing clerks; gaming cage workers; payroll and timekeeping clerks; procurement clerks; tellers

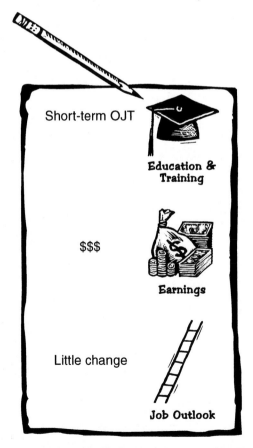

Short-term OJT

Education & Training

$$$

Earnings

Little change

Job Outlook

Bookkeeping, Accounting & Auditing Clerks

On the Job

Bookkeeping and accounting clerks keep records of all the money their company spends and receives. They prepare reports, post bank deposits, and pay bills. Auditing clerks check the financial records of other employees in an organization and correct any errors they find.

Subjects to Study

Math, office skills, computer skills, English, business, accounting

Discover More

Keep your own financial records. Use a notebook to record any money you receive from allowance, gifts, or chores. Then record how you spend your money. Keep your receipts and banking records in a file.

Related Jobs

Bill and account collectors; billing and posting clerks and machine operators; gaming cage workers; payroll and timekeeping clerks; procurement clerks; tellers

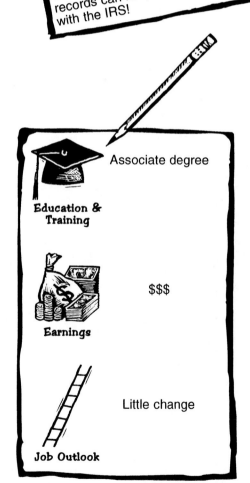

Education & Training — Associate degree

Earnings — $$$

Job Outlook — Little change

Gaming Cage Workers

On the Job

Gaming cage workers, also called cage cashiers, work in casinos and other gaming companies. The "cage" they work in is the central depository for money, chips, and paperwork. They do credit checks on people who want to open a casino credit account and sell gambling chips, tokens, and tickets. They use cash registers, adding machines, and computers to add up transactions.

Something Extra

Many people think of casinos as exotic, glamorous places. Some are, but many are not! Workers in gaming places must stand on their feet for long hours; deal with angry and upset customers—some of whom have had too much to drink—and breathe the smoke from other people's cigarettes. Turnover is high in this profession.

Subjects to Study

Math, business, English, foreign languages

Discover More

To learn about careers in the gaming industry, check out the Web site for the American Gaming Association: www.americangaming.org.

Related Jobs

Bill and account collectors; billing and posting clerks and machine operators; bookkeeping, accounting, and auditing clerks; payroll and time-keeping clerks; procurement clerks; tellers

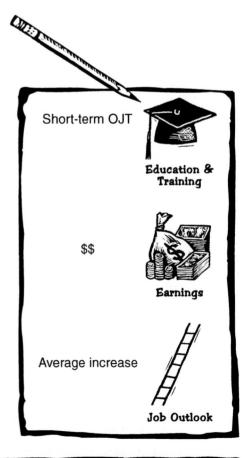

Short-term OJT

Education & Training

$$

Earnings

Average increase

Job Outlook

Payroll & Timekeeping Clerks

On the Job

Payroll and timekeeping clerks make sure that workers get their paychecks on time and that the checks are for the right amount. Timekeeping clerks collect timecards from employees and check them for errors. Payroll clerks figure a worker's pay by adding up the hours worked and subtracting taxes, insurance, and other deductions.

Subjects to Study

Math, office skills, computer skills, English

Discover More

Ask your parents to show you their paycheck stubs. Notice the difference between the "gross" and "net" earnings. Find out what costs (such as insurance, taxes, and savings plans) are taken out of the paycheck. These are called "deductions."

Related Jobs

Bill and account collectors; billing and posting clerks and machine operators; bookkeeping, accounting, and auditing clerks; gaming cage workers; procurement clerks; tellers

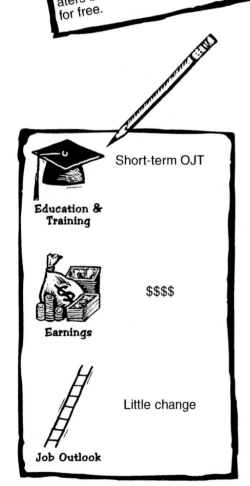

Short-term OJT

Education & Training

$$$$

Earnings

Little change

Job Outlook

Procurement Clerks

On the Job

Procurement clerks order the supplies and materials companies need to stay in business. They keep track of orders, making sure they arrive on schedule at the right price and meet the company's needs. These clerks perform inventory checks, keep spreadsheets, and place orders when stocks are short. They work in companies of all sizes and all kinds.

Something Extra

Procurement clerks used to be vital employees of most businesses. Today, however, with advances in technology, many clerks are being replaced by automated systems. Orders can be placed automatically as supplies get low. For example, many stores use cash registers that keep track of stock and place reorders whenever supplies go below a set level. Of course, some companies will always need a real, live human being to order inventory. But there are fewer today than yesterday.

Subjects to Study

Math, office skills, computer skills, English, foreign languages

Discover More

Try keeping track of inventory in your kitchen at home. Make a simple spreadsheet on graph paper, noting how much of each item your family has on hand. When you notice something is getting low, write it down on a list hanging on the refrigerator so that it gets bought on the next grocery trip.

Related Jobs

Bill and account collectors; billing and posting clerks and machine operators; bookkeeping, accounting, and auditing clerks; gaming cage workers; payroll and timekeeping clerks; tellers

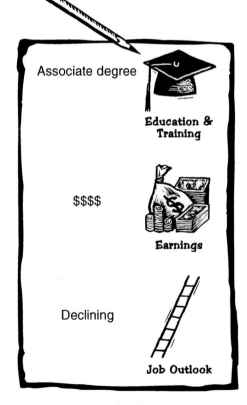

Associate degree

Education & Training

$$$$

Earnings

Declining

Job Outlook

Tellers

On the Job

Tellers work for banks, credit unions, and pension funds. They cash checks, make deposits and withdrawals, and accept loan payments. They use computers to keep records. Tellers begin work before the bank opens by counting the cash in their drawers and end the workday by accurately balancing their cash drawers with the day's receipts. They must be friendly with customers, even when customers are rude to them.

Subjects to Study

Math, English, communication skills, computer skills, typing, foreign languages, accounting, bookkeeping

Discover More

Open a savings or checking account at your local bank or credit union. Ask the teller to explain how to make deposits and withdrawals and how to use the ATM. Watch what the teller does as he or she helps you.

Related Jobs

Bill and account collectors; billing and posting clerks and machine operators; bookkeeping, accounting, and auditing clerks; gaming cage workers; payroll and timekeeping clerks; procurement clerks

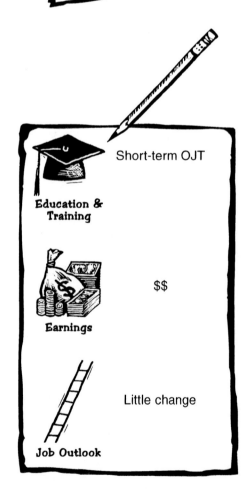

Short-term OJT

Education & Training

$$

Earnings

Little change

Job Outlook

Information & Record Clerks

On the Job

Information and record clerks might be called hotel clerks, receptionists, airline reservation agents, or travel clerks. All information and record clerks either get information from people or answer questions about their employer's services or products. Their workdays are filled with answering multi-line telephones, greeting visitors, helping customers, and using fax machines and computers.

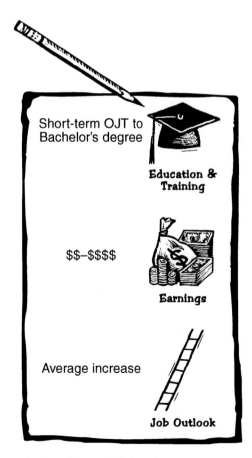

Something Extra

Information clerks use the telephone a lot in their work. You might use one a lot at home, too. But did you know that the telephone was originally invented for hearing-impaired people? Alexander Graham Bell was a teacher of the deaf. He was trying to find a way to help deaf people communicate when he invented the telephone in 1876.

Subjects to Study

English, communication skills, speech, computer skills, foreign languages, typing

Discover More

Do you know how your voice sounds on the telephone? Record a message in your normal speaking voice and play it back. If you don't like the way you sound, work on changing your voice and the way you speak.

Related Jobs

Customer service representatives, dispatchers, security guards and gaming surveillance officers, tellers, counter and rental clerks

Short-term OJT to Bachelor's degree

Education & Training

$$–$$$$

Earnings

Average increase

Job Outlook

Brokerage Clerks

On the Job

Brokerage clerks record the sale and purchase of stocks, bonds, and other investments. They may contact customers, take orders, and inform clients of changes in their accounts. Most workers assist two stock brokers, for whom they take calls from clients, write up order tickets, and process paperwork. Technology is changing their jobs today. Many now use special computer programs to process transactions.

Subjects to Study

Math, business, office skills, computer skills, English, foreign languages

Discover More

You can learn more about the investment industry by checking out these Web sites on the Internet:

The Young Investor
www.younginvestor.com
Kids' Money
www.kidsmoney.org
EduStock
http://library.thinkquest.org/3088/

Related Jobs

Credit authorizers, checkers, and clerks; file clerks; hotel, motel, and resort desk clerks; human resources assistants, except payroll and timekeeping; interviewers; library assistants, clerical; order clerks; receptionists and information clerks; reservation and transportation ticket agents and travel clerks

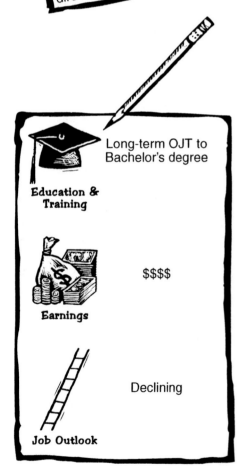

Education & Training
Long-term OJT to Bachelor's degree

Earnings
$$$$

Job Outlook
Declining

Credit Authorizers, Checkers & Clerks

On the Job

Credit clerks collect and confirm information that people give when they apply for credit. Sometimes they investigate further by verifying employment or financial information. Credit authorizers research credit records and decide whether customers have enough good credit to pay for what they want to buy.

Something Extra

Anyone who has a credit card or who has taken out a loan to buy something has a credit history. Credit bureaus keep track of these histories. You will start creating your credit history the first time you buy something on credit. If you don't pay your bills on time, your credit report will show that. If you make a habit of not paying your bills on time, you might not be able to buy a house or a car that you want.

Subjects to Study

English, communication skills, computer skills, math, typing

Discover More

Ask your parents if they know what information is in their credit histories. What credit cards do they have? Ask them if they have a house or car loan. How much do they owe on their loans?

Related Jobs

Brokerage clerks; file clerks; hotel, motel, and resort desk clerks; human resources assistants, except payroll and timekeeping; interviewers; library assistants, clerical; order clerks; receptionists and information clerks; reservation and transportation ticket agents and travel clerks

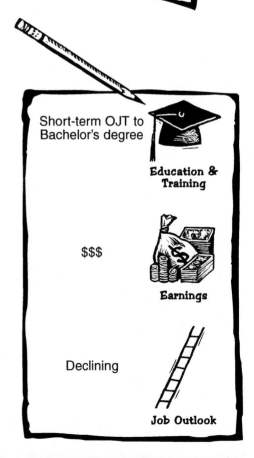

Short-term OJT to Bachelor's degree

Education & Training

$$$

Earnings

Declining

Job Outlook

File Clerks

On the Job

File clerks sort, store, retrieve, and update office records filed according to a company's system. They examine incoming information and mark it with a number or letter code. They store the information in a paper file or enter the information into a computer file. When someone in the company needs information from a file, the clerk retrieves it.

Subjects to Study

English, office skills, typing, computer skills

Discover More

Set up a filing system at home using a file cabinet, folders, or a simple cardboard box. Keep your report cards, medical records, information about sports and activities, and your financial records in it.

Related Jobs

Brokerage clerks; credit authorizers, checkers, and clerks; hotel, motel, and resort desk clerks; human resources assistants, except payroll and timekeeping; interviewers; library assistants, clerical; order clerks; receptionists and information clerks; reservation and transportation ticket agents and travel clerks

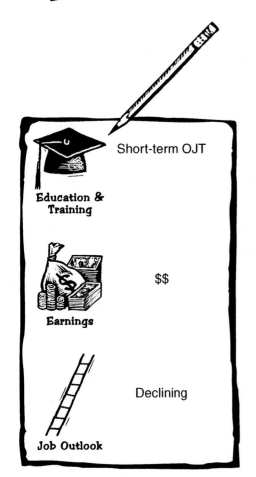

Education & Training
Short-term OJT

Earnings
$$

Job Outlook
Declining

Hotel, Motel & Resort Desk Clerks

On the Job

Hotel, motel, and resort desk clerks help guests check in and out of the inn, using computers to assign rooms. They answer questions about the local area and the establishment itself. They keep records of room assignments and collect payment from guests. In smaller motels, desk clerks may also act as bookkeepers and switchboard operators.

Something Extra

Someone once said, "If you want a real education in the ways of the world, work in a motel!" Hotel and motel desk clerks deal with all kinds of people from all over the world—many of whom are tired, lonely, or frustrated. Clerks must be friendly and courteous, even when a customer is yelling about lost reservations or bad service. They fix problems, answer questions, and soothe angry customers—and they must do it all with a smile.

Subjects to Study

Math, English, geography, psychology, communication skills, speech, typing, computer skills, foreign languages, bookkeeping

Discover More

If you were a desk clerk at a local hotel or motel, what places would you suggest that guests visit? Which restaurants would you recommend? Make a visitor's guide for your community.

Related Jobs

Brokerage clerks; credit authorizers, checkers, and clerks; file clerks; human resources assistants, except payroll and timekeeping; interviewers; library assistants, clerical; order clerks; receptionists and information clerks; reservation and transportation ticket agents and travel clerks

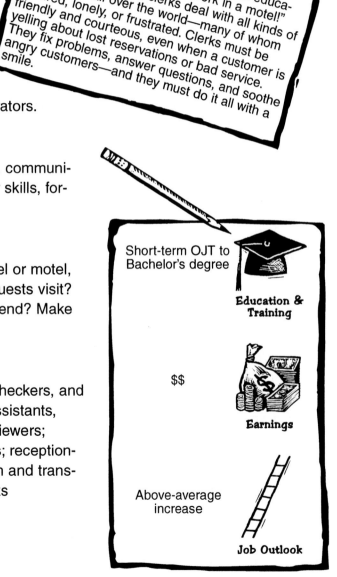

Short-term OJT to Bachelor's degree

Education & Training

$$

Earnings

Above-average increase

Job Outlook

Human Resources Assistants, Except Payroll & Timekeeping

On the Job

Human resources assistants work with people who are applying for jobs in their company as well as with newly hired workers. They explain company rules, dress codes, pay policies, and benefits. They also maintain employee records and notify employees of job openings in the company. When conflicts arise at work, human resources workers help mediate.

Subjects to Study

English, speech, communication skills, office skills, computer skills

Discover More

Get a job application from a business and look at the kind of information it asks for. Practice filling one out. If you can't get an application from a business, check the library for books with examples of job applications.

Related Jobs

Brokerage clerks; credit authorizers, checkers, and clerks; file clerks; hotel, motel, and resort desk clerks; interviewers; library assistants, clerical; order clerks; receptionists and information clerks; reservation and transportation ticket agents and travel clerks

Education & Training
Long-term OJT to Bachelor's degree

Earnings
$$$$

Job Outlook
Average increase

Interviewers

On the Job

Interviewers help people complete consumer surveys. New accounts clerks help people fill out bank account or charge card applications. They might work with people face to face, on the telephone, or by mail. Some interviewers get financial and medical information before admitting patients to a hospital. Others verify information or create new files.

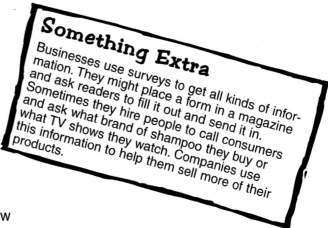

Something Extra

Businesses use surveys to get all kinds of information. They might place a form in a magazine and ask readers to fill it out and send it in. Sometimes they hire people to call consumers and ask what brand of shampoo they buy or what TV shows they watch. Companies use this information to help them sell more of their products.

Subjects to Study

English, spelling, typing, communication skills, math, psychology, foreign languages

Discover More

Take a survey to find out what books your friends are reading. Ask for each book's title and author. Has the person read other books by that author? What kinds of books are your friends reading?

Related Jobs

Brokerage clerks; credit authorizers, checkers, and clerks; file clerks; hotel, motel, and resort desk clerks; human resources assistants, except payroll and timekeeping; library assistants, clerical; order clerks; receptionists and information clerks; reservation and transportation ticket agents and travel clerks

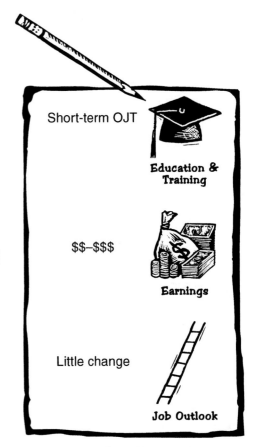

Short-term OJT

Education & Training

$$–$$$

Earnings

Little change

Job Outlook

Library Assistants, Clerical

On the Job

Library assistants help librarians by working at the desk that lends and collects books, issuing library cards, and repairing books. They may provide special help to people who can't see well or to students looking for assignment materials. They file books when they are returned or left out and collect fines for overdue books.

Subjects to Study

English, business math, computer skills, office skills, driver education

Discover More

Volunteer to clerk in your school library. Learn about the computer systems used in libraries to keep track of books, loans, overdue fines, and interlibrary loans. It's a long way from the old-fashioned card file.

Related Jobs

Brokerage clerks; credit authorizers, checkers, and clerks; file clerks; hotel, motel, and resort desk clerks; human resources assistants, except payroll and timekeeping; interviewers; order clerks; receptionists and information clerks; reservation and transportation ticket agents and travel clerks

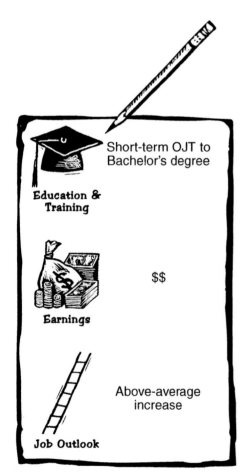

Education & Training
Short-term OJT to Bachelor's degree

Earnings
$$

Job Outlook
Above-average increase

Order Clerks

On the Job

Order clerks receive and fill requests for machine parts, movie rentals, clothing, foods, and all kinds of other items. After completing the order, they send it to the proper department to be filled. They may fill orders from other employees inside a business, from salespeople, or from customers. Most work regular workday hours, but some must work nights and weekends.

Something Extra

Do you like to shop by phone, ordering things from catalogs? If so, you deal with order clerks. More than half of all order clerks work in wholesale or retail sales, and many of them work in catalog sales. These clerks receive orders by mail, e-mail, fax, or phone. They also handle customer questions and complaints. And they must remember the old rule, "The customer is always right!"

Subjects to Study

Math, English, foreign languages, computer skills, office skills

Discover More

Look through a catalog and read the directions for placing an order. Fill out the order form for the products you'd like to buy. Make sure you give all the information asked for on the form. Figure out what your order would cost, including tax and shipping charges.

Related Jobs

Brokerage clerks; credit authorizers, checkers, and clerks; file clerks; hotel, motel, and resort desk clerks; human resources assistants, except payroll and timekeeping; interviewers; library assistants, clerical; receptionists and information clerks; reservation and transportation ticket agents and travel clerks

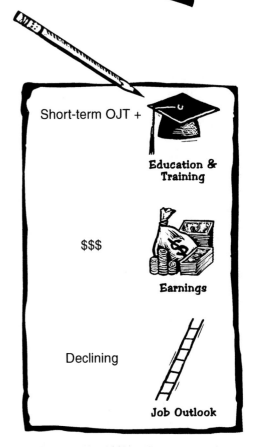

Short-term OJT +

Education & Training

$$$

Earnings

Declining

Job Outlook

Receptionists & Information Clerks

On the Job

Receptionists greet customers on the phone and in person and refer them to the proper person or department. Making a good first impression is an important part of this job, as the receptionist is the first person most customers or clients meet. Information clerks file papers, do basic data entry, and may also be asked to answer phones in the front office.

Subjects to Study

English, communication skills, spelling, speech, typing, computer skills, psychology, foreign languages, business

Discover More

Volunteer to be a greeter or an usher for a school play, a sports event, or a dance. Help people with their questions and concerns. Do you enjoy working with the public?

Related Jobs

Brokerage clerks; credit authorizers, checkers, and clerks; file clerks; hotel, motel, and resort desk clerks; human resources assistants, except payroll and timekeeping; interviewers; library assistants, clerical; order clerks; reservation and transportation ticket agents and travel clerks

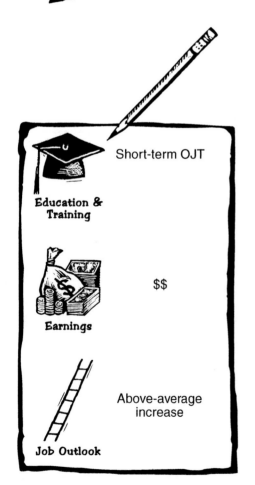

Education & Training
Short-term OJT

Earnings
$$

Job Outlook
Above-average increase

Reservation & Transportation Ticket Agents & Travel Clerks

On the Job

Reservation and transportation ticket agents make and confirm travel and hotel reservations, answer questions about rates and routes, and sell tickets. Travel clerks plan trips and offer travel suggestions. They tell their clients about tourist attractions, quality hotels, and good restaurants. These clerks and agents might work for travel clubs, airlines, hotels, or other businesses.

Something Extra

Many people belong to automobile clubs. Members contact the club when they are planning a trip. They tell the travel clerk where they want to go and when. Then the travel clerk maps out the most convenient route for the trip. The map provides information about roadwork, alternative routes, and scenic side trips. It also shows how many miles the trip will cover and how long it will take.

Subjects to Study

English, math, geography, communication skills, computer skills, foreign languages, psychology, typing, history

Discover More

Look through travel magazines or the travel section of a newspaper. Pick somewhere you would like to visit and send for information about it or look up sites on the Internet that have information about that place.

Related Jobs

Brokerage clerks; credit authorizers, checkers, and clerks; file clerks; hotel, motel, and resort desk clerks; human resources assistants, except payroll and timekeeping; interviewers; library assistants, clerical; order clerks; receptionists and information clerks

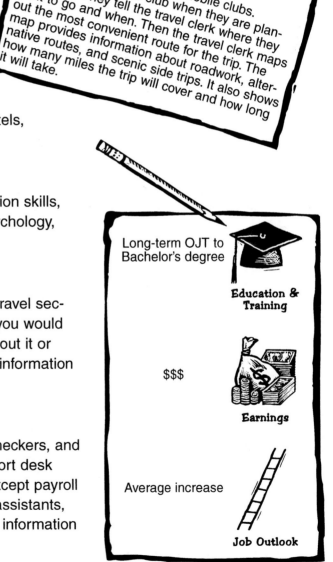

Long-term OJT to Bachelor's degree

Education & Training

$$$

Earnings

Average increase

Job Outlook

Material Recording, Scheduling, Dispatching & Distributing Occupations, Except Postal Workers

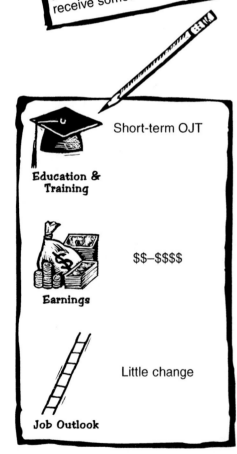

Education & Training

Short-term OJT

Earnings

$$–$$$$

Job Outlook

Little change

On the Job

Material recording, scheduling, dispatching, and distributing workers coordinate and keep track of orders for personnel, equipment, and materials. Clerks unpack, verify, and record arriving merchandise. Dispatchers working for utility companies or fire and police departments send crews where they are needed.

Subjects to Study

Math, computer skills, typing, communication skills, speech, English, physical education, psychology

Discover More

You need to be organized to keep track of materials. Make an inventory of the materials you use at school. What items do you need to restock?

Related Jobs

Cargo and freight agents; couriers and messengers; dispatchers; meter readers, utilities; production, planning, and expediting clerks; shipping, receiving, and traffic clerks; stock clerks and order fillers; weighers, measurers, checkers, and samplers, recordkeeping

Cargo & Freight Agents

On the Job

Cargo and freight agents sort cargo according to where it is going, determine shipping rates and other costs, then track the shipments. They take orders from customers and arrange for pickup of items for delivery to loading platforms. They also check on missing or damaged items.

Cargo and freight agents work for air and railroad carriers, trucking services, and department stores.

Something Extra

Do you love to travel? Do you want to visit far-away, exotic places? If so, being a freight agent with an airline might be the job for you. Many air carriers have overseas offices, and American employees work in some of those offices. And many airlines offer their employees free travel on their planes. Of course, you'll have to fly standby, but it's the best frequent-flyer deal you'll find!

Subjects to Study

Math, English, foreign languages, business, accounting, geography

Discover More

Call a freight service in your town and ask if you can spend a day shadowing a freight agent. Pay attention to the kinds of tasks he or she performs. Ask about the best and worst aspects of the job.

Related Jobs

Couriers and messengers; shipping, receiving, and traffic clerks; weighers, measurers, checkers, and samplers, recordkeeping; truck drivers and driver/sales workers; Postal Service workers

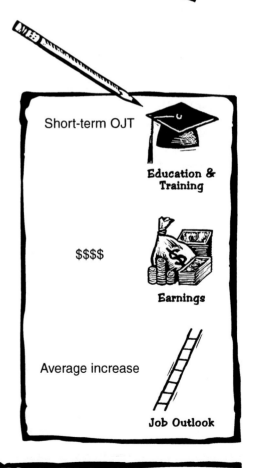

Short-term OJT

Education & Training

$$$$

Earnings

Average increase

Job Outlook

Couriers & Messengers

On the Job

Messengers and couriers drive, walk, or ride bicycles to pick up and deliver letters and packages that must be delivered quickly—usually within a single city. Most work for courier services, although 9 percent work for law firms and many others are self-employed and provide their own vehicles. Some messengers are paid by how many deliveries they make and how far they travel.

Subjects to Study

English, foreign languages, driver's education, geography

Discover More

Start your own local courier service. Offer to deliver letters and packages at your school, church, or local hospital. You will pick up your packages at the main office and deliver them to other rooms in the building, or perhaps to other buildings.

Related Jobs

Postal Service workers; truck drivers and driver/sales workers; shipping, receiving, and traffic clerks; cargo and freight agents

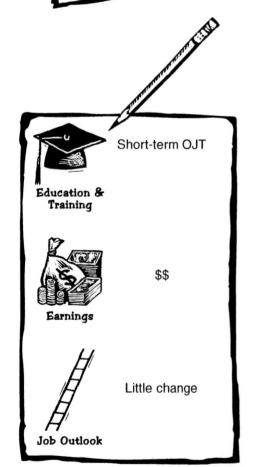

Education & Training — Short-term OJT

Earnings — $$

Job Outlook — Little change

Dispatchers

On the Job

Dispatchers receive emergency calls, find out where help is needed and how serious the situation is, and send police, firefighters, or ambulances to the scene. Dispatchers in transportation coordinate arrivals and departures of shipments to meet specific time schedules. All dispatchers keep records of the calls they receive and what they do about them.

Subjects to Study

English, computer skills, typing, communication skills, psychology, foreign languages

Discover More

Learn how to contact emergency help in your community. Visit a fire or police station and ask for permission to watch a dispatcher work.

Related Jobs

Air traffic controllers, communications equipment operators, customer service representatives, reservation and transportation ticket agents and travel clerks

Something Extra

Emergency dispatchers help save lives. Not only do they direct emergency services to the accident scenes, they sometimes play a direct role in saving lives. 911 operators tell children how to help a sick or injured parent, give instructions for helping people who are in shock, and tell callers how to prevent someone from losing too much blood before help arrives. Emergency dispatchers never know what will happen when they go to work, but they always make a real difference in people's lives.

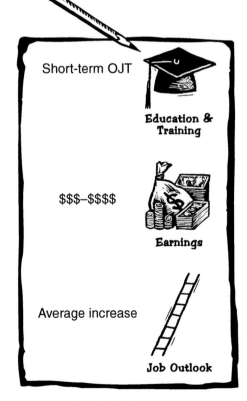

Short-term OJT

Education & Training

$$$–$$$$

Earnings

Average increase

Job Outlook

Meter Readers, Utilities

On the Job

Meter readers check electric, gas, water, or steam meters at businesses and houses, and record how much has been used. They also inspect the meters for damage, and contact repair workers if needed. They may turn off services if the customer does not pay the bill, and turn on services for new customers. These workers drive or walk on their routes and spend a lot of time outdoors.

Subjects to Study

Math, computer skills, business, bookkeeping

Discover More

Check the electric or gas meter on your own house or apartment. Track your family's use for one month. How much electricity or gas did you use? Now check the bill from the utility company. How much does the company charge per unit?

Related Jobs

Power plant operators, distributors, and dispatchers

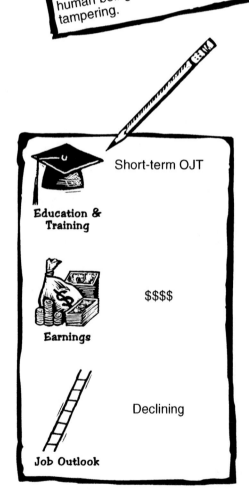

Education & Training — Short-term OJT

Earnings — $$$$

Job Outlook — Declining

Production, Planning & Expediting Clerks

On the Job

These clerks coordinate the flow of information, work, and materials within or among offices. They set and review schedules, estimate costs, keep inventory of materials, inspect and assemble materials, and order replacements when supplies are low. Most work in manufacturing companies and in wholesale trade or grocery stores.

Something Extra

Have you heard the term personnel supply services? Maybe you're more familiar with temp agencies. They perform the same function—supplying workers on a temporary basis to companies that don't want or need those workers on a full-time basis. Many production, planning, and expediting clerks are actually employed by temp agencies rather than the companies in which they do their work. This means less job security, of course, and often no benefits. But it's a good way to check out a job without making a long-term commitment.

Subjects to Study

Math, computer skills, business, bookkeeping, typing, English

Discover More

Visit your local grocery and ask if you can spend a day with the people who do this job. You might help take inventory, order new supplies, answer phones, or check on overdue shipments. Don't forget to ask lots of questions.

Related Jobs

Cargo and freight agents; shipping, receiving, and traffic clerks; stock clerks and order fillers; weighers, measurers, checkers, and samplers, recordkeeping

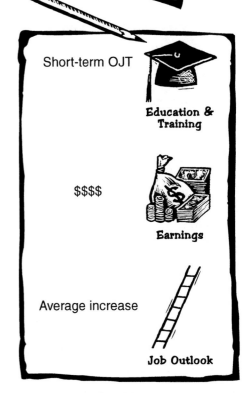

Short-term OJT

Education & Training

$$$$

Earnings

Average increase

Job Outlook

Shipping, Receiving & Traffic Clerks

On the Job

Traffic clerks keep records of all freight coming in and leaving a company and make sure the company is charged correctly. Shipping clerks keep records on all outgoing shipments. They fill orders from the stockroom and direct workers who load products onto trucks. Receiving clerks check materials coming into the warehouse, make sure they are in good condition, and send them to the right departments.

Subjects to Study

Math, computer skills, business, bookkeeping, typing

Discover More

Make a list of basic items you use every day, such as toothpaste, tissues, soap, and shampoo. Check your personal inventory. What items do you need to restock?

Related Jobs

Stock clerks and order fillers; production, planning, and expediting clerks; cargo and freight agents; Postal Service workers

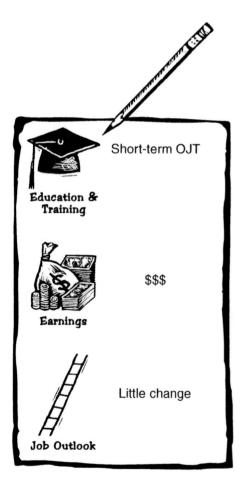

Short-term OJT

Education & Training

$$$

Earnings

Little change

Job Outlook

Stock Clerks & Order Fillers

On the Job

Stock clerks receive, unpack, and check materials into the stockroom. They keep records of items entering and leaving the stockroom and report damaged or spoiled products. Order fillers bring items to the sales floor and stock shelves. They also gather items for shipment in mail-order companies. Many stock clerks work for department or grocery stores.

Something Extra

An inventory is made up of all the products a business has on hand. A business must know what products it has if it is going to be successful. Bar-code systems are the most popular way to track inventory. Bar codes are the black stripes you see on items you buy. Stock clerks use hand-held scanners to read bar codes. This helps keep the inventory accurate. A bar code appears on the back of this book.

Subjects to Study

English, math, computer skills, physical education, bookkeeping

Discover More

Visit a grocery or warehouse-style store. Are there any stock clerks working on the floor? If so, notice how they organize products on the shelves. Ask what they like about the job.

Related Jobs

Shipping, receiving, and traffic clerks; production, planning, and expediting clerks; cargo and freight agents; procurement clerks

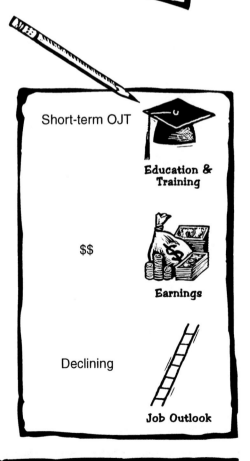

Short-term OJT

Education & Training

$$

Earnings

Declining

Job Outlook

Weighers, Measurers, Checkers & Samplers, Recordkeeping

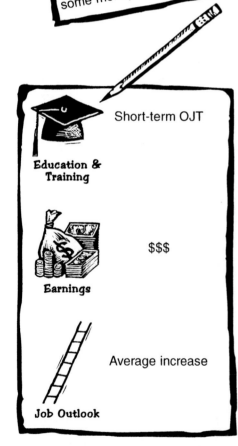

Education & Training
Short-term OJT

Earnings
$$$

Job Outlook
Average increase

On the Job

Just as the job titles imply, these workers weigh, measure, and check materials, supplies, and equipment to keep records. Most of their duties are clerical. They make sure that the amounts, quality, and value of things the company is buying matches what was ordered and paid for.

They use weight scales, counting tools, tally sheets, and calculators in their work.

Subjects to Study

Math, computer skills, business, bookkeeping, typing

Discover More

Go along on a grocery-shopping trip with your parents. Take a tally sheet and a calculator. Record the price listed on each item and check it against the amount the cashier rings up. Keep a running total on the calculator as you go and check that amount against the cashier's as well. When you get home, weigh the items to see that the amount listed on the packaging matches the actual amount you brought home.

Related Jobs

Cargo and freight agents; production, planning, and expediting clerks; shipping, receiving, and traffic clerks; stock clerks and order fillers; procurement clerks

Office & Administrative Support Worker Supervisors & Managers

On the Job

These supervisors and managers make sure their employees work efficiently. If supplies are low or equipment needs to be repaired, they order new supplies or contract with a repair service. They train new employees, plan their work, and check their progress. They evaluate their employees' work habits, recommend pay raises and promotions, and sometimes must fire a worker.

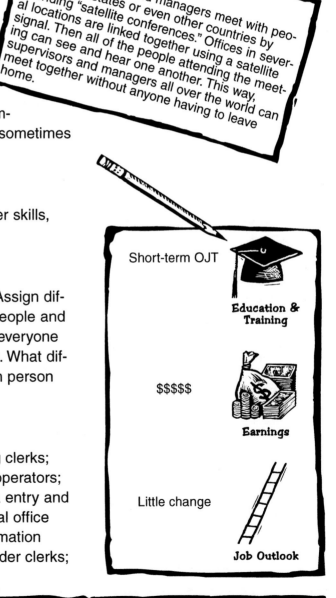

Something Extra

Many supervisors and managers meet with people in other states or even other countries by attending "satellite conferences." Offices in several locations are linked together using a satellite signal. Then all of the people attending the meeting can see and hear one another. This way, supervisors and managers all over the world can meet together without anyone having to leave home.

Subjects to Study

English, communication skills, computer skills, business, math, speech, psychology

Discover More

Volunteer to manage a group project. Assign different parts of the project to different people and check their progress. You'll notice that everyone has his or her own way of doing things. What differences do you notice in the way each person works?

Related Jobs

Bookkeeping, accounting, and auditing clerks; cashiers; communications equipment operators; customer service representatives; data entry and information processing workers; general office clerks, general; receptionists and information clerks; stock clerks and order fillers; order clerks; tellers

Short-term OJT

Education & Training

$$$$$

Earnings

Little change

Job Outlook

Office Clerks, General

On the Job

General office clerks work in all kinds of businesses, from doctors' offices to banks, from big law firms to small companies. Because a business's needs change from day to day, a clerk's job duties do, too. These workers file, type, keep records, prepare mailings, and proofread documents for mistakes. Senior clerks may be responsible for supervising other workers.

Subjects to Study

English, typing, word processing, computer skills, math, office practices, bookkeeping, accounting, business, spelling

Discover More

Can you type? Typing well is important in this and almost any other job. Many offices require clerks to type at least 60 words per minute. Take a typing class, practice, and become a good typist.

Related Jobs

Financial clerks, information and record clerks, secretaries and administrative assistants, data entry and information processing workers, cashiers, counter and rental clerks, food and beverage serving and related workers

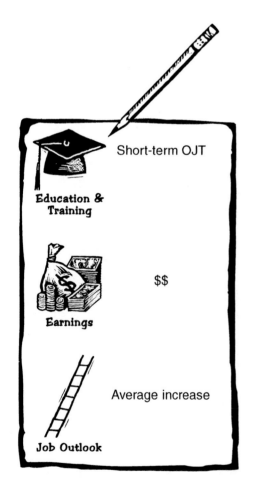

Education & Training
Short-term OJT

Earnings
$$

Job Outlook
Average increase

Postal Service Workers

On the Job

Postal workers sort mail for delivery, sell stamps, weigh packages, and help customers file claims for damaged packages. Mail carriers deliver the mail to homes and businesses on foot or by car. They also pick up mail from homes and businesses on their route.

Subjects to Study

English, physical education, driver education, communication skills, computer skills

Discover More

Find out who delivers your mail and talk to your carrier about his or her job. Does your carrier walk or drive? What are the working hours? What does your carrier like or dislike about the job?

Related Jobs

Cashiers; counter and rental clerks; file clerks; shipping, receiving, and traffic clerks; couriers and messengers; truck drivers and driver/sales workers; inspectors, testers, sorters, samplers, and weighers; material moving occupations

Something Extra

Optical character readers (OCRs) and bar-code sorters make sorting mail much easier and faster than it used to be. They also make it less likely that mail will go to the wrong address. How do they work? OCRs "read" the address line and the ZIP code at a speed of nine letters per second. A bar code is "sprayed" onto the mail, which is then sorted by as many as three different computers.

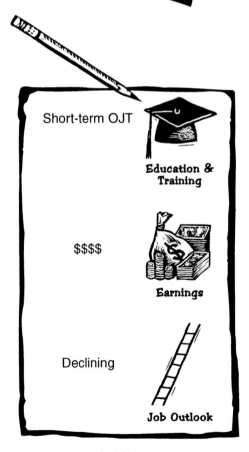

Short-term OJT

Education & Training

$$$$

Earnings

Declining

Job Outlook

Secretaries & Administrative Assistants

Education & Training
Short-term OJT to voc/tech training

Earnings
$$$–$$$$

Job Outlook
Declining

On the Job

Secretaries and administrative assistants help keep offices organized and running smoothly. They schedule appointments, maintain files, type correspondence, greet visitors, and answer telephone calls. They work with office equipment such as computers, fax machines, and copiers. They may supervise clerks and other office workers. Some, such as medical and legal secretaries, do highly specialized work.

Subjects to Study

English, spelling, grammar, speech, typing, computer skills, office skills, math

Discover More

Talk to the secretaries at your school about their training and job duties. Develop some office skills, such as typing, filing, and word processing.

Related Jobs

Bookkeeping, accounting, and auditing clerks; receptionists and information clerks; court reporters; human resources assistants, except payroll and timekeeping; computer operators; data entry and information processing workers; paralegals and legal assistants; medical assistants; medical records and health information technicians

Farming, Fishing & Forestry Occupations

Agricultural Workers

On the Job

Agricultural workers plant, grade, and sort farm products. Some work as inspectors, ensuring that the nation's food supply is safe. They work with food crops, animals, trees, and plants. They may work indoors or outdoors, in all kinds of working conditions. Many work long, irregular hours in plants and on farms. This is one of the most dangerous jobs in the U.S.

Subjects to Study

Physical education, shop courses, driver's education, biology, gardening

Discover More

Plant a garden in your yard or at a community plot. Try your hand at growing some food items: Broccoli, peppers, and tomatoes are easy starters. Look for nonchemical ways to control bugs and other pests. When your crop is ready, make a salad and treat your family to dinner!

Related Jobs

Fishers and fishing vessel operators; forest, conservation, and logging workers; grounds maintenance workers; animal care and service workers

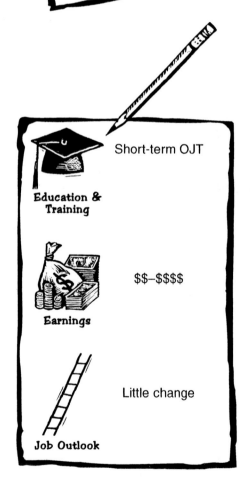

Education & Training
Short-term OJT

Earnings
$$–$$$$

Job Outlook
Little change

Fishers & Fishing Vessel Operators

On the Job

Fishers and fishing vessel operators catch and trap fish and seafood for the country's restaurants and grocery stores. The boat's captain plans and oversees the fishing, hires crew members, and arranges for the day's catch to be sold. The first mate is the captain's assistant and is in charge when the captain is not on duty. The boatswain helps the captain oversee the deckhands, who carry out the sailing and fishing operations. These workers may spend weeks or even months at sea, away from family and friends. The work is hard and sometimes dangerous, and employment can be seasonal.

Something Extra

Moby Dick, Herman Melville's classic book, tells the story of a sea captain's obsessive battle with a particularly vindictive great white whale. Ahab and his crew spend months chasing down the huge beast, and the final epic battle takes the captain's life. These days, whale-hunting is illegal for all but a few Native American groups. But sailors on fishing vessels still spend months at a time on the ocean, battling fatigue and the elements, if not "evil beasts."

Subjects to Study

Physical education, shop courses, mechanics, navigation, business math, first aid

Discover More

Take a boating-safety course to learn more about sailing. To find one near you, check out BoatSafe Kids at www.boatsafe.com/kids/index.htm, which has information on classes, online courses, books, and other Web sites.

Related Jobs

Water transportation occupations

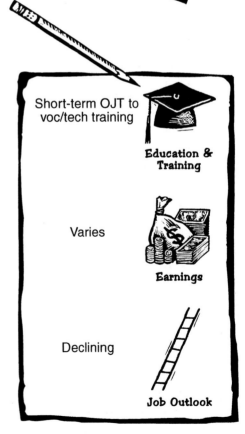

Short-term OJT to voc/tech training

Education & Training

Varies

Earnings

Declining

Job Outlook

Forest, Conservation & Logging Workers

On the Job

Forestry and conservation workers help develop and protect forests by planting new trees, fighting the pests and diseases that attack trees, and helping to control soil erosion.

Timber cutters and loggers cut down thousands of acres of forests each year for the timber that is used for wood and paper products. Forestry, conservation, and logging workers work outdoors in all kinds of weather. Their work is demanding and dangerous.

Subjects to Study

Physical education, first aid, mechanics

Discover More

Learn to identify the different kinds of trees in your area. Study a tree identification book and then visit a forest or park. How many trees can you identify?

Related Jobs

Conservation scientists and foresters; forest, conservation and logging workers; grounds maintenance workers; material moving occupations

Education & Training

Short-term OJT

Earnings

$$–$$$$

Job Outlook

Declining

Construction Trades & Related Workers

Boilermakers

On the Job

Boilermakers build boilers, vats, and other large tanks used for storing liquids and gases. Boilers supply steam for electric engines and for heating and power systems in buildings, factories, and ships. Because most boilers last for 35 years or more, repairing and maintaining them is a big part of a boilermaker's job.

These workers use dangerous equipment, lift heavy items, and may work on ladders or scaffolding.

Subjects to Study

Math, shop courses, blueprint reading, welding, machine metalworking

Discover More

Most boilermakers belong to labor unions. Find out which labor unions are active in your community. Contact one and ask about what the union does and how people become members.

Related Jobs

Assemblers and fabricators; machinists; industrial machinery installation, repair, and maintenance workers, except millwrights; millwrights; pipelayers, plumbers, pipefitters, and steamfitters; sheet metal workers; tool and die makers; welding, soldering, and brazing workers

Education & Training
Voc/tech training

Earnings
$$$$

Job Outlook
Little change

Brickmasons, Blockmasons & Stonemasons

On the Job

These workers lay sidewalks and patios, build fireplaces, and install ornamental exteriors on buildings. Brickmasons work with firebrick linings in furnaces and with bricks. Blockmasons work with concrete blocks. Stonemasons work with natural and artificial stones. They often build walls on churches, office buildings, and hotels. These workers are outdoors in all types of weather. They must be strong enough to move heavy materials. Many are self-employed.

Something Extra

You may have heard of Boy Scout Camp and church camp, but have you heard of Masonry Camp? Each year, the International Masonry Institute sponsors a Masonry Camp on Swan's Island in Maine. For one week each summer, architects, engineers, and masonry apprentices spend a week working together to design and build a challenging new project. This way, workers from several fields learn together how building plans translate from paper to actual bricks and mortar.

Subjects to Study

Business math, mechanical drawing, shop courses, art, physical education

Discover More

You can learn more about brick and stonework training programs by checking out the International Masonry Institute's Web site at www.imiweb.org. Or call the Institute at 1-800-562-7464.

Related Jobs

Carpet, floor, and tile installers and finishers; cement masons, concrete finishers, segmental pavers, and terrazzo workers; plasterers and stucco masons

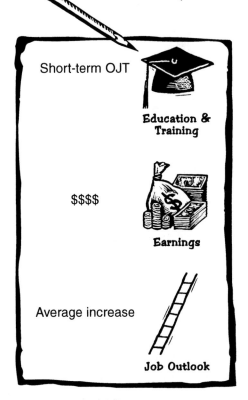

Short-term OJT

Education & Training

$$$$

Earnings

Average increase

Job Outlook

Carpenters

On the Job

Carpenters do all kinds of construction work, including woodworking, concrete work, drywall work, and many other jobs. They replace doors, windows, and locks; repair wooden furniture; hang kitchen cabinets; and install machinery. They work with hand and power tools and read blueprints. Carpenters form the largest group of building trade workers. Most work in new construction or remodeling. Others are self-employed.

Subjects to Study

Shop courses, mechanical drawing, carpentry, business math, first aid

Discover More

Try a simple carpentry project such as building a doghouse, a shelf, or a flower box. First, get a plan and gather the materials you need. Be sure you know how to use your tools safely before you begin.

Related Jobs

Brickmasons, blockmasons, and stonemasons; cement masons, concrete finishers, segmental pavers, and terrazzo workers; electricians; pipelayers, plumbers, pipefitters, and steamfitters; plasterers and stucco masons

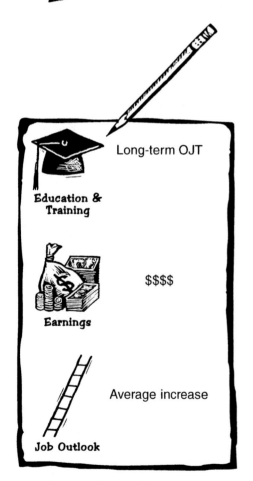

Education & Training — Long-term OJT

Earnings — $$$$

Job Outlook — Average increase

Carpet, Floor & Tile Installers & Finishers

On the Job

Carpet installers put carpet in new or old buildings and houses. Floor layers install flooring foundation materials such as rubber and linoleum, which act as sound dampers. Tilesetters use grout to apply ceramic tiles to floors and walls. All of these installers work regular daytime hours, but some work evenings. These workers spend their days kneeling, bending, stretching, and lifting heavy rolls of carpet.

Subjects to Study

Shop courses, driver's education, physical education, business math

Discover More

Carpet installers must measure rooms precisely. Using a tape measure and a calculator, measure a room in your house. Include nooks, bends, and closets. Take the total width of the room and multiply by the total length to get the square footage.

Related Jobs

Brickmasons, blockmasons, and stonemasons; carpenters; cement masons, concrete finishers, segmental pavers, and terrazzo workers; drywall installers, ceiling tile installers, and tapers; painters and paperhangers; roofers; sheet metal workers

Something Extra

Some people enjoy working 9 to 5 in an office. But others prefer traveling from place to place, working with their hands, and interacting with people. Carpet layers travel to people's homes and to office buildings, measure rooms for carpeting, pull out old carpets, and lay down new carpeting. It's hard physical work—carrying rolls of carpeting and stretching and nailing down a new carpet—but every day they are in a new place, working on a new job, and meeting new people.

Short-term OJT

Education & Training

$$$$

Earnings

Average increase

Job Outlook

Cement Masons, Concrete Finishers, Segmental Pavers & Terrazzo Workers

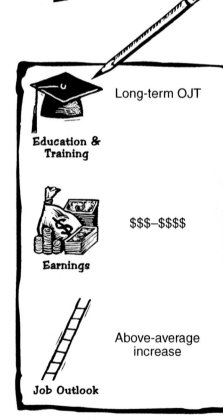

Education & Training
Long-term OJT

Earnings
$$$–$$$$

Job Outlook
Above-average increase

On the Job

Cement masons and concrete finishers use a mixture of cement, gravel, sand, and water to build home patios, huge dams, and miles of roads. They pour the concrete and smooth the finished surface. Terrazzo workers add marble chips to the surface of concrete to create decorative walls, sidewalks, and panels. These workers spend their days outdoors, bending, stooping, and kneeling. Most wear kneepads and water-repellent boots for protection.

Subjects to Study

Shop courses, blueprint reading, mechanical drawing, driver's education, physical education, business math

Discover More

The International Masonry Institute offers terrazzo training to apprentices and journeymen. Check out its Web site at www.imiweb.org. Or call the Institute at 1-800-562-7464.

Related Jobs

Brickmasons, blockmasons, and stonemasons; carpet, floor, and tile installers and finishers; drywall installers, ceiling tile installers, and tapers; plasterers and stucco masons

Construction & Building Inspectors

On the Job
Construction and building inspectors make sure that the country's buildings, roads, sewers, dams, and bridges are safe. They may check electrical or plumbing systems, elevators, or the beams and girders on sky-scrapers. They climb high ladders, crawl through underground tun-nels, and squeeze into tight spaces to do their jobs.

Something Extra
In 1989, a magnitude-6.8 earthquake hit Armenia in Central Asia. Thousands of buildings collapsed, killing more than 25,000 people. A year later, San Francisco was hit with an even larger earthquake, yet only 62 people died. Why the difference? Buildings, roads, and bridges in California must meet strict building codes. Those codes and the inspectors who enforce them saved thousands of lives.

Subjects to Study
Math, geometry, algebra, drafting, shop, computer skills

Discover More
Inspectors often use photographs in their reports. Practice your photography skills by taking pictures of building details in your neighborhood. Do you see anything that might be unsafe?

Related Jobs
Architects, except landscape and naval; construc-tion managers; civil engineers; cost estimators; drafters; engineering technicians; surveyors, car-tographers, photogrammetrists, and surveying technicians

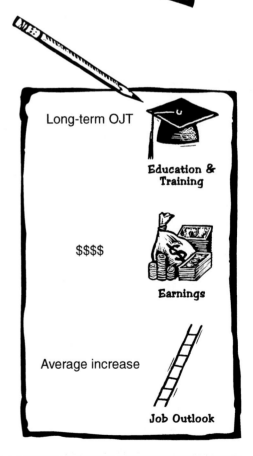

Long-term OJT

Education & Training

$$$$

Earnings

Average increase

Job Outlook

Construction Equipment Operators

On the Job

Construction equipment operators drive and operate the huge machinery used in building construction, road building and repair, and demolition. They might operate cranes, tractors, scrapers, backhoes, pavers, cement mixers, tamping machines, or hoists. They work outdoors in every kind of weather, at construction sites, shipping docks, airports, mines, and on the nation's highways. The pay for these jobs can be high, but the work may slow down in bad weather, reducing earnings.

Subjects to Study

Electronics, shop courses, science, mechanics, physical education

Discover More

To learn more about jobs operating these huge machines, check out the Web site of the International Union of Operating Engineers, which offers apprenticeships and training programs: www.iuoe.org

Related Jobs

Bus drivers; truck drivers and driver/sales workers; farmers, ranchers, and agricultural managers; agricultural workers; forest, conservation, and logging workers

Education & Training
Long-term OJT to Voc/tech training

Earnings
$$$$

Job Outlook
Average increase

Construction Laborers

On the Job

Construction laborers do a wide range of physically demanding jobs. They build skyscrapers and houses, roads, and mine shafts. They remove waste materials and help tear down buildings. The work can be dangerous when they work at great heights, remove hazardous chemicals, and work underground. Some work at construction only during the warmer months.

Something Extra

Who built the great pyramids of Egypt? If you answer the pharaohs, you are sadly mistaken. Certainly, the pharaohs funded the building of the pyramids. But it was construction laborers who did the actual building. Using only the technology of ancient times, these workers cut huge stones from quarries, shaped them into building blocks, moved them from the quarries to the building sites, then raised them hundreds of feet, layer upon layer. It's a building feat we still aren't sure how they accomplished.

Subjects to Study

Shop courses, carpentry, physical education, driver's education

Discover More

Offer your services to your family or neighbors the next time they are planning a construction project. You might help build a porch or deck, pave a driveway, or haul materials to and from the worksite.

Related Jobs

Material moving occupations; forest, conservation, and logging workers; grounds maintenance workers

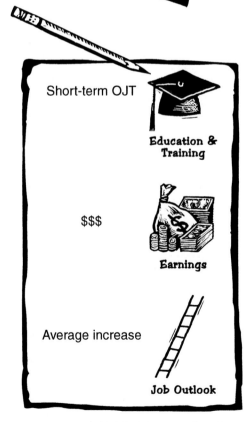

Short-term OJT

Education & Training

$$$

Earnings

Average increase

Job Outlook

Drywall Installers, Ceiling Tile Installers & Tapers

Something Extra

Most modern homes today have drywall interiors because drywall is such a versatile finish. This mix of gypsum and cardboard revolutionized the construction trade, and most people in today's market expect their walls to be finished in drywall. Drywall is a perfect surface for painting or wallpapering, and it holds up well under paneling, wainscoting, and today's decorative finishes.

On the Job

In most buildings, the walls and ceilings are made of drywall. Drywall and ceiling tile workers fasten drywall panels to a building's framework. Then they fill the joints between boards and prepare the wall for decorating. They may put metal or gypsum lath on walls, ceilings, and frameworks for support. These workers spend their days standing, reaching, and bending. They work on ladders and high scaffolding and wear masks so that they don't breathe in the dust from their work. Many are self-employed.

Subjects to Study

Shop courses, carpentry, physical education, business math

Discover More

Visit a hardware store or lumberyard and look at the drywall pieces. Ask the sales workers how the boards are cut and what tools drywall workers use.

Related Jobs

Carpenters; carpet, floor, and tile installers and finishers; insulation workers; plasterers and stucco masons

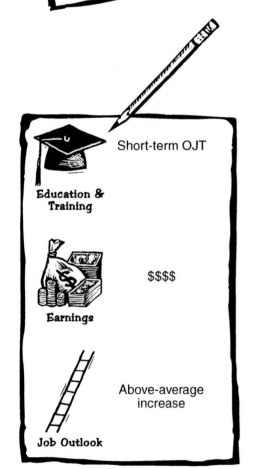

Education & Training — Short-term OJT

Earnings — $$$$

Job Outlook — Above-average increase

Electricians

On the Job

Electricians work with the systems that provide electricity to homes and businesses. They may install wiring, heating, and air-conditioning systems, or make repairs to such systems. They must follow government rules and building codes to ensure their safety and the safety of the buildings they work on. Electricians may work nights and weekends and be on call 24 hours a day. Many are self-employed.

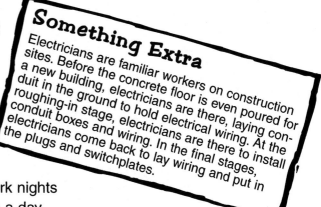

Something Extra

Electricians are familiar workers on construction sites. Before the concrete floor is even poured for a new building, electricians are there, laying conduit in the ground to hold electrical wiring. At the roughing-in stage, electricians are there to install conduit boxes and wiring. In the final stages, electricians come back to lay wiring and put in the plugs and switchplates.

Subjects to Study

Math, shop courses, electronics, mechanical drawing, science, blueprint reading, first aid

Discover More

Can you get power from a lemon? Try this experiment using a strip of copper, a strip of zinc, a small flashlight bulb, and a lemon. Insert the metal strips into the lemon, close together but not touching. Now put the end of the light bulb on the zinc and the end of the copper on the threads. The acid in the lemon should make the bulb light up.

Related Jobs

Heating, air-conditioning, and refrigeration mechanics and installers; line installers and repairers; electrical and electronics installers and repairers; electronic home entertainment equipment installers and repairers; elevator installers and repairers

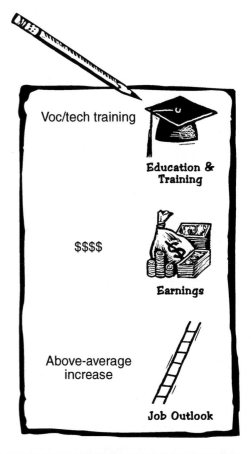

Voc/tech training

Education & Training

$$$$

Earnings

Above-average increase

Job Outlook

Elevator Installers & Repairers

On the Job

Elevator installers and repairers assemble, install, repair, and replace elevators and escalators. They repair and update older equipment and install new equipment. They also test the equipment to make sure it works properly. These workers must have a thorough knowledge of electricity and electronics. They may be on call 24 hours a day to help out in an emergency.

Subjects to Study

Math, shop courses, science courses, electronics, physics, first aid

Discover More

Learn about apprenticeship programs by visiting the Web site of the International Union of Elevator Constructors at www.iuec.org.

Related Jobs

Boilermakers; electricians; electrical and electronics installers and repairers; industrial machinery installation, repair, and maintenance workers, except millwrights; sheet metal workers; structural and reinforcing iron and metal workers

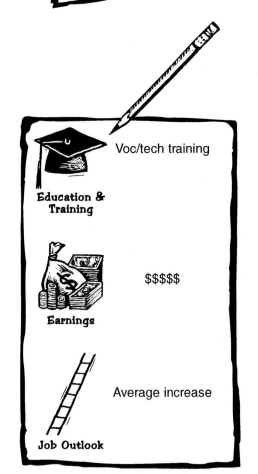

Education & Training
Voc/tech training

Earnings
$$$$$

Job Outlook
Average increase

Glaziers

On the Job

Glaziers cut, install, and remove all kinds of glass and plastics in doors, windows, showers, and baths. They often use glass that is precut and mounted in a frame. They may use cranes to lift large, heavy pieces into place. Once the glass is mounted, glaziers secure it with bolts, cement, metal clips, or wood molding. Glaziers work outdoors in all kinds of weather. They sometimes work on ladders and high scaffolding.

Something Extra

You've probably heard of or seen stained glass, but do you know how it's made? These days, only a small portion of glasswork in windows is actually "stained." Most stained glass today is actually clear glass that's been painted with silver oxide or pot-metal glass that's been colored in its molten state. The earliest colored glass we know about today is from 306 B.C., when builders in the Far East used it for windows in homes and public buildings.

Subjects to Study

Shop courses, business math, blueprint reading, mechanical drawing, general construction, first aid

Discover More

Make your own "stained glass" creation by getting a window-hanger kit from your local craft store. These kits contain metal frames and small, colored beads. You simply fill the frame with beads and then put it in the oven to melt the beads so that they look like glass.

Related Jobs

Brickmasons, blockmasons, and stonemasons; carpenters; carpet, floor, and tile installers and finishers; cement masons, concrete finishers, segmental pavers, and terrazzo workers; painters and paperhangers; automotive body and related repairers

Short-term OJT to voc/tech training

Education & Training

$$$$

Earnings

Average increase

Job Outlook

Hazardous Materials Removal Workers

On the Job

These workers identify, remove, package, transport, and dispose of materials that are dangerous to human beings. They might deal with asbestos, lead, or radioactive materials. They wear protective clothing, including coveralls, gloves, shoe covers, face shields, and respirators. They must follow strict safety guidelines, and the work may require climbing or crawling into tight spaces. They may be called on to work overtime to meet deadlines and in emergencies.

Subjects to Study

Math, chemistry, general science, biology, physical education

Discover More

Do you know what kinds of hazardous materials are present in your community? To find out, check out Environmental Defense's Scorecard at www.scorecard.org. Just type your ZIP code and you'll get a complete list of what pollutants are being released into the environment near you and who is releasing them.

Related Jobs

Painters and paperhangers; insulation workers; sheet metal workers; power plant operators, distributors, and dispatchers; water and liquid waste treatment plant and system operators

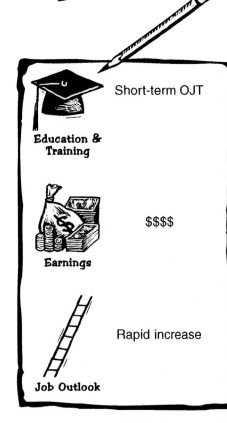

Education & Training
Short-term OJT

Earnings
$$$$

Job Outlook
Rapid increase

Insulation Workers

On the Job

Builders put insulation in buildings to save energy by keeping the heat in during the winter and the heat out during the summer. Insulation workers cement, staple, wire, tape, or spray insulation between the inner and outer walls or under the roof of a building. They often use a hose or blowing machine to spray a liquid insulation that dries into place. These workers must wear protective suits, masks, and respirators. Many are self-employed.

Subjects to Study

Shop courses, blueprint reading, general construction, physical education, driver's education

Discover More

Head to your local hardware store and check out the different kinds of insulation. Ask the sales worker about each kind. Ask your parents what kind of insulation your home has. If you live in an apartment building, ask the building manager.

Related Jobs

Carpenters; carpet, floor, and tile installers and finishers; drywall installers, ceiling tile installers, and tapers; roofers; sheet metal workers

Something Extra

Have you ever heard of asbestos? It's a material that was once widely used for insulation in homes and buildings across America. It is fire-resistant and very effective. Unfortunately, it also causes cancer in people exposed to it. Insulation workers who deal with asbestos must wear special protective clothing, gloves, and masks to prevent asbestos contamination. This safety clothing keeps them safe from cancer.

Short-term OJT

Education & Training

$$$$

Earnings

Average increase

Job Outlook

Painters & Paperhangers

On the Job

Painters and paperhangers make walls look clean and attractive by applying paint or wallpaper to them. They paint outside walls with special paints that protect the walls from weather damage. Painters mix paints to match colors, then brush and roll the paints onto surfaces. Sometimes they rag-roll, splatter, or sponge on a second coat of paint in a different color. Paperhangers apply sizing and wallpapers and add decorative borders. Many are self-employed and work outdoors or seasonally.

Subjects to Study

Shop courses, art courses, business math, art, physical education

Discover More

Try your painting skills by refinishing an old piece of furniture. First, sand off the old finishing. Then clean the surface completely. Apply two or three even coats of a new color and then coat the surface with a clear finish.

Related Jobs

Carpenters; carpet, floor, and tile installers and finishers; drywall installers, ceiling tile installers, and tapers; painting and coating workers, except construction and maintenance; plasterers and stucco masons

Education & Training
Voc/tech training

Earnings
$$$$

Job Outlook
Average increase

Pipelayers, Plumbers, Pipefitters & Steamfitters

On the Job

Plumbers install and repair water, waste disposal, drainage, and gas pipe systems in homes and other buildings. They also install showers, sinks, toilets, and appliances. Pipelayers, pipefitters, and steam-fitters install and repair the pipe systems used in manufacturing, creating electricity and heating and cooling buildings. These workers may work nights and weekends, or be on call 24 hours a day. They must be strong enough to lift heavy pipes. Many are self-employed.

Subjects to Study

Shop courses, drafting, blueprint reading, physics, physical education, business math

Discover More

Tour your home or school and look at the pipe work in the bathrooms and kitchen. Are the pipes lead, stainless steel, or copper? Are the joints taped or welded? Are there other kinds of piping in the building?

Related Jobs

Boilermakers; electricians; elevator installers and repairers; heating, air-conditioning, and refrigeration mechanics and installers; industrial machinery installation, repair, and maintenance workers, except millwrights; millwrights; sheet metal workers; stationary engineers and boiler operators

Something Extra

Did you ever hear of the "White House Plumbers"? These men were employed by President Richard Nixon to spy on opponents. They broke into a psychiatrist's office and into the headquarters of the Democratic National Committee at the Watergate Hotel. Why were they called plumbers? Because their job was to "plug leaks" in Nixon's administration. They may be the only plumbers in history to bring down a president.

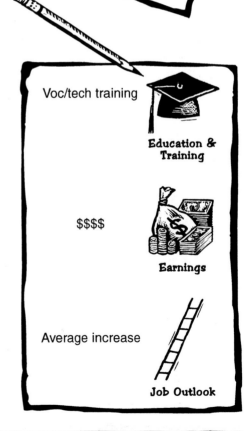

Voc/tech training

Education & Training

$$$$

Earnings

Average increase

Job Outlook

Plasterers & Stucco Masons

On the Job

Plasterers apply plaster to walls and ceilings to make them fire-resistant and more soundproof. They also apply insulation to the outside of new or old buildings. They create smooth or textured finishes using trowels and combs. Skilled plasterers sometimes specialize in complicated decorative work. Stucco masons apply stucco finishes to exterior walls. Many plasterers and stucco masons are self-employed. Their work is physically demanding. Some of the materials they use may irritate the eyes and skin.

Subjects to Study

Mechanical drawing, shop courses, art, drafting, blueprint reading, physical education, business math

Discover More

Make garden stones for your home or school. Mix plaster of paris and pour it into a flat, round mold. Place marbles, beads, and small shells in patterns in the wet plaster. Allow the plaster to dry and then remove the mold.

Related Jobs

Brickmasons, blockmasons, and stonemasons; cement masons, concrete finishers, segmental pavers, and terrazzo workers; drywall installers, ceiling tile installers, and tapers

Education & Training
Long-term OJT to voc/tech training

Earnings
$$$$

Job Outlook
Average increase

Roofers

On the Job

Roofers install roofs made of tar or asphalt and gravel, rubber, metal, and other materials. They may install or repair the tiles on private home roofs, or repair old roofs on other buildings. Some also waterproof concrete walls and floors. These workers do physically demanding work outdoors, including lifting, climbing, and stooping. They risk injury from slips, falls, and burns. The roofing industry has the highest accident rate of all construction work.

Subjects to Study

Shop courses, mechanical drawing, physical education, business math

Discover More

Make a survey of roofing materials in your neighborhood. How many houses and buildings have asphalt-shingled roofs? Are there any buildings in your area with metal roofs or wooden shingles?

Related Jobs

Carpenters; carpet, floor, and tile installers and finishers; cement masons, concrete finishers, segmental pavers, and terrazzo workers; drywall installers, ceiling tile installers, and tapers; plasterers and stucco masons

Something Extra

In the 1970s, James Taylor re-recorded a song called "Up on the Roof." In it, Taylor sang about escaping from the worries of the world and sitting on the rooftop, just relaxing. In reality, rooftops can be steep, slippery, scary places. They're not a good place for daydreaming, and roofing is not a good job for those who are careless or afraid of heights.

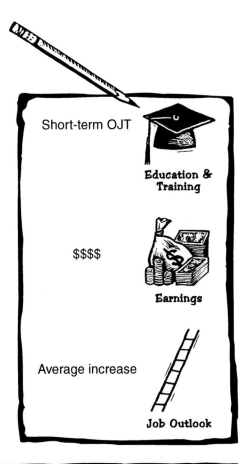

Short-term OJT

Education & Training

$$$$

Earnings

Average increase

Job Outlook

Sheet Metal Workers

On the Job

Sheet metal workers use large sheets of metal to make ductwork for air-conditioning and heating systems. They also make roofs, rain gutters, skylights, outdoor signs, and other products. They install and maintain these products as well. They usually work in shops or at the job site. They must be strong enough to lift heavy, bulky items. They wear safety glasses to protect their eyes, and they cannot wear jewelry or loose-fitting clothing around the machinery they use.

Subjects to Study

Algebra, geometry, mechanical drawing, shop courses, physical education

Discover More

To learn more about this job, write to the International Training Institute for the Sheet Metal and Air Conditioning Industry, 601 N. Fairfax St., Suite 240, Alexandria, VA 22314; www.sheetmetal-iti.org.

Related Jobs

Assemblers and fabricators; machinists; machine setters, operators, and tenders—metal and plastics; tool and die makers; glaziers; heating, air-conditioning, and refrigeration mechanics and installers

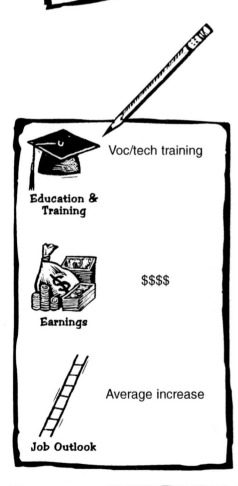

Education & Training — Voc/tech training

Earnings — $$$$

Job Outlook — Average increase

Structural & Reinforcing Iron & Metal Workers

On the Job

These workers build the steel frames used to strengthen bridges, high-rise buildings, highways, and other structures. They install metal stairways, window frames, decorative ironwork, and other metal products. Some erect metal storage tanks and other pre-made buildings. Structural and reinforcing metalworkers work outdoors in extremely high places, on scaffolding and beams. They must be strong enough to lift heavy pieces of metal.

Subjects to Study

Shop courses, mechanical drawing, blueprint reading, business math, physical education

Discover More

You can learn more about the physics of bridge building by making your own bridge. Stack four books in two piles that are the same height, four inches apart. Now use an index card as a bridge between the stacks. How many pennies can you put on the card before the "bridge" collapses? Now move the books closer and arch your bridge. Will it hold more pennies?

Related Jobs

Assemblers and fabricators; boilermakers; civil engineers; cement masons, concrete finishers, segmental pavers, and terrazzo workers; welding, soldering, and brazing workers

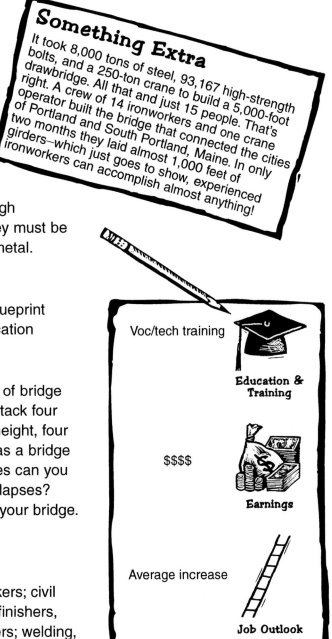

Something Extra

It took 8,000 tons of steel, 93,167 high-strength bolts, and a 250-ton crane to build a 5,000-foot drawbridge. All that and just 15 people. That's right. A crew of 14 ironworkers and one crane operator built the bridge that connected the cities of Portland and South Portland, Maine. In only two months they laid almost 1,000 feet of girders—which just goes to show, experienced ironworkers can accomplish almost anything!

Voc/tech training

Education & Training

$$$$

Earnings

Average increase

Job Outlook

Installation, Maintenance & Repair Occupations

Computer, Automated Teller & Office Machine Repairers

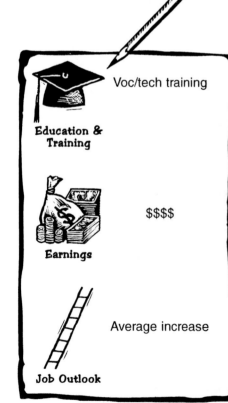

Voc/tech training

Education & Training

$$$$

Earnings

Average increase

Job Outlook

On the Job

Computer repairers install and fix computers, equipment used with computers, and word-processing systems. Office machine repairers work on copiers, typewriters, cash registers, and mailing equipment. Some repairers work on both computers and office equipment. Automated teller repairers install and fix ATMs at banks and credit unions. These repairers work in many industries, and some are on call 24 hours a day to make emergency repairs.

Subjects to Study

Math, computer science, physics, shop courses, electronics

Discover More

Do you know how to hook up a computer? Ask the teacher in your school's computer lab to show you how to connect a computer's cables to the printer or scanner. Ask whether the school uses a power-surge protector to prevent electrical overload.

Related Jobs

Broadcast and sound engineering technicians and radio operators; electronic home entertainment equipment installers and repairers; electrical and electronics installers and repairers; industrial machinery installation, repair, and maintenance workers, except millwrights; radio and telecommunications equipment installers and repairers

Electrical & Electronics Installers & Repairers

On the Job

These workers install and repair equipment in factories. About one-third of them work for the federal government, many for the Department of Defense. They install radar, missile controls, and communication systems on ships, on aircraft, on tanks, and in buildings. Other electronic equipment repairers work for telephone companies, at hospitals, and in repair shops.

Subjects to Study

Math, physics, science courses, shop courses, electronics

Discover More

You can work on electronics projects in a science club or 4-H club. Ask your teacher whether one of these clubs meets at your school.

Related Jobs

Computer, automated teller, and office machine repairers; electronic home entertainment equipment installers and repairers; radio and telecommunications equipment installers and repairers; industrial machinery installation, repair, and maintenance workers, except millwrights

Something Extra

Since the first bands of nomads started arguing over territory, armies have been coming up with new ways to throw weapons at their enemies. During the Middle Ages, warriors used catapults to launch stones, dead horses, and even manure into enemy camps. Gunpowder and the first guns brought that kind of warfare to an end. Today's warriors use computers to guide missiles to their targets—which is a lot cleaner than loading manure onto a catapult!

Voc/tech training

Education & Training

$$$–$$$$$

Earnings

Little change

Job Outlook

Electronic Home Entertainment Equipment Installers & Repairers

On the Job

These workers install and repair radios, TV sets, stereos, cameras, video games, and other home electronic equipment. They run tests to find problems and adjust and replace parts. They sometimes use complicated equipment to help them detect problems. Most work in repair shops or in service departments at larger stores. They may make home visits to fix equipment. Some are self-employed.

Subjects to Study

Math, science courses, shop courses, electronics, physics

Discover More

Visit a VCR repair shop in your area. Ask the technicians whether you can watch as they make repairs and run tests.

Related Jobs

Broadcast and sound engineering technicians and radio operators; computer, automated teller, and office machine repairers; electrical and electronics installers and repairers; radio and telecommunications equipment installers and repairers

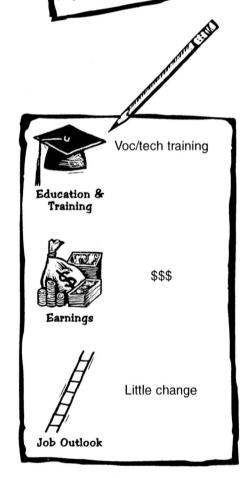

Education & Training
Voc/tech training

Earnings
$$$

Job Outlook
Little change

Radio & Telecommunications Equipment Installers & Repairers

On the Job

These workers install, repair, and maintain complex telephone and radio equipment. Most work either in a phone company's central office or in the field at customers' homes or offices. Others work on equipment for cable TV companies, railroads, or airlines. Some work nights and weekends, and they may be on call to handle emergencies.

Subjects to Study

Math, science courses, shop courses, electronics, physics

Discover More

Take apart an old telephone and look at its insides. Can you follow the wires to their sources? Can you figure out what the different parts do? Now, can you put it back together?

Related Jobs

Broadcast and sound engineering technicians and radio operators; computer, automated teller, and office machine repairers; electronic home entertainment equipment installers and repairers; electrical and electronics installers and repairers; line installers and repairers; engineering technicians

Something Extra

Communications equipment has changed a lot in the last 100 years. Before 1876, if you wanted to get in touch with people across town, you had to write a letter or go to their house. Today, you can connect with people in Mongolia or Zimbabwe instantly by phone or through the Internet. We have, indeed, become a global village.

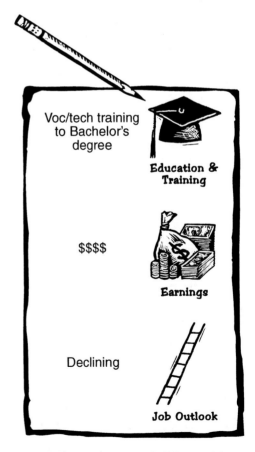

Voc/tech training to Bachelor's degree

Education & Training

$$$$

Earnings

Declining

Job Outlook

Aircraft & Avionics Equipment Mechanics & Service Technicians

On the Job

Aircraft and avionics mechanics and service technicians inspect airplanes for problems. They make repairs and test equipment to make sure it is working properly. Some work on several different types of planes, whereas others specialize in just one type. Some mechanics even specialize in one part of an aircraft, such as the engine or electrical system of a DC-10. Sometimes they work inside, but often they work outdoors.

Subjects to Study

Math, physics, chemistry, electronics, computer science, mechanical drawing

Discover More

To find out more about aircraft mechanics, write to the Flight Safety Foundation, 601 Madison Street, Suite 300, Alexandria, VA 22314. Or visit its Web site at www.flightsafety.org.

Related Jobs

Electricians, electrical and electronics installers and repairers, elevator installers and repairers

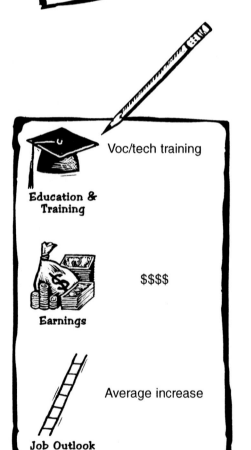

Education & Training — Voc/tech training

Earnings — $$$$

Job Outlook — Average increase

Automotive Body & Related Repairers

On the Job

Automotive body repairers fix cars and trucks damaged in accidents. They straighten bent bodies, hammer out dents, and replace parts that can't be fixed. Their supervisors usually decide which parts to fix, which ones to replace, and how long the job should take. In large shops, some repairers specialize in one type of repair, such as installing glass or repairing doors.

Something Extra

Did you know that some cars have parts made from plastic? If these parts are damaged, a body repairer can use heat from a hot-air welding gun or simply put the damaged part in very hot water to make the plastic soft. Then the repairer can mold the softened part into its original shape and put it back on the car.

Subjects to Study

Shop courses, automotive body repair, science courses, math

Discover More

A model car has many of the same body parts as a real car. Buy a model car kit and build and paint the model. Can you customize the car so that it reflects your personality?

Related Jobs

Automotive service technicians and mechanics; diesel service technicians and mechanics; painting and coating workers, except construction and maintenance

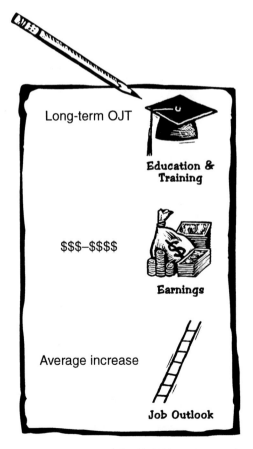

Long-term OJT

Education & Training

$$$–$$$$

Earnings

Average increase

Job Outlook

Automotive Service Technicians & Mechanics

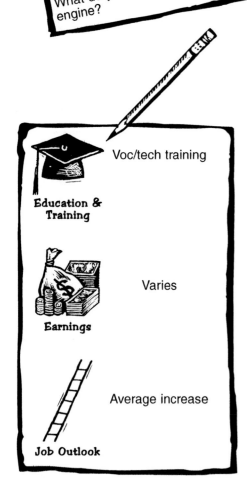

Voc/tech training

Education & Training

Varies

Earnings

Average increase

Job Outlook

On the Job

Automotive mechanics and service technicians repair and service cars, trucks, and vans that have gas engines. Mechanics must be quick and accurate when they are diagnosing mechanical problems. During routine service work, mechanics inspect, adjust, and replace vehicle parts. They usually follow a checklist to make sure they examine parts that might cause a future breakdown. Some mechanics are self-employed.

Subjects to Study

Math, shop courses, automotive mechanics, electronics, physics, chemistry, computer skills

Discover More

Do you know someone who works on cars? Ask that person whether you can help or just watch while he or she works on a car. You can learn a lot by watching and listening as a mechanic works. You might even be able to help by handing him or her tools.

Related Jobs

Automotive body and related repairers, diesel service technicians and mechanics, small engine mechanics

Diesel Service Technicians & Mechanics

On the Job

Diesel mechanics and service technicians repair and maintain diesel engines in heavy trucks, buses, and other equipment such as tractors, bulldozers, and cranes. They spend a lot of time doing preventive maintenance to make sure that the equipment operates safely, to prevent wear and tear, and to reduce expensive breakdowns. Most work in repair shops, but some work outdoors to repair equipment at construction sites.

Subjects to Study

Math, shop courses, automotive repair, electronics, computer skills

Discover More

Do you know the differences between gas engines and diesel engines? You can find out by reading about engines and how they work. Check out some science books from the library and learn about both kinds of engines.

Related Jobs

Aircraft and avionics equipment mechanics and service technicians, automotive service technicians and mechanics, heavy vehicle and mobile equipment service technicians and mechanics, small engine mechanics

Something Extra

Diesel engines are heavier and last longer than gas engines. They're also more efficient because a diesel engine compresses its fuel—so it uses less to do more. This means that more fuel is available to power the engine. Large trucks, buses, trains, and even some cars have diesel engines these days. But although diesel fuel is more efficient, it might be harder to find at your local gas station.

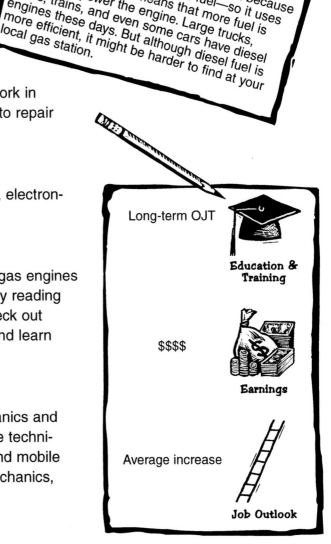

Long-term OJT

Education & Training

$$$$

Earnings

Average increase

Job Outlook

Heavy Vehicle & Mobile Equipment Service Technicians & Mechanics

On the Job

Mobile heavy equipment mechanics and technicians repair the machinery used in construction, logging, and mining. They fix and maintain motor graders, trenchers, backhoes, bulldozers, and cranes. They service and repair diesel engines and other machine parts. They may also repair the hydraulic lifts used to raise and lower scoops and shovels. These workers are outdoors in all kinds of weather.

Subjects to Study

Math, automobile mechanics, science courses, physics, chemistry

Discover More

Visit a construction site and watch how the equipment moves and works. Talk to a construction worker about what happens when a machine breaks down.

Related Jobs

Aircraft and avionics equipment mechanics and service technicians; automotive service technicians and mechanics; diesel service technicians and mechanics; heating, air-conditioning, and refrigeration mechanics and installers; small engine mechanics

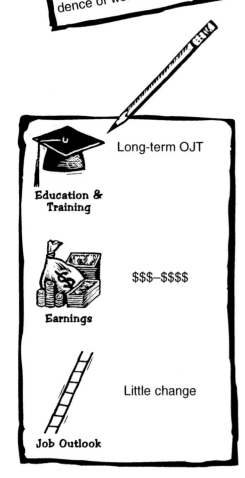

Education & Training
Long-term OJT

Earnings
$$$–$$$$

Job Outlook
Little change

Small Engine Mechanics

On the Job

Small engine mechanics do routine engine checkups and repair everything from chainsaws to yachts. The mechanic first talks with the owner to try to understand the problem. Then he or she runs tests to find the source of the problem. In some areas, mechanics may work much more during the summer than they do in the winter. Many of these workers are self-employed.

Something Extra

If you take a job in a restaurant, you wouldn't expect to bring your own pots and pans, would you? But mechanics often must provide their own hand tools for their work. Most beginning mechanics start out with the basics, such as wrenches, pliers, screwdrivers, and power drills. As they gain experience, they collect more tools. Experienced mechanics might have thousands of dollars invested in tools.

Subjects to Study

Business math, small-engine repair, shop courses, science, electronics

Discover More

Ask your parents or neighbor whether you can help them prepare the lawnmower for spring use or winter storage. As you work, ask about the various parts of the motor.

Related Jobs

Automotive service technicians and mechanics, diesel service technicians and mechanics, heavy vehicle and mobile equipment service technicians and mechanics

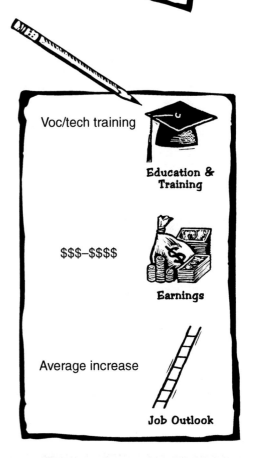

Voc/tech training

Education & Training

$$$–$$$$

Earnings

Average increase

Job Outlook

Coin, Vending & Amusement Machine Servicers & Repairers

On the Job

These servicers and repairers check coin-operated machines that offer entertainment, soft drinks, snacks, sandwiches, and other items for sale. They retrieve money, stock the machines, and make sure the machines are clean and working properly. They also keep records and order parts. These workers travel from place to place to make repairs. They may be outside in all kinds of weather.

Subjects to Study

Driver's education, shop courses, electronics, machine repairs, math

Discover More

The next time you see someone servicing a vending machine, stop and talk with him or her. Ask about the best and worst parts of the job. How much time does the repairer spend on the road?

Related Jobs

Electrical and electronics installers and repairers; electronic home-entertainment equipment installers and repairers; heating, air-conditioning, and refrigeration mechanics and installers; home appliance repairers

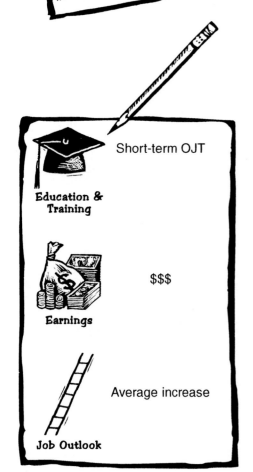

Education & Training — Short-term OJT

Earnings — $$$

Job Outlook — Average increase

Heating, Air-Conditioning & Refrigeration Mechanics & Installers

On the Job

These mechanics help keep people comfortable by installing and repairing heating systems and air conditioners. They also help protect food and medicine that must be kept refrigerated. These workers maintain, diagnose, and correct problems within entire heating or cooling systems. They may work for large companies or be self-employed.

Something Extra

People working in this job can have a strong impact on the environment. CFCs are coolants used in older air-conditioning and refrigeration systems. Particles of CFCs are dangerous if they escape into the atmosphere. Escaped CFCs eat away at the ozone layer that protects plants, animals, and people from too much radiation. Nothing on Earth will survive if the ozone layer is completely destroyed. Responsible technicians are careful to protect the environment from CFCs.

Subjects to Study

Shop courses, math, electronics, mechanical drawing, physics, chemistry, blueprint reading, physical education

Discover More

Visit your local supermarket and ask to talk with someone who works in the frozen-food or dairy section. Ask how repairs are made to the cooling systems.

Related Jobs

Boilermakers; home appliance repairers; electricians; sheet metal workers; pipelayers, plumbers, pipefitters, and steamfitters

Voc/tech training

Education & Training

$$$$

Earnings

Above-average increase

Job Outlook

Home Appliance Repairers

Something Extra

Do you enjoy working on your own? Do you like being your own boss? Home appliance and power tool repairers often work on their own, without a boss looking over their shoulders. Many people choose this job because they enjoy the freedom of being self-employed. Self-employed appliance and tool repairers work from their own homes or workshops. Others might work through appliance and tool stores.

On the Job

These workers repair ovens, washers, dryers, refrigerators, and other home appliances. They may also repair power tools such as saws and drills. First, they find the problem. Then they replace or repair faulty parts. At the same time, they tighten, clean, and adjust other parts if needed. They must keep good records, prepare bills, and collect payments.

Subjects to Study

Shop courses, electronics, math, science courses

Discover More

Call a repair shop in your area and ask whether you can help in the shop for a day or two. Watch how the repairer works and help out by bringing tools, waiting on customers, or cleaning the shop.

Related Jobs

Electrical and electronics installers and repairers; electronic home entertainment equipment installers and repairers; small engine mechanics; coin, vending, and amusement machine servicers and repairers; heating, air-conditioning, and refrigeration mechanics and installers

Education & Training
Short-term OJT to voc/tech training

Earnings
$$$$

Job Outlook
Little change

Young Person's Occupational Outlook Handbook, © JIST Works, Inc.

Industrial Machinery Installation, Repair & Maintenance Workers, Except Millwrights

On the Job

Industrial machinery workers install and maintain the machines in factories or plants to keep the work on schedule. Their work includes keeping machines and their parts oiled, tuned, and cleaned. When repairs are needed, the repairer must work quickly so that production is not delayed, which might cause the company to lose money. Sometimes this means making emergency repairs at night or on weekends.

Subjects to Study

Mechanical drawing, math, blueprint reading, science courses, physics, electronics, physical education, computer skills

Discover More

Contact the office of a factory in your area and ask for a tour. Watch the machinery used in production. Ask your guide what would happen to the production schedule if an important piece of machinery broke down.

Related Jobs

Aircraft and avionics equipment mechanics and service technicians; automotive service technicians and mechanics; diesel service technicians and mechanics; elevator installers and repairers; millwrights; small engine mechanics

Something Extra

Industrial machine repairers must be able to spot and fix little problems before they cause major breakdowns. If a machine has a vibration that shouldn't be there, mechanics must find the source of the problem, such as a worn belt or loose bearing. The more repairs they make at early stages, the more money they save their employers down the road. After all, it's a lot cheaper to replace a worn belt than to repair an engine damaged by one.

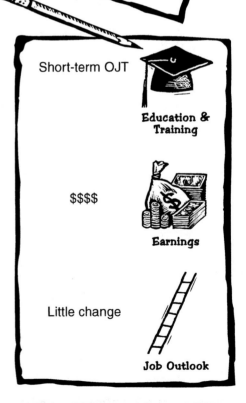

Short-term OJT

Education & Training

$$$$

Earnings

Little change

Job Outlook

Line Installers & Repairers

On the Job

Line installers and repairers lay the wires and cables that bring electricity, phone service, and cable TV signals into our homes. They clear lines of tree limbs, check them for damage, and make emergency repairs when needed. This job can be dangerous because installers and splicers work underground, high above ground, and with various chemicals and electricity.

Subjects to Study

Math, physical education, shop courses, science, electronics

Discover More

Contact the human resources department of your local electric company, telephone company, or cable TV company. Ask about the kinds of jobs they have and what kind of training they require.

Related Jobs

Broadcast and sound engineering technicians and radio operators, electricians, radio and telecommunications equipment installers and repairers

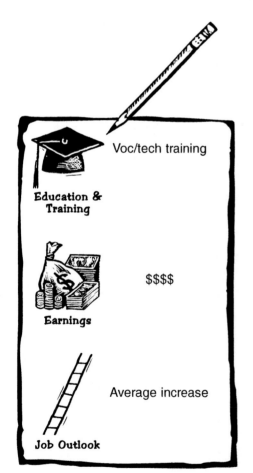

Education & Training — Voc/tech training

Earnings — $$$$

Job Outlook — Average increase

Maintenance and Repair Workers, General

On the Job

General maintenance and repair workers have skills in many different crafts. They repair and maintain machines, mechanical equipment, and buildings and work on plumbing, electrical, and air-conditioning and heating systems. They build partitions, make plaster or drywall repairs, and fix or paint roofs, windows, doors, floors, woodwork, and other parts of building structures. They also maintain and repair specialized equipment and machinery found in cafeterias, laundries, hospitals, stores, offices, and factories.

Subjects to Study

Mechanical drawing, electricity, woodworking, blueprint reading, science, math, computers

Discover More

Spend a day on the job with your school custodian. You'll find that they do much more than sweep the halls. They are responsible for making sure all the machinery in your school building works properly.

Related Jobs

Carpenters; pipelayers, plumbers, pipefitters, and steamfitters; electricians; heating, air-conditioning, and refrigeration mechanics and installers; coin, vending, and amusement machine servicers and repairers

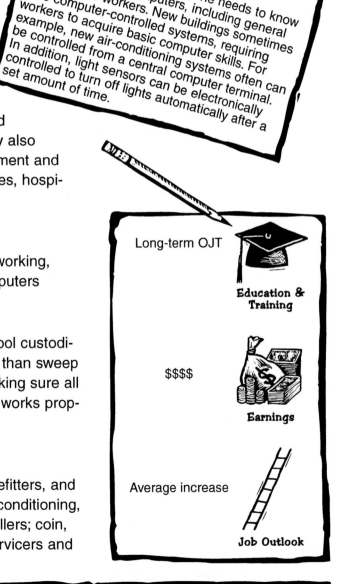

Something Extra

These days, just about everyone needs to know something about computers, including general maintenance workers. New buildings sometimes have computer-controlled systems, requiring workers to acquire basic computer skills. For example, new air-conditioning systems often can be controlled from a central computer terminal. In addition, light sensors can be electronically controlled to turn off lights automatically after a set amount of time.

Long-term OJT

Education & Training

$$$$

Earnings

Average increase

Job Outlook

Millwrights

On the Job

Millwrights install, repair, replace, and take apart the machinery and heavy equipment used in many industries. The wide range of facilities and the development of new technology require millwrights to keep their skills up-to-date—from blueprint reading and pouring concrete to diagnosing and solving mechanical problems.

Subjects to Study

Science, math, mechanical drawing, computers, machine shop practice

Discover More

To see what kind of topics generally concern people who work as millwrights, go to the National Tooling and Machining Association Web site at www.ntma.org. Click on Resource Center, then Discussion Forum. This is where millwrights can share ideas and ask each other for advice to problems they have on the job.

Related Jobs

Industrial machinery installation, repair, and maintenance workers, except millwrights; aircraft and avionics equipment mechanics and service technicians; structural and reinforcing iron and metal workers; assemblers and fabricators; heavy vehicle and mobile equipment service technicians and mechanics

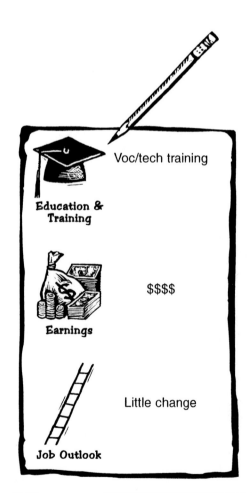

Education & Training — Voc/tech training

Earnings — $$$$

Job Outlook — Little change

Precision Instrument & Equipment Repairers

On the Job

This job title covers a wide range of jobs. Precision instrument and equipment repairers fix watches and clocks, cameras, medical equipment, and even musical instruments. They use hand instruments and must have good eye-hand coordination and pay attention to details. Many are self-employed and work in small workshops. Instrument repairers often must travel to the site of the instrument.

Something Extra

A piano tuner's tools include pliers, wire cutters, and various kinds of scrapers. Using a tuning fork, the tuner tightens or loosens the "A" string until it sounds like the tuning fork. Then he or she sets the pitch of each of the strings in relation to that "A" string. Tuning a piano takes about an hour and a half and requires a good ear.

Subjects to Study

Shop courses, carpentry, physical education, business math

Discover More

Ask your band or orchestra teacher whether you can watch the next time he or she tunes the instruments or has a repairer come to work on them. Offer to help maintain the instruments.

Related Jobs

Computer, automated teller, and office machine repairers; coin, vending, and amusement machine servicers and repairers; dental laboratory technicians; ophthalmic laboratory technicians; industrial machinery installation, installation, repair and maintenance workers, except millwrights; jewelers and precious stone and metal workers; electronic home entertainment equipment installers and repairers

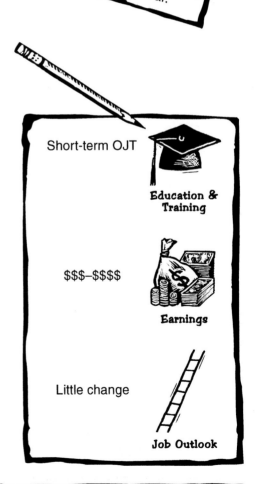

Short-term OJT

Education & Training

$$$–$$$$

Earnings

Little change

Job Outlook

Production Occupations

Assemblers & Fabricators

Something Extra

Automation and robotics have eliminated some manufacturing jobs, but certain jobs are beyond a robot's abilities. A lot of precision assembly work is done in hard-to-reach places, such as inside gearboxes. Because robots are not flexible enough for such jobs, precision assemblers are less likely to be replaced by robots than other manufacturing workers.

On the Job

Assemblers and fabricators are experienced and trained workers who put together complicated products such as computers, appliances, and electronic equipment. Their work is detailed and must be done accurately. They follow directions from engineers and use several tools and precise measuring instruments. Some work in clean, well-lit, dust-free rooms, while others work around grease, oil, and noise. They may have to lift and fit heavy objects.

Subjects to Study

Math, science, computer education, shop courses, electronics

Discover More

Get a kit from an electronics store and assemble a radio or another piece of electronic equipment.

Related Jobs

Welding, soldering, and brazing workers; machine setters, operators, and tenders—metal and plastics; inspectors, testers, sorters, samplers, and weighers

Education & Training
Short-term OJT to voc/tech training

Earnings
$$–$$$

Job Outlook
Declining

Food Processing Occupations

On the Job

Food processing workers work in grocery stores and production plants. They may work in a small market, in a large refrigerated room, or on an assembly line. Their work areas must be clean, but they are often cold and damp. Bakers produce cakes, breads, and other baked goods. Deli workers make salads and other side dishes. Butchers and meat, poultry, and fish cutters cut animal meat into small pieces to be sold to customers. These workers have the highest rate of work-related injuries and illnesses of any industry.

Subjects to Study

Health, nutrition, home economics, food preparation

Discover More

Learn about the different cuts of meat, fish, and poultry. Visit the meat department of a grocery store near you to see the different cuts. Talk to the butcher and ask about the job.

Related Jobs

Chefs, cooks, and food preparation workers

Something Extra

In the 1800s, a Swiss naturalist connected two facts. First, the brain contains phosphorus. Second, phosphorus is found in fish. Therefore, he decided that eating fish helps develop the brain. Actually, phosphorus is found in most foods, so eating fish before a test isn't a guarantee of passing a class or getting an A. But it couldn't hurt!

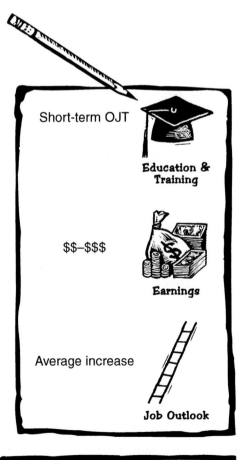

Short-term OJT

Education & Training

$$-$$$

Earnings

Average increase

Job Outlook

Computer-Control Programmers & Operators

Something Extra

Many metal and plastics workers learn their trades through an apprenticeship program. They start out by learning from and working with a professional, making little money but gaining invaluable experience. When the apprenticeship is finished, the new workers become tradesmen or journeymen, a title that lets people know they have a certain set of skills. Apprenticeships are a time-honored way to learn a profession. No one knows for certain when they began, but they are mentioned in many ancient texts, including the Bible.

On the Job

These workers use special computer-controlled machines to cut and shape products such as car parts, machine parts, and compressors. They use lathes, spindles, and milling machines following blueprints from engineers. While they work they must constantly monitor readouts from the computer to make sure parts are being made properly. Because of the machinery they use, this can be a dangerous job.

Subjects to Study

Math, shop courses, blueprint reading, drafting, physics, mechanical drawing, computer skills, electronics

Discover More

Visit a machining shop in your community and watch the programmers and operators at work. You may even be able to help by watching monitors and carrying parts.

Related Jobs

Machinists; tool and die makers; machine setters, operators, and tenders—metal and plastics; welding, soldering, and brazing workers; computer programmers

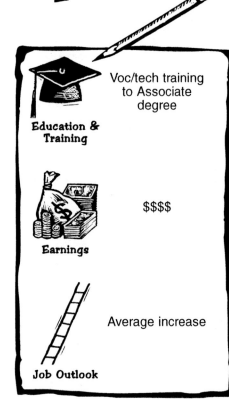

Education & Training
Voc/tech training to Associate degree

Earnings
$$$$

Job Outlook
Average increase

Machinists

On the Job

Machinists make metal parts using lathes, drill presses, and milling machines. They often make specialized parts or one-of-a-kind items for companies that produce everything from cars to computers. Most work in machine shops and wear safety glasses and earplugs. Because of the machinery they use and the coolants and lubricants for the machine, this can be a dangerous job.

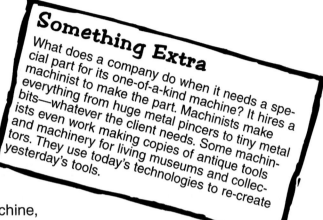

Something Extra

What does a company do when it needs a special part for its one-of-a-kind machine? It hires a machinist to make the part. Machinists make everything from huge metal pincers to tiny metal bits—whatever the client needs. Some machinists even work making copies of antique tools and machinery for living museums and collectors. They use today's technologies to re-create yesterday's tools.

Subjects to Study

Math, shop courses, blueprint reading, drafting, physics, mechanical drawing, computer skills, electronics

Discover More

Visit a machine shop in your community. High school shops and vocational schools are some places you can find metalworking machines. Ask the instructor to show you how the machines work.

Related Jobs

Tool and die makers; machine setters, operators, and tenders—metal and plastics; computer-control programmers and operators; welding, soldering, and brazing workers

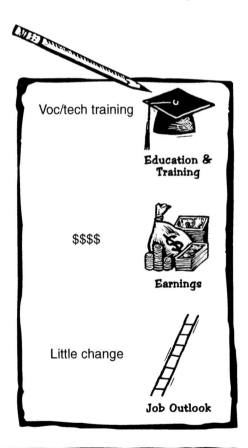

Voc/tech training

Education & Training

$$$$

Earnings

Little change

Job Outlook

Machine Setters, Operators & Tenders—Metal & Plastics

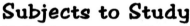

On the Job

These workers fall into two groups: those who set up machines for operation, and those who tend the machines while they work. They may work with drilling and boring machines, milling and planing machines, or lathe and turning machines. They work according to blueprints and other instructions to turn out metal and plastic parts for everything from toasters to trucks.

Subjects to Study

Math, shop courses, blueprint reading, drafting, physics, mechanical drawing, computer skills, electronics

Discover More

Take apart an old appliance at home, such as a toaster or alarm clock. Separate the appliance into as many individual pieces as possible. Now look at the variety of shapes and sizes. Each individual part was made by machine setters and tenders.

Related Jobs

Machinists; tool and die makers; assemblers and fabricators; computer-control programmers and operators; welding, soldering, and brazing workers; inspectors, testers, sorters, samplers, and weighers

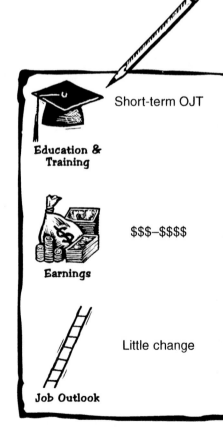

Education & Training

Short-term OJT

Earnings

$$$–$$$$

Job Outlook

Little change

Tool & Die Makers

On the Job

Tool and die makers are highly skilled workers. Toolmakers create tools that cut, shape, and form metal and other materials. Die makers make dies, which are the forms used to shape metal in stamping and forging machines. Tool and die makers must know about machining operations, mathematics, and blueprint reading. They must follow safety rules and wear protective clothing on the job. They spend a good part of the day standing and must be able to lift heavy items.

Subjects to Study

Math, shop courses, blueprint reading, metalworking, drafting, machine shop, mechanical drawing

Discover More

Using pen and paper, design a new tool to do something useful. Or think up a new use for an old tool. Can you convert an egg slicer to cut bagel chips?

Related Jobs

Machinists; computer-control programmers and operators; machine setters, operators, and tenders—metal and plastics; welding, soldering, and brazing workers

Something Extra

Today's tool and die makers are on the cutting edge of technology. They use computer-aided design (CAD) programs to draw and test new parts and tools on the computer drawing board. Then they send the design to a computer-controlled machine that makes the actual part or tool. These workers also use special microscopes, micrometers, grinders, mills, and furnaces to do their jobs.

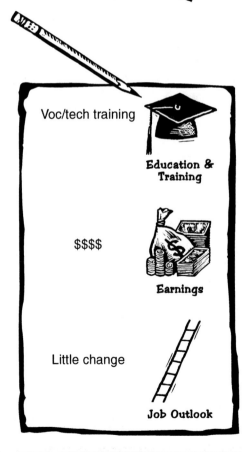

Voc/tech training

Education & Training

$$$$

Earnings

Little change

Job Outlook

Welding, Soldering & Brazing Workers

On the Job

These workers use the heat from a torch to permanently join metal parts. Because of its strength, welding is used to build ships, cars, aircraft, and even the space shuttle. Welders may use a hand torch or a welding machine. They also use torches to cut and dismantle metal objects.

Welders must wear protective gear to prevent burns and injuries. Some work outdoors on ladders or scaffolding.

Subjects to Study

Shop courses, blueprint reading, shop math, mechanical drawing, physics, chemistry

Discover More

To learn more about this occupation, write to the American Welding Society, 550 N.W. LeJeune Rd., Miami, FL 33126-5699; or check out their Web site at www.aws.org.

Related Jobs

Machinists; machine setters, operators, and tenders—metal and plastics; computer-control programmers and operators; tool and die makers; sheet metal workers; boilermakers; assemblers and fabricators

Education & Training
Short-term OJT to voc/tech training

Earnings
$$$$

Job Outlook
Average increase

Bookbinders & Bindery Workers

On the Job

Bookbinders and bindery workers use machines to "bind" the pages of books and magazines in a cover. These machines fold, cut, gather, glue, stitch, sew, trim, and wrap pages to form a book. Bindery work is physically hard. Workers stand, kneel, lift, and carry heavy items. Many work on assembly lines. Some work in hand binderies, and a few are self-employed.

Something Extra

Did you know that some rare old books are worth thousands of dollars? So what does a library or museum do when one of these treasures starts to fall apart? They call in a bookbinder. These workers use special tools and chemicals to restore pages. Then they rebind the book by hand, using needle and thread.

Subjects to Study

Math, English, art, history, shop courses

Discover More

Bind your own book. First make an "end paper" by folding a sheet of heavy paper over your pages. Sew the pages into the end paper, using a heavy thread and needle. Paste each end paper to a heavy cardboard square. Now paste the squares onto a sheet of wallpaper. Cut the wallpaper to leave one inch of trim. Fold the trim over the cardboard squares and paste them down.

Related Jobs

Prepress technicians and workers; printing machine operators; machine setters, operators, and tenders—metal and plastics

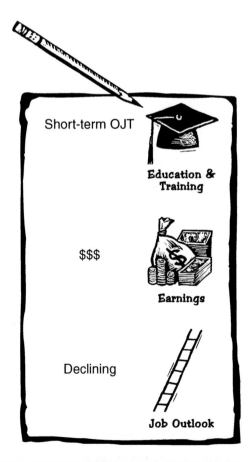

Short-term OJT

Education & Training

$$$

Earnings

Declining

Job Outlook

Prepress Technicians & Workers

On the Job

Prepress technicians and workers prepare materials for printing presses. They do typesetting, design page layouts, take photographs, and make printing plates. With personal computers, customers can now show workers how they want their printed material to look. Prepress workers have different titles depending on their jobs. Most work at video monitors, and some work with harmful chemicals.

Subjects to Study

English, writing skills, electronics, computer skills, art, photography, typing

Discover More

Learn how to use word processing and graphics programs on a computer. Industry standards include Microsoft Word®, Corel WordPerfect®, Adobe PageMaker® and Photoshop®, and Quark®. Design your own greeting card or brochure.

Related Jobs

Artists and related workers, designers, desktop publishers, data entry and information processing workers, printing machine operators

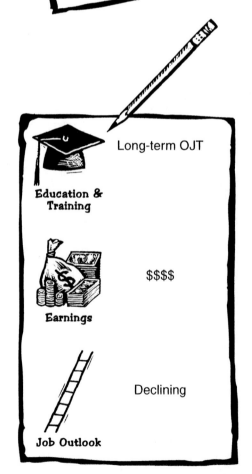

Education & Training
Long-term OJT

Earnings
$$$$

Job Outlook
Declining

Printing Machine Operators

On the Job

Printing machine operators prepare, run, and maintain the printing presses in a pressroom. They check the paper and ink, make sure paper feeders are stocked, and monitor the presses as they are running. Computerized presses allow operators to make adjustments at a control panel by simply pressing buttons. These workers are on their feet most of the time. The work can be physically hard. Most wear earplugs around the presses.

Something Extra

Before the Middle Ages, few people could read. That's because manuscripts had to be copied by hand. A group of workers called scribes were employed by monasteries to copy books. It was a time-consuming and expensive process. When a man named Gutenberg made the first printing press in 1456, he put a lot of scribes out of work. But he made books available to the common man for the first time in history.

Subjects to Study

Math, English, communication skills, computer science, chemistry, electronics, physics

Discover More

Try printing your own greeting cards with a woodblock printing kit. These kits are available at craft and hobby stores.

Related Jobs

Machine setters, operators, and tenders—metal and plastics; bookbinders and bindery workers

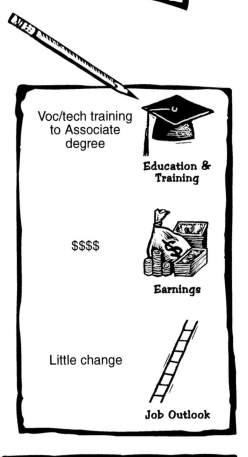

Voc/tech training to Associate degree

Education & Training

$$$$

Earnings

Little change

Job Outlook

Textile, Apparel & Furnishings Occupations

On the Job

Textile workers care for and operate the machines that make textile goods. These goods are then used in all kinds of products, from clothing to materials in tires. Apparel workers make cloth, leather, and fur into clothing and other products. They may also repair torn or damaged items, or resew them to fit a customer better. Upholsterers are skilled craft workers who make new furniture or repair old furniture.

Subjects to Study

Home economics, sewing, upholstery, shop courses, woodworking, art, business math, computer skills

Discover More

Get a pattern for a simple sewing project. Follow the pattern directions to make something you can wear.

Related Jobs

Assemblers and fabricators, dental laboratory technicians, food-processing occupations, jewelers and precious stone and metal workers, woodworkers

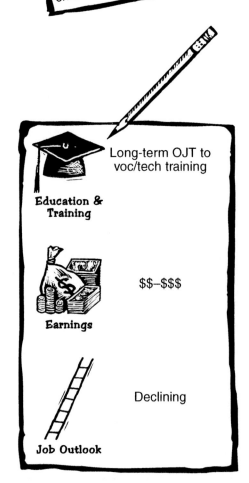

Education & Training — Long-term OJT to voc/tech training

Earnings — $$–$$$

Job Outlook — Declining

Woodworkers

On the Job

Woodworkers make things from wood and work in many stages of the production process. They use machines that cut, shape, assemble, and finish wood to make doors, cabinets, paneling, and furniture. Precision woodworkers use hand tools to make rare or customized items. Most woodworkers handle heavy materials, stand for long periods, and risk exposure to dust and air pollutants. Some operate dangerous equipment.

Something Extra

If you think woodworkers make only furniture, think again! Woodworkers make a huge variety of items, from cabinets and rocking chairs to fishing decoys and jewelry. Some specialize in musical instruments such as guitars and banjoes. Others make knickknacks such as wooden flowers and jewelry boxes. Woodworkers even make machines from wood—imagine a wooden paper shredder. In fact, if you can dream it, a woodworker can probably make it.

Subjects to Study

Math, science, computer skills, shop courses, woodworking, blueprint reading, mechanics

Discover More

Ask an adult to help you with a woodworking project, such as building a shelf or a wooden toy. You can get plans for these projects at your local hardware store.

Related Jobs

Carpenters, sheet metal workers, structural and reinforcing iron and metal workers, computer-control programmers and operators, machinists, tool and die makers

Long-term OJT

Education & Training

$$–$$$

Earnings

Little change

Job Outlook

Power Plant Operators, Distributors & Dispatchers

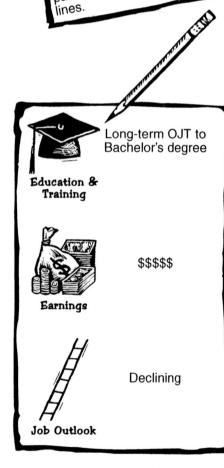

Something Extra

Why would a power plant dispatcher need to know the weather forecast? Because dispatchers must plan ahead to meet people's needs for electricity. During a heat wave, when everyone in town is running an air conditioner, the plant must provide more electricity. During blizzards, it must provide enough power to run heaters that are working overtime. Dispatchers must also be prepared for emergencies such as downed power lines.

Education & Training

Long-term OJT to Bachelor's degree

Earnings

$$$$$

Job Outlook

Declining

On the Job

Power plant operators control the machinery that generates electricity. They start or stop generators as power requirements change. Power distributors and dispatchers make sure that users receive enough electricity. They plan for times when more electricity is needed and handle emergencies. These workers often work nights, weekends, and holidays.

Subjects to Study

Math, physics, electronics, computer science, shop courses, English

Discover More

Talk to someone at the public relations department of your local electric company. Find out where your electricity is generated. Can you take a field trip to see the plant?

Related Jobs

Stationary engineers and boiler operators; water and liquid waste treatment plant and system operators

Stationary Engineers & Boiler Operators

On the Job

Stationary engineers and boiler operators operate and maintain equipment that provides air-conditioning, heat, and ventilation to large buildings. This equipment may supply electricity, steam, or other types of power. These workers may work weekends and holidays. They are exposed to heat, dust, dirt, and noise from the equipment. Hazards of the job include burns, electric shock, and injury from moving machinery parts.

Subjects to Study

Math, computer science, mechanical drawing, shop courses, chemistry, physical education

Discover More

Learn how to maintain and care for machines in your home such as the lawnmower and electric tools. Learn what tools to use, how to oil the machines, and how to keep them in good repair.

Related Jobs

Power plant operators, distributors, and dispatchers; water and liquid waste treatment plant and system operators; industrial machinery installation, repair, and maintenance workers, except millwrights; millwrights

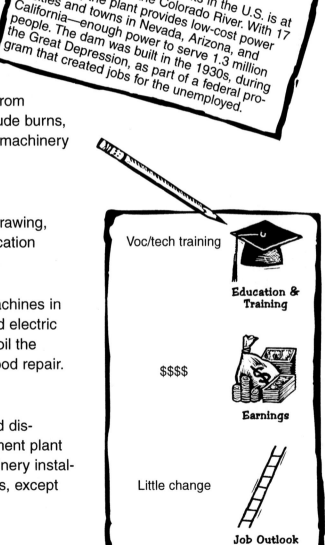

Something Extra

One of the largest power plants in the U.S. is at the Hoover Dam on the Colorado River. With 17 generators, the plant provides low-cost power to cities and towns in Nevada, Arizona, and California—enough power to serve 1.3 million people. The dam was built in the 1930s, during the Great Depression, as part of a federal program that created jobs for the unemployed.

Voc/tech training

Education & Training

$$$$

Earnings

Little change

Job Outlook

Water & Liquid Waste Treatment Plant & System Operators

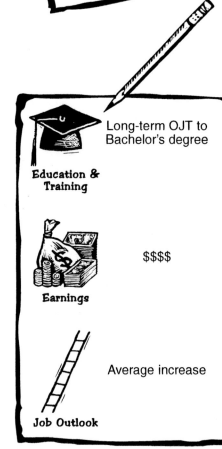

Education & Training
Long-term OJT to Bachelor's degree

Earnings
$$$$

Job Outlook
Average increase

On the Job

Water treatment plant operators make sure that the water you drink is safe. Wastewater plant operators remove harmful pollution from wastewater. They read meters and gauges and adjust controls. They take water samples, perform analyses, and test and adjust chemicals in the water, such as chlorine. They work both indoors and outdoors and may be exposed to dangerous gases. They may work day, evening, or night shifts, weekends, and holidays.

Subjects to Study

Math, chemistry, biology, shop courses, health, environmental sciences

Discover More

Call the water company in your community and ask whether your class can participate in a water-testing program. Many companies will send a representative to your school to teach a class on how to test the water at school and in your home for pollutants such as lead and harmful bacteria.

Related Jobs

Power plant operators, distributors, and dispatchers; stationary engineers and boiler operators

Dental Laboratory Technicians

On the Job

Dental laboratory technicians make the products dentists use to replace decayed teeth. Using dentists' directions and molds of patients' mouths, they make dentures (false teeth), crowns, and bridges. These workers usually have their own workbenches in clean, well-lit areas. Their work is very delicate and takes a lot of time. Salaried technicians usually work 40 hours a week, but self-employed technicians often work longer hours.

Subjects to Study

Sciences, art, metal and wood shop, drafting, business math, management courses

Discover More

Invite an orthodontist to speak to your class. Ask how he or she decides when someone needs braces, how to measure the patient's mouth, and how the braces are made.

Related Jobs

Dentists; opticians, dispensing; ophthalmic laboratory technicians; precision instrument and equipment repairers

Something Extra

What did people do before they had porcelain dentures? You've probably heard that George Washington had wooden teeth. But did you know that when Elizabeth I was queen of England (1558–1603), she lost all her front teeth to decay? To make her face appear fuller, Elizabeth put pieces of cloth under her lips. Other members of the royal court had ornamental teeth made from silver or gold.

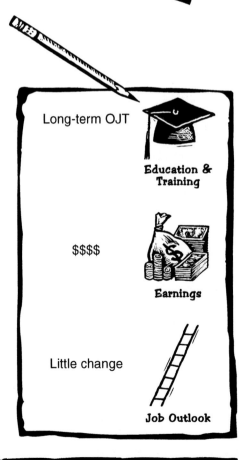

Long-term OJT

Education & Training

$$$$

Earnings

Little change

Job Outlook

Inspectors, Testers, Sorters, Samplers & Weighers

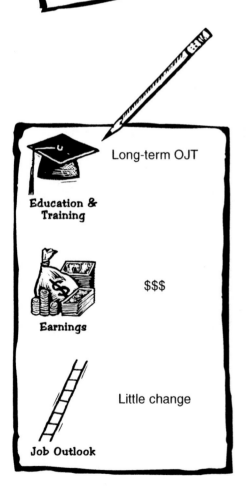

Education & Training

Long-term OJT

Earnings

$$$

Job Outlook

Little change

On the Job

These workers examine and sort products before releasing them to consumers. They may test by looking, listening, feeling, tasting, weighing, or smelling. Products must meet certain quality standards. Inspectors may reject a product, send it back to be fixed, or fix the problem themselves. Inspectors work in all kinds of industries. Some move from place to place. Others sit on an assembly line all day.

Subjects to Study

English, math, shop courses, blueprint reading, mechanics

Discover More

Learn how to contact a company if you are not satisfied with a product. Check the packaging of some products in your home for a consumer telephone number or an address.

Related Jobs

Construction and building inspectors, occupational health and safety specialists and technicians

Jewelers & Precious Stone & Metal Workers

On the Job

These workers use precious metals and stones such as gold and diamonds to make necklaces, rings, bracelets, and other jewelry. Some specialize in one area, such as buying, designing, cutting, repairing, selling, or appraising jewels. This work requires a high degree of skill and attention to detail. Jewelers use chemicals, sawing and drilling tools, and torches in their work. Some are self-employed.

Something Extra

One of the most famous jewels in the world is the Hope Diamond. This 451-carat blue diamond was found in the early 1600s and has crossed oceans and continents and passed from kings to commoners. It has been stolen and recovered, sold and resold, cut and recut. But its fame is due to the bad luck it seems to bring its owners. More than 20 deaths have been blamed on the gem. Through the years, several of its owners have been killed by wild dogs, beheaded, and committed suicide.

Subjects to Study

Math, art, mechanical drawing, chemistry, computer skills, blueprint reading

Discover More

Take a jewelry-making class at school or your local craft store. Try designing and selling your own jewelry pieces.

Related Jobs

Precision instrument and equipment repairers; welding, soldering, and brazing workers; woodworkers; artists and related workers; designers; retail salespersons; sales representatives, wholesale and manufacturing

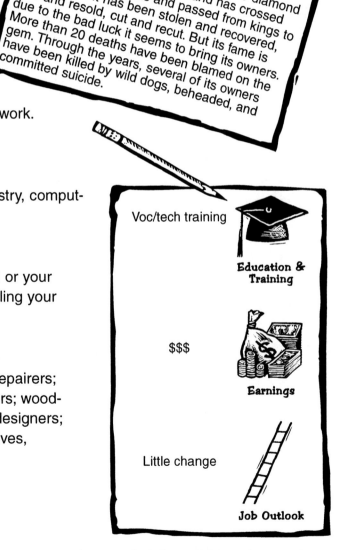

Voc/tech training

Education & Training

$$$

Earnings

Little change

Job Outlook

Ophthalmic Laboratory Technicians

On the Job

Ophthalmic laboratory technicians make the lenses for eyeglasses. Some make lenses for instruments such as telescopes and binoculars. They read the directions from eye doctors and mark the lenses to show where to grind the curves. Then they polish the lenses to remove the rough edges and put them in frames.

They wear goggles to protect their own eyes while grinding the glass for lenses.

Subjects to Study

Math, science, English, shop courses, art

Discover More

Visit an optical store at your local mall. Most have ophthalmic labs on site. Ask whether you can watch the technician work on a pair of glasses. Try on some frames while you're there.

Related Jobs

Dental laboratory technicians; opticians, dispensing; precision instrument and equipment repairers

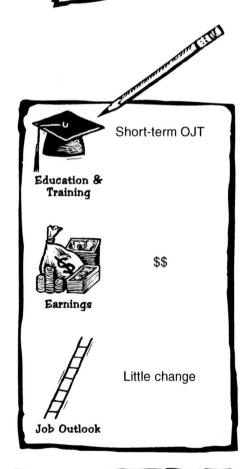

Education & Training — Short-term OJT

Earnings — $$

Job Outlook — Little change

Painting & Coating Workers, Except Construction & Maintenance

On the Job

Painting and coating machine operators cover everything from cars to candy with paints, plastics, varnishes, chocolates, or special solutions. The most common methods of applying paints and coatings are spraying and dipping. These workers must wear respirators over their noses and mouths to protect themselves from dangerous fumes. Most work in factories, but self-employed car painters may own their own shops.

Subjects to Study

Shop courses, art

Discover More

An auto body repair shop is one place you can watch spray painting in action. Call a shop and ask if you can watch the painters. You will probably have to watch from a distance because of the fumes.

Related Jobs

Painters and paperhangers; woodworkers; machine setters, operators, and tenders—metal and plastics

Something Extra

You probably can think of things that are painted—cars, toys, bikes, and wicker furniture. But what does a coating machine do? Well, paper-coating machines spray the glossy finish on paper products. Silvering applicators spray a mix of silver, copper, and tin onto glass to make mirrors. And enrobing machines coat bakery goods with melted chocolate, sugar, or cheese.

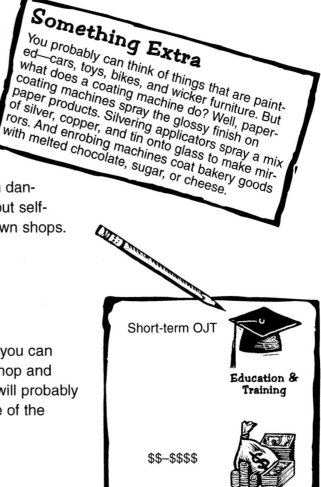

Short-term OJT

Education & Training

$$–$$$$

Earnings

Average increase

Job Outlook

Photographic Process Workers & Processing Machine Operators

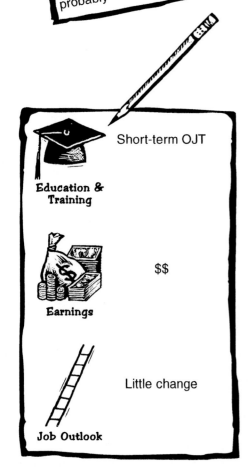

Short-term OJT

Education & Training

$$

Earnings

Little change

Job Outlook

On the Job

Photographic process workers and processors develop film, make picture prints and slides, and enlarge and retouch photographs. They also restore damaged and faded photographs. Most of these workers operate machines to complete their tasks. They are exposed to chemicals and must wear gloves and aprons for protection. Some work in large labs, while others work in one-hour mini-labs.

Subjects to Study

Math, art, computer science, photography

Discover More

Does your school have a darkroom? If so, find out who develops the photos for the school newspaper and yearbook. Ask if you can watch them do their work.

Related Jobs

Clinical laboratory technologists and technicians, computer operators, jewelers and precious stone and metal workers, prepress technicians and workers, printing machine operators, science technicians

Semiconductor Processors

On the Job

Semiconductors, also known as microchips, are the tiny brains inside today's computers. Semiconductor processors are the workers who make these microchips. They work in sterile areas and wear special coveralls called "bunny suits" to keep any dust away from the chips. Operators use special equipment to imprint information on tiny silicon wafers. Technicians maintain the equipment and check the chips for flaws. Semiconductor plants operate around the clock, seven days a week, so shift work is common.

Subjects to Study

Math, general science, physics, chemistry, computer science, electronics, shop courses

Discover More

To learn more about semiconductors and computers, check out the Electronics Hobbyist: www.eskimo.com/~billb/amateur/elehob.html#here. This site has links to cool sites on everything from camps to experiments you can do at home.

Related Jobs

Assemblers and fabricators, engineering technicians, electrical and electronics engineers, except computer, science technicians

Something Extra

Semiconductor processor is a job that didn't exist just a few years ago. It's hard to imagine, but until the 1980s most people had never even seen a computer. Today, computer technology is one of the fastest-growing industries in the U.S., and microchip processing is the only manufacturing job expected to grow rapidly in the coming years. In addition, it's one of the safest jobs available. Because microchips must be produced in a sterile environment, workers spend their days in absolutely clean rooms free of the conditions that cause job-related illnesses and accidents.

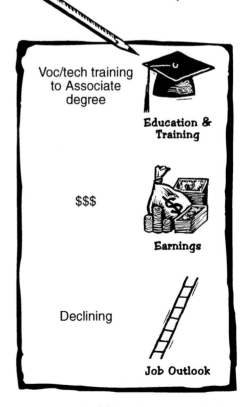

Voc/tech training to Associate degree

Education & Training

$$$

Earnings

Declining

Job Outlook

Transportation & Material Moving Occupations

Aircraft Pilots & Flight Engineers

On the Job

Aircraft pilots fly airplanes and helicopters, test aircraft, and sometimes fight forest fires. Pilots may work for large airlines, charter services, the government, or private businesses. They must plan flights, check the aircraft and weather conditions, and keep records of each flight. Flight engineers act as a third pilot on large aircraft, monitoring and operating many of the instruments and systems.

Subjects to Study

English, math, computer skills, electronics, geography, physics, physical education, foreign languages

Discover More

To learn more about aviation and piloting, check out the Federal Aviation Authority's student Web site at www.faa.gov/education/destined.htm. It has lots of great links to other sites for future pilots as well.

Related Jobs

Air traffic controllers

Education & Training
Bachelor's degree +

Earnings
$$$$–$$$$$

Job Outlook
Average increase

Air Traffic Controllers

On the Job

Air traffic controllers are responsible for the safe movement of airport traffic both in the air and on the ground. Using radar and visual observation, they direct landings, takeoffs, and ground movement of aircraft. They keep planes a safe distance apart during flights and tell pilots of current weather conditions. In emergencies they may search for missing aircraft. This can be a very stressful job.

Something Extra

Do you like computer games in which you have to keep track of a lot of small, moving objects? Imagine each of those objects as a real-life aircraft, carrying real-live human beings. Your job is to keep track of them, ensure they remain safely apart, and stay aware of changing conditions that affect them. Air traffic controllers must be able to track several aircraft, monitor weather and traffic, and stay calm under sometimes extreme stress. People's lives depend on them!

Subjects to Study

English, math, computer skills, physics, shop and technology courses, foreign languages, electronics

Discover More

Call the U.S. Job Information Center in your area and ask for a copy of the *Air Traffic Controller Announcement,* which describes this job more fully. You can find the number in your Yellow Pages under U.S. Government, Office of Personnel Management. Or you can check the Web site for the National Air Traffic Controllers Association at www.natca.org.

Related Jobs

Aircraft pilots and flight engineers

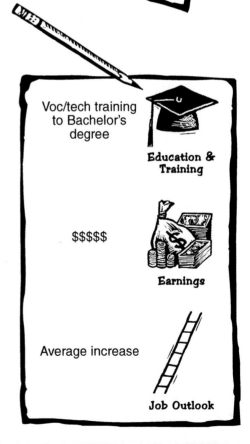

Voc/tech training to Bachelor's degree

Education & Training

$$$$$

Earnings

Average increase

Job Outlook

Bus Drivers

On the Job

Bus drivers transport people from place to place following a time schedule and a specific route. Some drive people long distances within a state or throughout the country. Others drive only locally. School bus drivers drive students to and from school. These workers deal with heavy traffic and many passengers, often in bad weather. Some work nights, weekends, and holidays; others travel overnight away from their homes. Many school bus drivers work part-time.

Subjects to Study

English, communication skills, math, driver's training, first aid

Discover More

Take a ride on a city bus and talk to the bus driver about this job. What tests does your state require? Is special training required? Watch what the driver does to communicate with passengers and care for the bus.

Related Jobs

Taxi drivers and chauffeurs, truck drivers and driver/sales workers

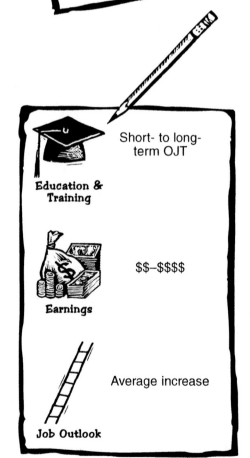

Education & Training
Short- to long-term OJT

Earnings
$$–$$$$

Job Outlook
Average increase

Taxi Drivers & Chauffeurs

On the Job

Taxi drivers and chauffeurs drive people in cars, limousines, and vans. Taxi drivers drive people to airports, hotels, or restaurants. Chauffeurs pamper their passengers by providing extras like newspapers, drinks, music, and television. These workers must lift heavy luggage and packages, drive in all kinds of weather and traffic, and sometimes put up with rude customers. Most taxi drivers and chauffeurs work nights and weekends.

Something Extra

Are you a night owl? Do you love to be on the road? If so, being a chauffeur might be just your ticket. Chauffeurs working for limousine companies often drive at night. They take people to concerts and parties, to dances and clubs, and sometimes to weddings. Many chauffeurs tell stories of driving famous folks in town for concerts or plays. Who knows? You could pick up your favorite actor at the airport and get an autograph along with a fare!

Subjects to Study

English, business math, physical education, driver's education

Discover More

Take a taxi ride and talk to the driver. Ask about the best and worst parts of the job. Has he or she ever driven anyone famous?

Related Jobs

Bus drivers, truck drivers and driver/sales workers

Short-term OJT

Education & Training

$$

Earnings

Above-average increase

Job Outlook

Truck Drivers & Driver/Sales Workers

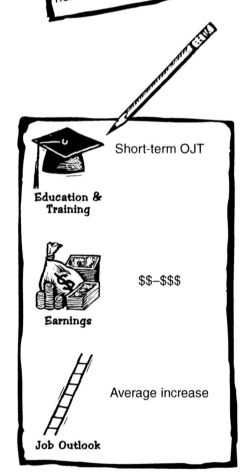

Something Extra

Long-distance trucking runs might last for several days or even weeks. Drivers stop only for gas, food, and loading and unloading. On such long runs, two drivers might work together. One driver sleeps in a berth built into the truck while the other drives. Sometimes married couples work as team drivers on long hauls. They aren't at home a lot, but they get plenty of time to talk!

Short-term OJT

Education & Training

$$–$$$

Earnings

Average increase

Job Outlook

On the Job

Truck drivers move and deliver goods between factories, terminals, warehouses, stores, and homes. They maintain their trucks, check for fuel and oil, make sure their brakes and lights work, and make minor repairs. They also load and unload the goods they transport. They drive in heavy traffic and bad weather. Some self-employed truckers may spend 240 days a year on the road.

Subjects to Study

Business math, driver's education, physical education, accounting

Discover More

Call a truck-driver training school in your area. Ask whether you can visit the school and see the rigs they drive. Maybe an instructor will take you for a ride.

Related Jobs

Bus drivers, taxi drivers and chauffeurs

Rail Transportation Occupations

On the Job

This job includes railroad workers as well as subway and streetcar operators. Railroad engineers operate locomotives that transport passengers and cargo. Conductors are responsible for the cargo and passengers on trains. Brakemen remove cars and throw switches to allow trains to change tracks. Railroads operate around the clock, seven days a week. Employees work nights, weekends, and holidays. Some spend several nights a week away from home.

Something Extra

In the late 1800s, when the railroad was the only way to travel, wealthy people sometimes bought their own railroad cars. These cars were usually decorated with rich, expensive materials. Some even had luxury items such as sunken bathtubs, barbers' chairs, and pipe organs. When they wanted to travel, these wealthy folks simply had their cars hitched to a train and traveled in style. Most employed their own maids, chefs, and waiters to serve them on the trip.

Subjects to Study

Math, mechanics, geography, driver's education, physical education

Discover More

Visit a railroad station or ride a train or subway and watch the different workers. If they have free time, ask them about their jobs. What are the best and worst parts? Do they get to ride for free when they are off-duty?

Related Jobs

Bus drivers, truck drivers and driver/sales workers, water transportation occupations

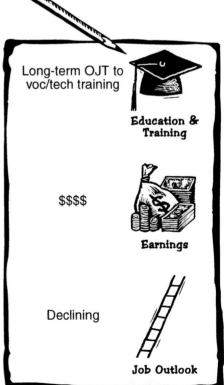

Long-term OJT to voc/tech training

Education & Training

$$$$

Earnings

Declining

Job Outlook

Water Transportation Occupations

On the Job

Workers in water transportation use all kinds of boats on oceans, the Great Lakes, rivers, canals, and other waterways. Captains or masters are in charge of a vessel and the crew. Deck officers or mates help the captain. Seamen and deck hands do maintenance, steer, and load and unload cargo. Pilots guide ships through harbors and narrow waterways. These workers are outdoors in all kinds of weather. Many spend long periods away from home. Working on ships can be dangerous and lonely.

Subjects to Study

Math, physical education, swimming, first aid

Discover More

Water transportation workers must be comfortable both on and in the water. Take swimming lessons at your local park or YMCA. Then sign up for a water-safety or first-aid course.

Related Jobs

Fishers and fishing vessel operators, job opportunities in the armed forces

Education & Training — Voc/tech training

Earnings — $$$$$

Job Outlook — Little change

Material Moving Occupations

On the Job

Material moving equipment operators and laborers load and unload trucks and ships using cranes, bulldozers, and forklifts. They move construction materials, logs, and coal around factories, warehouses, and construction sites. They sometimes set up, clean, and repair equipment. Most work outdoors in all kinds of weather. Others work inside warehouses or factories. The machinery may be noisy and dangerous.

Something Extra

Crane safety is a big concern today. That's because there are so many cranes operating on construction sites around the country, and they can be very dangerous equipment. In 2004, a crane collapsed on a Toledo interstate highway, killing four people. That's why cranes are inspected regularly, and operators receive special safety training.

Subjects to Study

Shop classes, auto mechanics, driver's education, first aid

Discover More

Look for material moving machines in your community. What do they move? Are they used in any work except construction? How do the operators control the machines?

Related Jobs

Bus drivers; construction equipment operators; machine setters, operators, and tenders—metal and plastics; rail transportation occupations; truck drivers and driver/sales workers; agricultural workers; building cleaning workers; construction laborers; forest, conservation, and logging workers; grounds maintenance workers

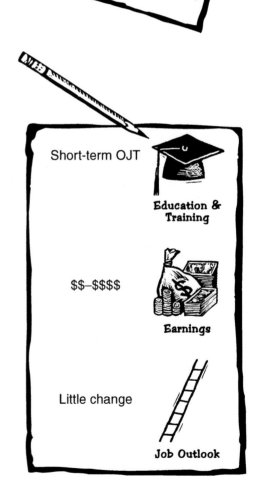

Short-term OJT

Education & Training

$$–$$$$

Earnings

Little change

Job Outlook

Job Opportunities in the Armed Forces

Job Opportunities in the Armed Forces

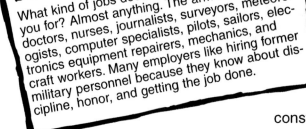
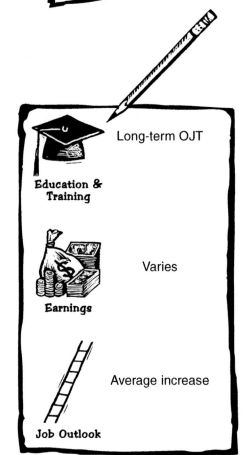

Education & Training
Long-term OJT

Earnings
Varies

Job Outlook
Average increase

On the Job

The U.S. armed forces is the country's largest employer. Maintaining a strong defense requires many activities, such as running hospitals, repairing helicopters, programming computers, and operating nuclear reactors. Military jobs range from clerical work to professional positions to construction work. People in the military must serve for a specified time and can be moved from one base to another. Many work nights, weekends, and holidays, and combat duty is always possible.

Subjects to Study

Math, English, business, sciences, shop courses, physical education

Discover More

Do you think you would enjoy military life? Talk to people who have served in the armed forces. Contact a recruiter to find out about a particular branch of the military. (Remember, though, that a recruiter's job is to get people to join.) Check the Military Careers Web site at www.militarycareers.com to learn about specific jobs within the military, as well as information about all five branches of the military (Army, Navy, Air Force, Marines, Coast Guard).

Related Jobs

Nearly any civilian job

Appendix: More Job Information on the Web

The Internet is a great place to find out more about jobs that interest you. Here are some Web sites that will get you started.

Management and Business and Financial Operations Occupations

American Association of Advertising Agencies
www.aaaa.org

American Board of Funeral Service Education
www.abfse.org/index.html

American College of Health Care Administrators
www.achca.org

American Council for Construction Education
www.acce-hq.org

American Institute of Certified Public Accountants
www.aicpa.org

American Management Association
www.amanet.org

American Purchasing Society
www.american-purchasing.com

American Society of Farm Managers and Rural Appraisers
www.asfmra.org

Association for the Advancement of Cost Engineering
www.aacei.org

Association of Higher Education Facilities Officers
www.appa.org

Association of Management Consulting Firms
www.amcf.org

Association of University Programs in Health Administration
www.aupha.org

Community Associations Institute
www.caionline.org

Financial Management Association International
www.fma.org

Financial Planning Association
www.fpanet.org

Institute of Certified Professional Managers
http://cob.jmu.edu/icpm

Institute of Internal Auditors
www.theiia.org

Institute of Real Estate Management
www.irem.org

Insurance Information Institute
www.iii.org

Insurance Institute of America
www.aicpcu.org

International Claim Association
www.claim.org

International Council on Hotel,
Restaurant, and Institutional Education
www.chrie.org

International Facility Management
Association
www.ifma.org

Mortgage Bankers Association of
America
www.mbaa.org

National Association of Elementary
School Principals
www.naesp.org

National Association of Secondary
School Principals
www.nassp.org

National Association of State Budget
Officers
www.nasbo.org

National Funeral Directors Association
www.nfda.org

National Restaurant Association
Educational Foundation
www.nraef.org

Society for Human Resource
Management
www.shrm.org

Professional & Related Occupations

Aerospace Industries Association
www.aia-aerospace.org

Alliance of Cardiovascular Professionals
www.acp-online.org

American Academy of Actuaries
www.actuary.org/index.htm

American Academy of Environmental
Engineers
www.aaee.net

American Academy of Forensic Sciences
www.aafs.org

American Academy of Physician
Assistants Information Center
www.aapa.org

American Anthropological Association
www.aaanet.org

American Association for Laboratory
Animal Science
www.aalas.org

American Association for Respiratory
Care
www.aarc.org

American Association of Bioanalysts
www.aab.org

American Association of Colleges of
Pharmacy
www.aacp.org

American Association of Petroleum Geologists
www.aapg.org

American Association of Pharmaceutical Scientists
www.aaps.org

American Bar Association
www.abanet.org

American Board of Opticianry
www.abo.org

American Chemical Society
www.acs.org

American Congress on Surveying and Mapping
www.acsm.net

American Correctional Association
www.aca.org

American Counseling Association
www.counseling.org

American Dental Association
www.ada.org

American Design Drafting Association
www.adda.org

American Dietetic Association
www.eatright.org

American Geological Institute
www.agiweb.org

American Health Information Management Association
www.ahima.org

American Historical Association
www.theaha.org

American Institute of Architects
www.aia.org

American Institute of Biological Sciences
www.aibs.org

American Institute of Chemical Engineers
www.aiche.org

American Institute of Graphic Arts
www.aiga.org

American Institute of Physics
www.aip.org

American Library Association
www.ala.org

American Mathematical Society
www.ams.org

American Meteorological Society
www.ametsoc.org/AMS

American Nuclear Society
www.ans.org

American Occupational Therapy Association
www.aota.org

American Physical Society
www.aps.org

American Physical Therapy Association
www.apta.org

American Planning Association
www.planning.org

American Podiatric Medical Association
www.apma.org

American Political Science Association
www.apsanet.org

American Probation and Parole Association
www.appa-net.org

American Psychological Association
www.apa.org

American Society for Clinical Pathology
www.ascp.org/bor

American Society for Engineering Education
www.asee.org

American Society for Microbiology
www.asm.org

American Society of Agricultural Engineers
www.asae.org

American Society of Agronomy
www.agronomy.org

American Society of Civil Engineers
www.asce.org

American Society of Health-System Pharmacists
www.ashp.org

American Society of Landscape Architects
www.asla.org

American Society of Mechanical Engineers
www.asme.org

American Society of Radiologic Technologists
www.asrt.org

American Society of Safety Engineers
www.asse.org

American Sociological Association
www.asanet.org

American Speech-Language-Hearing Association
www.asha.org

American Statistical Association
www.amstat.org

American Therapeutic Recreation Association
www.atra-tr.org

American Translators Association
www.atanet.org

American Veterinary Medical Association
www.avma.org

Archaeological Institute of America
www.archaeological.org

Association for Career and Technical Education
www.acteonline.org

Association for Computing Machinery
www.acm.org

Association of American Colleges and Universities
www.aacu-edu.org

Association of American Geographers
www.aag.org

Association of American Medical Colleges
www.aamc.org

Association of Computer Support Specialists
www.acss.org

Association of Schools and Colleges of Optometry
www.opted.org

Association of Surgical Technologists
www.ast.org

Biomedical Engineering Society
www.bmes.org

Council of American Survey Research Organizations
www.casro.org

Council on Chiropractic Education
www.cce-usa.org

Division of Education, American Dental Hygienists' Association
www.adha.org

Hartford Institute for Religion Research: Official Denominational Websites
www.hirr.hartsem.edu/org/
faith_denominations_homepages.html

Institute for Operations Research and Management Science
www.informs.org

Institute of Electrical and Electronics Engineers
www.ieee.org

Institute of Electrical and Electronics Engineers Computer Society
www.computer.org

Institute of Industrial Engineers
www.iienet.org

Junior Engineering Technical Society (JETS-Guidance)
www.jets.org

Marketing Research Association
www.mra-net.org

Materials Research Society
www.mrs.org

Minerals, Metals, & Materials Society
www.tms.org

National Accrediting Agency for Clinical Laboratory Sciences
www.naacls.org

National Association for Business Economics
www.nabe.com

National Association for Practical Nurse Education and Service
www.napnes.org

National Association for the Education of Young Children
www.naeyc.org

National Association of Broadcasters
www.nab.org

National Association of Emergency Medical Technicians
www.naemt.org

National Association of Legal Assistants
www.nala.org

National Association of Schools of Art and Design
http://nasad.arts-accredit.org

National Association of Schools of Dance
http://nasd.arts-accredit.org

National Association of Schools of Music
http://nasm.arts-accredit.org

National Association of Schools of Public Affairs and Administration
www.naspaa.org

National Association of Schools of Theater
http://nast.arts-accredit.org

National Association of Social Workers
www.socialworkers.org

National Center for State Courts
www.ncsconline.org

National Clearinghouse for Professions in Special Education
www.special-ed-careers.org

National Court Reporters Association
www.ncraonline.org

National Federation of Paralegal Associations
www.paralegals.org

National High School Athletic Coaches Association
www.hscoaches.org

National League for Nursing
www.nln.org

National Organization for Human Service Education
www.nohse.org

National Workforce Center for Emerging Technologies
www.nwcet.org

Pharmacy Technician Certification Board
www.ptcb.org

Professional Photographers of America
www.ppa.com

Public Relations Society of America
www.prsa.org

Society for American Archaeology
www.saa.org

Society for Mining, Metallurgy, and Exploration
www.smenet.org

Society for Technical Communication
www.stc.org

Society of American Archivists
www.archivists.org

Society of Broadcast Engineers
www.sbe.org

Society of Diagnostic Medical Sonography
www.sdms.org

Society of Nuclear Medicine
www.snm.org

Society of Petroleum Engineers
www.spe.org

System Administrators Guild
www.sage.org

U.S. Department of Education, Office of Vocational and Adult Education
www.ed.gov/about/offices/list/ovae/index.html?src=mr

U.S. Department of Labor, Occupational Safety and Health Administration
www.osha.gov

Service Occupations

American Association of Medical Assistants
www.aama-ntl.org

American Association for Medical Transcription
www.aamt.org

American Council on Exercise
www.acefitness.org

American Dental Assistants Association
www.dentalassistant.org

American Gaming Association
www.americangaming.org

American Jail Association
www.corrections.com/aja/

Association of American Pesticide Control Officials
http://aapco.ceris.purdue.edu

Federal Bureau of Investigation (FBI)
www.fbi.gov

Humane Society of the United States
www.hsus.org

International Association of Firefighters
www.iaff.org

International Executive Housekeepers Association
www.ieha.org

National Animal Control Association
www.nacanet.org

National Association for Home Care
www.nahc.org

National Child Care Information Center
www.nccic.org

National Cosmetology Association
www.salonprofessionals.org

National Dog Groomers Association of America
www.nationaldoggroomers.com

National Restaurant Association
www.restaurant.org

Professional Lawn Care Association of America
www.plcaa.org

Tree Care Industry Association
www.TreeCareIndustry.org

Sales & Related Occupations

American Rental Association
www.ararental.org

American Society of Travel Agents
www.astanet.com

Independent Insurance Agents of America
www.iiaa.org

Insurance Vocational Education Student Training (InVEST)
www.investprogram.org

International Fabricare Institute
www.ifi.org

International Foodservice Distributors Association
www.ifdaonline.org

Manufacturers' Agents National Association
www.manaonline.org

Manufacturers' Representatives Educational Research Foundation
www.mrerf.org

National Association of Convenience Stores
www.nacsonline.com

National Association of Health Underwriters
www.nahu.org

National Association of Realtors
www.realtor.org

National Automobile Dealers Association
www.nada.org

National Retail Federation
www.nrf.com

Retail, Wholesale, and Department Store Union
www.rwdsu.org

Securities Industry Association
www.sia.com

Office & Administrative Support Occupations

Air Transport Association of America
www.airlines.org

American Institute of Professional Bookkeepers
www.aipb.org

Association of Computer Operations Management (AFCOM)
www.afcom.com

Association of Credit and Collection Professionals
www.acainternational.org

Association of Public Safety Communications Officials
www.apco911.org

Association for Suppliers of Printing, Publishing and Converting Technologies
www.npes.org/education/index.html

Communications Workers of America
www.cwa-union.org

Council on Library/Media Technicians
http://colt.ucr.edu

Educational Institute of the American Hotel and Lodging Association
www.ei-ahma.org

Graphic Arts Information Network
www.gain.net

International Association of Administrative Professionals
www.iaap-hq.org

Legal Secretaries International
www.legalsecretaries.org

National Academies of Emergency Dispatch
www.emergencydispatch.org

National Management Association
www.nma1.org

United States Postal Service
www.usps.com/about/

Farming, Fishing & Forestry Occupations

American Forest & Paper Association
www.afandpa.org

Forest Resources Association
www.forestresources.org

Marine Technology Society
www.mtsociety.org

National FFA Organization
www.ffa.org

New England Small Farm Institute
www.smallfarm.org/newoof/newoof.html

Society of American Foresters
www.safnet.org

U.S. Forest Service
www.fs.fed.us

Construction Trades & Related Workers

American Society of Home Inspectors
www.ashi.org

Associated General Contractors of America
www.agc.org

Association of Construction Inspectors
www.iami.org/aci

Brotherhood of Boilermakers
www.boilermakers.org

Floor Covering Installation Contractors Association
www.fcica.com/index2.html

International Association of Bridge, Structural, Ornamental, and Reinforcing Iron Workers
www.ironworkers.org

International Association of Electrical Inspectors
www.iaei.org

International Masonry Institute
www.imiweb.org

International Union of Elevator Constructors
www.iuec.org

International Union of Operating Engineers
www.iuoe.org

International Union of Painters and Allied Trades
www.iupat.org

Laborers' International Union of North America

www.liuna.org

Laborers—AGC Education and Training Fund

www.laborerslearn.org

National Association of Home Builders

www.nahb.org

National Association of Plumbing-Heating-Cooling Contractors

www.phccweb.org

National Center for Construction Education and Research

www.nccer.org

National Concrete Masonry Association

www.ncma.org

National Electrical Contractors Association (NECA)

www.necanet.org

National Glass Association

www.glass.org

National Insulation Association

www.insulation.org

National Joint Apprenticeship Training Committee (NJATC)

www.njatc.org

National Roofing Contractors Association

www.nrca.net

Operative Plasterers' and Cement Masons' International Association of the United States and Canada

www.opcmia.org

Painting and Decorating Contractors of America

www.pdca.org

Sheet Metal Workers International Association

www.smwia.org

United Brotherhood of Carpenters and Joiners of America

www.carpenters.org

Installation, Maintenance & Repair Occupations

ACES International (Fiber Optics, Electronics, and Communications Professionals)

www.acesinternational.org

Air-Conditioning Contractors of America (ACCA)

www.acca.org

Association of Equipment Management Professionals

www.equipment.org

Automotive Service Association

www.asashop.org

Automotive Youth Educational Systems (AYES)

www.ayes.org

Computing Technology Industry Association

www.comptia.org

Custom Electronic Design and Installation Association
www.cedia.org

International Brotherhood of Electrical Workers
www.ibew.org

International Society of Certified Electronics Technicians
www.iscet.org

ISA—The Instrumentation, Systems, and Automation Society
www.isa.org

National Automatic Merchandising Association
www.vending.org

National Tooling and Machining Association
www.ntma.org

Professional Aviation Maintenance Association
www.pama.org

SkillsUSA-VICA
www.skillsusa.org

Production Occupations

American Public Power Association
www.appanet.org

American Society for Quality
www.asq.org

American Textile Manufacturers Institute
www.atmi.org

American Water Works Association
www.awwa.org

American Welding Society
www.aws.org

Graphic Communications Council
www.teched.vt.edu/gcc

Manufacturing Jewelers and Suppliers of America
mjsa.polygon.net

National Association of Dental Laboratories
www.nadl.org

Precision Machine Products Association
www.pmpa.org

Precision Metalforming Association Educational Foundation
www.pmaef.org

Semiconductor Industry Association
www.semichips.org

Woodworker's Central
www.woodworking.org

Transportation & Material Moving Occupations

A Career Afloat
www.marad.dot.gov/acareerafloat/index.htm

Air Line Pilots Association
www.alpa.org

American Public Transportation Association
www.apta.com

American Trucking Association
www.trucking.org

Association of American Railroads
www.aar.org

Federal Aviation Administration
www.faa.gov

National Limousine Association
www.limo.org

National School Transportation Association
www.schooltrans.com

United Motorcoach Association
www.uma.org

Job Opportunities in the Armed Forces

U.S. Department of Defense
Defense Manpower Data Center
Military Career Guide Online

www.todaysmilitary.com